RENEWALS 458-4574

DATE DUE

GAYLORD			PRINTED IN U.S.A.

The Autonomy of Literature

Also by Richard Lansdown

BYRON'S HISTORICAL DRAMAS

The Autonomy of Literature

Richard Lansdown
Lecturer in English
James Cook University
Cairns
Queensland
Australia

First published in Great Britain 2001 by
MACMILLAN PRESS LTD
Houndmills, Basingstoke, Hampshire RG21 6XS and London
Companies and representatives throughout the world

A catalogue record for this book is available from the British Library.

ISBN 0–333–92134–8

First published in the United States of America 2001 by
ST. MARTIN'S PRESS, LLC,
Scholarly and Reference Division,
175 Fifth Avenue, New York, N.Y. 10010

ISBN 0–333–92134–8

Library of Congress Cataloging-in-Publication Data
Lansdown, Richard, 1961–
    The autonomy of literature / Richard Lansdown.
        p.   cm.
    Includes bibliographical references and index.
    ISBN 0–333–92134–8
    1. Criticism—History—20th century. 2. Criticism—United States–
    –History—20th century. 3. Criticism—Great Britain—History—20th
    century. 4. Literature, Modern—20th century—History and criticism.
    I. Title.

PN94 .L36 2000
801'.95—dc21
                                                    00–041517

This book is printed on paper suitable for recycling and made from fully managed and sustained forest sources.

10   9   8   7   6   5   4   3   2   1
10   09   08   07   06   05   04   03   02   01

Printed and bound in Great Britain by
Antony Rowe Ltd, Chippenham, Wiltshire

for my mother and my father

Contents

Acknowledgements   viii

Introduction   1

1 **Institutionalism and Ideality**   12
2 **'A New Spin on the Old Words': Criticism
   and Philosophy**   49

   2.1 Richard Rorty   51
   2.2 Alasdair MacIntyre and Charles Taylor   63
   2.3 Martha Nussbaum   78

3 **'These Shafts Can Conquer Troy, These Shafts
   Alone': Criticism and Psychoanalysis**   95

   3.1 Freud   98
   3.2 Object relations   120
   3.3 'The Secret Sharer'   128

4 **'A Province of Truth': Criticism and History**   145

   4.1 R.G. Collingwood   146
   4.2 New Historicism   150
   4.3 Hayden White and Paul Ricoeur   176

5 **Four Objections**   201

   5.1 'Approaching' literature   201
   5.2 What institutionalists say and what they mean   211
   5.3 Who, we? Effects on readers   215
   5.4 Derrida again   222

Notes   239

Index   261

Acknowledgements

It is a pleasure to thank the people who have given their time so generously and helped in the writing of this book: especially Jane Adamson, Bill Arfin, Rosemary Ashton, Simon Haines, Seumas Miller, the late Ralf Norrman, Peter Pierce, Stephen Torre, and Susan Tridgell. As the reader will discover, two individuals have had a particularly powerful influence over the argument presented here. Sam Goldberg saw only a fraction of the book before his death in 1991, but his work and example remained an inspiration long after, and remain so still. His friend Dan Jacobson, by contrast, saw the book coming and saw it through to the very end, reading, commenting, and corresponding indefatigably. He has been doing the same job for this particular writer now for twenty years.

Special acknowledgement must also be made to Nick Royle and Alex Segal, who responded to earlier versions of my discussion of Derrida in Chapter 1 with tact, with exemplary patience, and with invaluable suggestions for further reading. They are responsible for the argument presented there only in the sense that it would have been worse without their help.

A special thanks is also due to the staff and students of the School of English Philology at the University of Tampere, in which calm and conducive environment the groundwork for the study was laid, many years ago.

At Macmillan, and under Macmillan's auspices, two people expressed a faith in the project without which it might never have seen the light: Charmian Hearne and Professor John Sutherland.

My wife Angela has stood by, understood, and put up with these obsessions; without her it could not have been done. As for Sam and Holly: well, if the truth were told, you delayed this book – but in doing so, you made it better, too.

Trinity Beach, Queensland

viii

Introduction

Any future historian of literary criticism and theory in the English-speaking world during the second half of the twentieth century will have a long and complex tale to tell, no doubt. But the basic lines of development will be clear enough. In Britain and its erstwhile colonies and in the United States two very different but generally dominant critical practices – the school of Leavis and the New Criticism – came increasingly under pressure from traditions of thought and analytic procedures essentially new to both of them, and derived from Continental philosophy and social science. In the years after the Second World War certain Continental intellectual traditions, of French origin particularly, re-invented and re-deployed themselves, with lasting effect on 'the languages of criticism and the sciences of man'.

The words just quoted are taken from the title of a famous conference at Johns Hopkins University in 1966, where the structuralist revolution was formally introduced to American academia. Essential to Leavis himself and the New Critics had been the arriving at judgements of moral and aesthetic value by way of 'close reading' of literary texts. The structuralists, by contrast, had little patience with those concerns; they concentrated instead on trying to illustrate the general laws through which all systems of communication – languages, literatures, styles of clothing, indeed all modes of human expression – sought to order experience. Subsequently structuralism of this kind, associated with Lévi-Strauss, Roman Jakobson, and the 'early' Barthes, gave way to the post-structuralism that had been at work within and alongside it for many years and which, with its even more radical scepticism about any conceivable stability of meaning, selfhood, or 'closure', looked back to such thinkers as Nietzsche and Heidegger.

Indeed, Jacques Derrida himself had been one of the star performers at the 1966 conference mentioned above, and it was there that he gave a paper now regarded as a positive cornerstone of post-structuralism: 'Structure, Sign and Play in the Discourse of the Human Sciences'. Derrida was a crucial figure in the post-structuralist transformation, but he was not alone: Gilles Deleuze's *Nietzsche et la philosophie* had appeared as early as 1962; Foucault's even more epoch-marking *Folie et déraison* a year earlier still. In the mid- to late-sixties, and after the 1966 conference in Maryland, the movement massively extended and consolidated the territory it had apparently conquered: Foucault's *Les Mots et les Choses* appeared in 1966, Lacan's *Écrits* in the same year, and Derrida's *annus mirabilis* came in 1967, with *De la Grammatologie*, *Écriture et la différance*, and *La Voix et la phénomène*. Over the years immediately following, Foucault and Derrida produced further major works, as did Julia Kristeva, Luce Irigaray, and Hélène Cixous. Finally, Jean-François Lyotard's *La Condition postmoderne*, published in 1979, gave the whole group a veritable kick into cyber-space.

Naturally there were delays in the spread of this revolution in the English-speaking world, indicated as often as not by the gaps intervening between the appearance of these books in their original language and in English translation. *Folie et déraison* was published in 1961, translated in 1967; *Les Mots et les Choses* waited from 1966 to 1970; *Écrits* from 1966 to 1977; *De la Grammatologie* from 1967 to 1976. (Deleuze's book on Nietzsche had to wait until 1983.) There was a perceptible time-lag, therefore; and it is probably true to say that it was not until the mid-seventies that the movement really began to come into its own in the English-speaking literary and philosophical worlds, to generate its English-speaking disciples, and to attract heavyweight English-speaking critical notice. Nor of course was it the case that Derrida single-handedly produced the Yale School of deconstruction simply by working there: individuals connected with Yale University such as Paul de Man and Geoffrey Hartman had been thinking along similar lines before his arrival, though clearly his presence served as an irreplaceable catalyst.

For various reasons the rate and extent of the uptake of this new thinking was markedly different in Britain and America. Many more Continental thinkers and academics went to America after the Second World War than went to Britain. (No one comparing England in 1946 with California at the same time would be surprised by that.) Those thinkers and academics, naturally enough, fostered and sustained links with colleagues in Europe who were then invited to the States for longer or shorter periods of time. Cultural conditions in America generally, but especially in American academic and intellectual life, also strongly encouraged this development. Some of the fostering conditions were very broad indeed: they can perhaps best be indicated by the fact that the representative literary intellectual of nineteenth-century Britain was Matthew Arnold, whereas his American counterpart, one would have to say, was Ralph Waldo Emerson. The British, in other words, had a long tradition of empiricism; the Americans of idealism. Other conditions were more specific and historically quantifiable, however: the German university system, for example, had had a preponderant influence on the American one in the period of revolution and enlargement in the years following the Civil War.

In any event and for whatever reason the intellectual atmosphere in the two countries – or two centres of influence – has been very different, though a common language and a close social and political relationship perhaps combines to obscure the fact. If we take an intellectual discipline as far removed from literary criticism as possible, while still being one of the humanities – Anthropology, say – there were great differences of intellectual approach separating British social anthropologists inspired originally by Malinowski (himself an expatriate Pole) and their American counterparts inspired originally by Boas (himself an expatriate German). In psychoanalysis, there are similar differences between the Object Relations school associated with Melanie Klein and the ego-psychology practised by Hartmann, Erickson, and others. In literary–critical terms there grew up in America a *wissenschaftliche* interest in interpretation – increasingly embodied in the New Criticism as it evolved in the years leading up to the Second World War. In Britain this subject has never been so eagerly pursued.

For these reasons (and there are of course many others) the new departures in Continental thought, and especially Francophone thought, had a deeper, broader, and more rapid impact in America than in Britain. But then, as has happened before in the history of American universities – we might think of Irving Babbitt and the neo-humanism he sought to deploy against the Germanic professionalization of university life mentioned above – a sudden change of emphasis made itself felt. The energy of the post-structuralist, deconstructionist movement began noticeably to run down, whereas the energy building up within its opponents suddenly flared into activity. Without doubt a decisive event here was the revelation in 1987 of Paul de Man's wartime activities on behalf of, or at the very least his intellectual collusion with, the pro-Nazi Belgian government. To the de Man scandal many other moral and ethical doubts about certain post-structuralists' personal and professional lives attached themselves, however loosely and in however anecdotal or gossipy a fashion: Lacan's professional idiosyncrasies; Foucault's Maoism and his apparent support for Pol Pot; even Althusser's having murdered his wife; and so on. But there were other concerns at issue, too, regarding the very basis of the post-structuralist, deconstructionist, post-modernist project. In particular exception was taken to its suppressing, ignoring, or debunking of the ethical dimension of human life – which then came back, after the de Man revelations, to haunt the project with a vengeance. Deconstruction was now seen to be insufficiently political, in the affirmative or practical sense, and also insufficiently focused on history.

In short, as some critics began to suggest, America had performed her old trick of seducing the European; and the New Criticism, by dragging the newcomer back into the constraints of 'close reading', had transformed deconstruction at least as much as it had itself been transformed. The response of the deconstructionist movement to these accusations – basically to assert that, contrary to appearances, it was *more* ethical, *more* political, and *more* historical than anybody or anything else – only seemed to underline its desperation. And soon the inevitable happened: books appeared (by writers generally sympathetic to deconstruction I hasten to add) with titles like *In the Wake of Theory* (Paul Bové, 1992), *Beyond Deconstruction* (Howard Felperin, 1985), *The Wake of Deconstruction* (Barbara Johnson, 1994), *After Derrida* (Nick Royle, 1995), etc. Then even they dried up.

What emerged in the wake of deconstruction – that is to say, the most radical wing of the post-structuralist movement – had been predicted by one of its American elder statesmen, J. Hillis Miller, in a Presidential Address (the very notion is inconceivable in Britain!) given to the Modern Language Association of America in 1986, the year before the de Man catastrophe. Miller could see the writing on the wall, and what the moving finger spelled out was that the highly refined, literary–philosophical episteme of Derrida and Yale was inexorably giving way to the socio-historical one of Foucault and California. The representative figures and tutelary spirits of American literary study were no longer Miller himself, Geoffrey Hartman, or Barbara Johnson, but Stephen Greenblatt and Edward Said. 'As everyone knows', Miller said,

> literary study in the past few years has undergone a sudden, almost universal turn away from theory in the sense of an orientation toward language as such and has made a corresponding turn toward history, culture, society, politics, institutions, class and gender conditions,

the social context, the material base in the sense of institutionalization, conditions of production, technology, distribution, and consumption of 'cultural products,' among other products. This trend is
so obvious everywhere as hardly to need description. How many symposia, conferences, scholarly convention sessions, courses, books, and
new journals recently have had the word *history*, *politics*, *society*, or
culture in their titles?[1]

The velvet revolution described by Hillis Miller in 1986 has gone on
unabated to this day; and what is more to the point perhaps is that this
time the British have not lagged behind. If the Americans in the mid-
eighties suddenly discovered (in Hillis Miller's words) 'the impatience
to get on with it, that is, not to get lost in the indefinite delays of
methodological debates but to make the study of literature *count* in
our society' (my italics), the British had possessed just such a tradition
of thought ever since the fifties. It may have been unglamorous
and neglected by comparison with Sartre, Paris, and '68, but writers
like Raymond Williams, Richard Hoggart, and Stuart Hall had been
steadily plugging away, finding aid and succour in historians like
E.P. Thompson, Eric Hobsbawm, and Christopher Hill, and ultimately
establishing an institutional home for their own preoccupations in the
Centre for Contemporary Cultural Studies in Birmingham.

Even here, though, there are important differences between Britain
and America, which principally have their origin in the two countries'
wholly different leftist traditions. New Historicism, for all the worthy
aims Hillis Miller ascribed to it in 1986, seems almost irretrievably academic by comparison with Hoggart's surveys of working-class literacy.
It is hard to see how a displaced bonnet once belonging to Cardinal
Wolsey – the subject of an essay of Stephen Greenblatt's in *Learning to
Curse* – is likely to make the study of literature count in our society.
That much said, it is also true that the British socialist tradition has in
recent years itself lost much of its own *élan*; and while there is Cultural
Studies in Britain (and Australia) there are also plenty of writers – and a
research industry more generally speaking – virtually indistinguishable
from American New Historicism.

For the first time, then, a degree of consensus has arisen, right across
the English-speaking academic literary world. The preoccupations which
Hillis Miller anticipated have indeed come to dominate the field.
It is not that theory has died; far from it – Miller's presidential address
was called 'The Triumph of Theory' after all. But it has been shoul-
dered aside by a cuckoo in the nest. Deconstruction goes on; radical

post-structuralism and psychoanalysis goes on: but the overwhelming bulk of literary work in the contemporary English-speaking university is oriented as Miller suggested. Around the amorphous body of historicism – which may not even call itself either historicism or cultural studies – hang all the other critical subcultures hoping, in some way or another, 'to make the study of literature count in our society': post-colonialism, gender studies, feminism, Marxism, 'queer lit.', and so on. All this in fact marks the triumph of theory. When Hillis Miller lists the things newly on offer in 1986 – 'history, culture, society, politics, institutions, class and gender conditions, the social context, the material base in the sense of institutionalization, conditions of production, technology, distribution, and consumption of "cultural products"' – we know that it was the French who put them there, or put them there in that fashion. The great ziggurat of structuralist and post-structuralist thought, however – from Lévis-Strauss, Barthes, and Althusser, to Foucault, Lacan, and Derrida – has become not much more than a kind of scaffolding, ready to be kicked away. An interest in structures has given way to an interest in *institutions*, and the transition has thus been effected to the quasi-pluralist consensus we have today – namely, that literature is itself no more than one institution among many others and, like all other institutions, it is ultimately shaped as a cultural product by the socio-political and ideological forces to which it is subjected.

The existence of the consensus I have just tried to describe is nowhere made more clear than in its hostility to one intellectual tradition in particular. The various organs of an institutional persuasion may argue with each other, may compare and contrast their 'approaches' or 'perspectives' – the plenitude of their own, the limitations of others – but to one member of the family they never accord even this degree of civility. The house of theory has many mansions, with room for all the languages of criticism and the sciences of man: but no room can be made in it for the reprobate to which the derogatory term 'liberal humanism' has been assigned. He is the Joseph, stripped of his coat and thrown down the well.

These are the circumstances in which the present work seeks to establish its place. The decent and praiseworthy institutionalist objective of making the study of literature count almost invariably involves making it count *in a particular way* (in a queer way, in a feminist way, in a post-colonialist way, in a liberal Marxist-cum-leftist 'committed' sort of a way), and therein lies the rub. Even in hailing the new consensus in 1986 Hillis Miller was careful to place a thorn within the bouquet he was holding out to it. 'I have great sympathy for this shift,' he said: 'but not when it takes the form of an exhilarating experience of liberation from the obligation to read, carefully, patiently, with nothing taken for granted beforehand.' In other words, the compulsion to make literature count in one particular way can have the effect of reducing its ability to count at all.[2]

This book is written in the belief that literature has a life of its own, but one which is not in opposition to all other forms of life. On the contrary, the life that literature evinces comes from its ever-shifting modes of dealing with and transforming whatever lies outside it. Every individual work of literature seeks to address us in its own manner and for its own ends, of that we may be sure: with the artist breathing down both its neck and (often enough) our own. But there need be nothing either naïve or ideologically collusive in insisting, in response, on those features of the work which institutionalism cannot assimilate and digest, and which for want of better words we had better call its imaginative, formal, and moral elements. That is what this book wants to argue, at least: that the institutionalist consensus is inadequate and that something like the position outlined in the pages that follow is necessary, not to vanquish the modern consensus in one more bout of the theory wars, but to supplement it. But I should say here immediately that this study will not directly confront the great shift of literary–critical interest and focus described by Hillis Miller. Institutionalism has a long life and takes many forms, and the intention here, for the most part at least, is to consider its more sophisticated and intellectually ambitious variants in certain intellectual disciplines aside from criticism itself. The point of departure is Hillis Miller's recognition of how things stand in the study of English just recently and just now; but the intention of the study is something broader than polemic alone.

The first chapter of this study clears some room for the concept of autonomy advanced and illustrated in the book as a whole. In particular, it considers the view of literature advanced by those I have begun to characterize as 'institutionalists': those who see literature as the more or less passive recipient of institutional influence. (I mean by this influences derived most obviously from social institutions such as the media or the state; but I also use the term in a broader sense to refer to the historical context of a work, for example, or the individual writer's psychological disposition and settled philosophical preconceptions.) Jacques Derrida and Pierre Macherey are discussed in this connection.

At the same time the chapter follows the institutionalists in general and Derrida in particular in rejecting the notion that literature possesses 'ideality', some kind of essential philosophical, literary, or aesthetic quality which is its permanent guardian and guarantor. Thus the first chapter and the study as a whole defend a notion of autonomy similar to that which can be put forward with respect to human individuals: that a person is autonomous to the degree that what he or she thinks and does cannot be explained without reference to his or her own activity of mind.

This idea of literary activity – analogous but not identical to human mental activity – is distinguished from both mere chance and the myth of inspiration, and is seen instead in terms of dialogue and dialectic. There is the dialogue between the literary text and what lies outside it on the one hand, and there is the dialogue the text establishes with its author and its readers about itself: a dialogue in which sometimes the text and sometimes the author appears to have the upper hand. Finally, therefore (and to 'even the scores' if you like), the chapter comments on the theory of literary activity advanced by T.S. Eliot in 'Tradition and the Individual Talent'. If one of the effects of Derrida's thought has been for critics to overemphasize the weakness of the literary text in the face of the contaminatory, institutional influences which surround it, then Eliot tends to overemphasize its strength, *vis-à-vis* the virtually passive author. Somewhere between these two positions, this study argues, the truth about literature's autonomy lies.

There then follow three chapters which are in varying degrees both 'theoretical' (forensic and 'negative') and 'practical' (descriptive, and 'positive') in orientation. In each case the institutional claims made on literature by some practitioners within a particular intellectual discipline are analysed. Philosophy is the subject of Chapter 2, Psychoanalysis of Chapter 3, and History – or at least historical and narratological theories of literature – is the subject of Chapter 4. Such practitioners need not necessarily be institutionalists by conviction; but as often as not they are.

These three chapters are largely self-explanatory, but two important issues about their manner of proceeding should be raised in advance. First, The New Historicist critics and historical narratologists discussed in Chapter 4 are a fairly representative group. Similarly, Chapter 3 discusses Sigmund Freud as well as some important figures in the Object Relations school of psychoanalysis: so this chapter, too, covers some highly representative psychoanalytical writers. (The great exception here, needless to say, is the contribution of Jacques Lacan, which cannot be discussed in detail for lack of space.) But Chapter 2 really does limit itself to a small – though at present highly significant – area of Philosophy's dealings with literature: a group of North American Aristotelians with avowed literary interests. None of these chapters is intended to be a complete discussion of criticism's institutional negotiations with the fields concerned – even if such a discussion could ever be achieved – but only a fair and reasonable picture of significant aspects of them.

The second issue is this: each of these chapters, as I have said, tends to adopt a forensic and on occasion a frankly polemical attitude. But as I say repeatedly in what follows, the intention is by no means to forbid philosophers, psychoanalysts, and history theorists from reading literature, or to cultivate a 'hands-off literature' attitude, or to use some notional authority vested in the literary critic to banish illegal immigrants. I end up disagreeing with all my invited guests: but I do not disagree *entirely* with any of them, and credit is given wholeheartedly where it is due. 'Those who wish to turn the page on philosophy', Derrida has suggested (see p. 243, footnote 49), 'only end up doing philosophy badly.' I do not think literary criticism need or should be nearly so sanctimonious about its nature and activities. The study acknowledges the vital and irreplaceable contributions made to literary study – again and again, and for all time – by 'outsiders'. There are occasions when I think Freud, or Richard Rorty, or Hayden White are plain wrong; but overall and in the end the differences are mostly ones of emphasis (however crucial emphasis can be): cases where, in my view, partial accounts of literature are presented as complete ones, or certain factors – historical or psychological causation, for example – are dogmatically and reductively presented as being of primary importance.

So much for the theoretical, forensic, and negative side of these three central chapters. In each case, however, as and when space and opportunity permit, the pendulum swings to other but intimately related concerns, or the argument sees the same concerns from other points of view. First and foremost, negative or polemical theoretical discussion in almost every case is accompanied by the introduction and furthering of a positive theory of literature, and this is where my debt to the authorities I have criticized becomes particularly clear: for I could not have gone on to improve (if I may say so) Richard Rorty's or Martha Nussbaum's or Sigmund Freud's or Stephen Greenblatt's accounts of literature if those accounts had not been available in the first place. So it is that the theoretical problems I see in other writers encourage me gradually and intermittently to spell out a positive theory of literature of my own: that literature is more morally problematic and unpredictable than the American Aristotelians allow, for example; or that the artist's practice in at once exercising and foregoing creative control over the work is a more important critical principle than wish-fulfilment and the return of the repressed dwelt upon by Freud and others; or that the distinction between history and literature on the grounds of truth is in certain key respects unreliable (for they are evidently both true, only in different ways); and so on.

On each occasion, moreover, the attempt is made – again, subject to space and opportunity – to see the issues raised from literature's point of view, as it were. The three central chapters contain a variety of literary examples – albeit mostly, necessarily, brief ones. Sometimes I use these in order to make a forensic or polemical point, to be sure; but I also use my literary examples to further positive discussion. Thus *Lolita*, *Middlemarch*, *Wuthering Heights*, Henry James, and Daniel Defoe come to my aid in Chapter 2; Dickens, Jane Austen, and Charlotte Brontë – but above all Joseph Conrad and William Wordsworth – are volunteered in Chapter 3; and Emily Dickinson, *King Lear*, and *Northanger Abbey* perform similar services in Chapter 4. The reader will recognize these discussions as being broadly 'traditional', in literary–critical terms: tending unquestionably, in some respects at least, towards the moral, the formalist, and the liberal–humane end of the spectrum.

But – as I began to suggest at the end of the first section of this Introduction – the study is also quite clearly not altogether happy with that particular concatenation of attitudes, long-lived as it certainly has been in the English critical tradition. The literature I have worked with encourages me to reconsider moralism, formalism, and liberal humanism (above all and in particular) often quite radically. In fact it demands that I do so. It may well be, for example, that the critical writers examined in the theoretical discussions would not in fact disagree with the practical analyses presented alongside them. But that is not as important as it sounds: the important issue is that my intention is to present textual analyses which my chosen theoreticians could not themselves have provided, their foci of interest being what they are. The aim in this respect is twofold: to suggest in practical terms the many forms literature's autonomy can take; and to justify a mode of criticism that responds accordingly.

There remain four issues that are central to the case I seek to present, but which do not fit neatly into the chapters outlined above. In order to engage the reader and to outline these issues directly and economically, I have written of them in an adversarial mode as 'Four Objections': but the chapter makes it quite clear that there is no attempt on my part to forestall or disarm every criticism which such a study will attract. The four objections raised are those which, being answered, might most successfully advance the argument as a whole. The aim is to draw together the various strands of the book and attempt to provide a more comprehensive account of the relations between reader, writer and the world at large than those described and criticized in previous pages.

1
Institutionalism and Ideality

1.1

In defending his *thèse d'état* at the Sorbonne in 1980, Jacques Derrida offered something of a summary of his career to date, and reviewed those published works which comprised the thesis he was to defend. 'I have to remind you somewhat bluntly and simply,' he told his audience, 'that my most constant interest, coming even before my philosophical interest I should say, if this is possible, has been directed towards literature, towards that writing which is called literary.'[1] His first research topic, Derrida admitted, had been registered in 1957; that topic was 'The ideality of the literary object'.

The word 'ideality' was one he had inherited from Husserl, as Derrida went on to explain. I am going to use it here in its more everyday sense: specifically, the possibility of seeing literature in abstract, generalizable, 'Platonic' terms by virtue of its possessing certain essential attributes. Derrida's attitude to such a possibility is clear. 'Logocentrism', he writes, 'is...fundamentally, an idealism. It is the matrix of idealism. Idealism is its most direct representation, the most constantly dominant force. And the dismantling of logocentrism is simultaneously – *a fortiori* – a deconstitution of idealism or spiritualism in all their variants.'[2] On the basis of comments like these it is fair to say that Derrida's work as a whole is anti-idealist where literature (and indeed anything else) is concerned. On 'the enterprise of returning "strategically," ideally, to an origin or to a "priority" held to be simple, intact, normal, pure, standard, self-identical, in order *then* to think in terms of derivation, complication, deterioration, accident, etc.', for example, Derrida has this to say:

> Although this exigency is...essentially 'idealistic' I do not criticize it as such, but rather ask myself what this idealism is, what its force

and its necessity are, and where its intrinsic limit is to be found. Nor is this idealism the exclusive property of those systems commonly designated as 'idealistic.' It can be found at times in philosophies that proclaim themselves to be anti-idealistic, in 'materialisms.' Or in discourses that declare themselves alien to philosophy.[3]

Discourses, that is to say, like literary criticism.

Derrida's anti-idealism has proved immensely influential over the last twenty-five years, in literary theory above all other disciplines. 'Deconstruction', he writes, 'is neither a theory nor a philosophy. It is neither a school nor a method. It is what happens, what is happening today in what they call society, politics, diplomacy, economics, historical reality, and so on and so forth. Deconstruction is the case.'[4] In saying this, Derrida is surely right to acknowledge that deconstruction has spread far beyond his own work and that of his admirers. Deconstruction, in its many incarnations and varieties, but in particular as that 'new theory of literature' Derrida began to pursue in 1957 ('TT' 37), 'is the case', and the new theory of literature for which, ultimately, it provides the philosophical rationale or substrate has as a direct result a hostility towards idealism. As I suggested in the Introduction, far from being the specialist, rarefied, hyper-refined field it may appear to outsiders, some *kind* of deconstruction is at work in almost every contemporary critical idiom, from feminism to New Historicism, and from post-colonialism to cultural studies. So the form it takes and the influence it exerts demand treatment here before rest of the study can be embarked upon.

In thinking about the topic he had chosen for his thesis, Derrida began to ask himself a series of questions long familiar to those who consider the ideality of the literary object:

> What is literature? And first of all what is it to 'write'? How is it that the fact of writing can disturb the very question 'what is?' and even 'what does it mean?' To say this in other words – and here is the *saying otherwise* that was of importance to me – when and how does an inscription become literature and what takes place when it does? To what and to whom is this due? ('TT' 37–8)

This set of questions, then, contains some important traditional elements – though Derrida, even as he framed his enquiry, began to move in a direction quite his own: towards 'saying otherwise' in fact. Such questions, we must imagine, have occupied the minds of all those who have thought critically about literature from Plato onwards. But only a simpleton would imagine that such questions can be answered when framed in so stark a form, and certainly Derrida did not believe that they could. Like other critics he sought a second group of questions, related to the first, that he could hope to answer. 'What takes place', he immediately asked himself, 'between philosophy and literature, science and literature, politics and literature, theology and literature, psychoanalysis and literature?' ('TT' 38.)

Of course no secondary, 'answerable' group of questions such as these will ever be a simple restatement of the original line of enquiry from which they derive: they themselves restrict the focus of or otherwise transform questions like 'what is literature?' or 'to what or to whom is it due?' For Derrida one particular focus of his enquiry into the ideality of literature was the *institution* of literature and the form that institution takes. This led to the university – ineluctably linked, as he puts it, 'with the ontological and logocentric onto-encyclopedic system' ('TT' 43) – which in turn and in time led to the institution of the thesis itself. Consideration of the institution of the university and its relation to 'a certain metaphysics' took him by a more or less direct progression, as his account has it, to 'an interpretation of the Hegelian theory of the sign, of speech and of writing in Hegel's semiology' ('TT' 43). So in 1967 Hegel's semiology was registered as his second research topic.

I do not want to use Derrida's academic career as an illustration of the well-known fact that people's thesis topics change over time. Nor do I think it at all self-evident that between 1957 and 1967 he forfeited an interest in literature for an interest in philosophy. The account he gives in 'The Time of a Thesis' is not one of sudden transformations or conversions on the road to Damascus but of a growing recognition of his need to approach the question 'what is literature?' by the only avenue available to him. By a series of radical enquiries he was brought full circle: from a thesis on the ideality of literature he came to question not only literature's ideality but, as a direct result, the institution of the thesis and all the academic apparatuses it both serves and crowns. An interest in ideality brought him to an interest in institutions. Derrida is no iconoclast. On the contrary, his interest in institutions can be highly traditional. But most of his work does suggest that the question 'what is literature?' is one to be answered only in institutional terms, and that this fact itself renders the ideality of literature, as it might loosely be defined in Platonic or quasi-Platonic terms, impossible.

'[T]here is no text which is literary *in itself*', he argues: 'Literarity is not a natural essence, an intrinsic property of the text. It is the correlative of an intentional relation to the text, an intentional relation which integrates in itself, as a component or an intentional layer, the more or less implicit consciousness of rules which are conventional or institutional – social, in any case.'[5] This is why Derrida's response to the question 'what is literature?', as we have seen, is likely to be either '*to what* is the literary effect due?', or 'what takes place *between* literature and (say) science?' Literature's ideality is fatally compromised by its institutional affiliations.[6]

As I have suggested, Derrida's influence where this point is concerned has extended far beyond his acknowledged admirers in deconstruction. Many contemporary critics – Marxists, feminists, New Historicists, postcolonialists, et al. – disagree sharply with Derrida over the specificities of his thought: 'the linked series', as he calls it, 'formed by the trace, *différance*, undecidables, dissemination, the supplement, the graft, the hymen, the parergon, etc.' ('TT' 45–6). On the more general and basic question of whether or not literature is able to retain the quality of being ideal, however, such critics owe a great deal to Derrida's 'institutional' view, whether they are aware of such a debt or not. Indeed some critical schools (in particular the New Historicist one) go much further with Derrida's new theory than Derrida himself. Anything remotely approximating to the ideality of literature is something they emphatically repudiate; nor is that repudiation a mere incidental in their critical work but the very cornerstone of it.[7]

It is not, however, the *ideality* of literature that is defended in this study. It is not my wish either to praise or to bury such a thing, conceived of as a natural essence or an intrinsic property of a text. The better word for my purposes is *autonomy*. But may I make it clear: when I use the word I have no wish to evoke the boy-stood-on-the-burning-deck, last-stand-at-the-Alamo attitude adopted by some. 'I feel quite alone these days', writes Harold Bloom, 'in defending the autonomy of the aesthetic'. 'Aesthetic criticism', he goes on in this lone and palely loitering mood, 'returns us to the autonomy of imaginative literature and the sovereignty of the solitary soul, the reader not as a person in society but as the deep self, our ultimate inwardness.'[8] This study gives a wide berth to the solitary soul, the deep self, and the ultimate inwardness, in the belief that literature itself has concerned itself with those things only to the extent of demonstrating their unreality. It also gives a wide berth to 'the autonomy of the aesthetic', for reasons which will become clear.

Autonomy, Gerald Dworkin suggests, is a concept to be 'character-ized' rather than defined.[9] With the aim of suggesting its ubiquity and lack of definition, Dworkin provides a 'brief catalogue of uses of the term', drawn from a variety of sources in moral and political philosophy, as well as related fields. Of these uses, Joel Feinberg's statement, 'I am autonomous if I rule me, and no one else rules I', is far too categorical for what I have in mind. Even if we employ a strictly etymological def-inition (*auto-nomos*, self-ruled) it is clear that literature derives its own rules in large part from seeing what rules are arrived at by *other* forms of discourse. To believe it rules itself will not get us very far. The pre-sent purpose is better served by a formulation such as R.F. Dearden's:

> A person is 'autonomous' to the degree that what he thinks and does cannot be explained without reference to his own activity of mind.[10]

For Geoffrey Bennington, autonomy is 'giving-oneself-the law' – a notion he rightly regards as naïve. ('The law one gives oneself retains an irreducible relation to the law received before the law.') 'What we have said about writing and the trace', he argues, 'shows that no *autos* is possible without an inscription of alterity, no inside without a rela-tion to an outside which cannot be simply outside but must remark itself on the inside', which 'implies fatally that autonomy is de jure impossible.'[11] Certainly 'giving-oneself-the-law' is not what is intended in this study. The kinds of critics and readers whom I most want to convince are prone to making arguments of an *aut Caesar aut nihil* kind: that those who consider something to be typically human are in fact making a claim for its being essentially human; or that those unwilling to describe the human subject as an effect of language are therefore committed to a principle of metaphysical foundationalism; or that those who do not believe literature to be wholly infiltrated by institutional influence must therefore believe literature to be an unadulterated essence along the lines of 'I rule me, and no one else rules I'. This book will argue that there is a defensible position between these last two extremes: a position that involves an attempt to compre-hend literature's 'own activity', even if it should prove that that activ-ity is itself a response to institutional influence.

Still, many traditional or conventional defences of the autonomy of literature take the view that that which essentially separates literary or artistic objects from others is their self-referentiality: the fact that works of literature are 'ends in themselves' rather than instrumental means to ends outside. (R.G. Collingwood turns up on two occasions in this study, and in *The Principles of Art* he distinguished between art and magic on grounds similar to these. Similar distinctions have been drawn between art and advertizing, for example, or art and pornography.) But one of the reasons I value R.F. Dearden's emphasis on *activity*, and make that (rather than self-sufficiency, say, or self-referentiality) the basis for the definition of autonomy that is offered here, is that I do not believe the traditional distinction between means and ends is of much value in this area. In *The Idea of a University* Cardinal Newman famously attacked the distinction between learning as a means of vocational preparation, and learning as an end in itself. He pointed out that learning is both: like good health, it is an end in itself and also a means to other things. Something of the same is true of literature. No one who reads ideologically explicit authors like Milton, Pope, Jane Austen, or D.H. Lawrence (never mind Harriet Beecher Stowe or Ezra Pound) could deny that these writers are putting their work to 'ends': religious, social, or ideological. Nor is there any work of literature imaginable which does not, to some degree or other, pursue such ends: anti-religious, anti-social, anti-ideological ones, even. But literature is also a means to ends of quite another kind. In so far as every work of literature is to some degree a compensatory fantasy (individual or collective), it enacts all sorts of developments its author would like to see or fears to see enacted in reality, and this is an 'end', too. Indeed, a moment's reflection will suggest that a work of literature which was an end in itself, or wholly self-referential, would be a sterile and meaningless exercise for both the writer and the reader.

Both those who wish to preserve and those who wish to undermine the autonomy of literature employ 'institutional' arguments: the former to distinguish literature from, say, history, and by these means circumscribe both activities; the latter to blur or efface such distinctions and by those means to reveal, say, the literary element in historical narratives or the historical embeddedness of poems, plays, and novels. The primary consideration as far as this study is concerned is not so much whether inter-institutional relations exist (for they surely do), but whether or not any work of literature possesses or preserves 'its own activity' amidst the institutional influences to which it is unquestionably subject. Very few people nowadays would seek to prove 'that literature is a field with indivisible and simply assignable limits'.[12] It may be that very few people have ever in fact sought to prove such a thing. But it is a kind of activity nonetheless.

Derrida is not the first person who has sought to clarify the autonomy of literature. It may help to approach this issue of literature's 'activity' from another direction, or from another intellectual source. 'The specificity of the work', writes Pierre Macherey, 'is also its autonomy':

> in so far as it is self-elaborating it is a law unto itself and acknowledges only an intrinsic standard, an autonomous necessity. This is why literary works ought to be the object of a *specific science*: otherwise they will never be understood. And though various disciplines such as linguistics, the theory of art, the theory of history, the theory of ideologies, the theory of unconscious formations, must all collaborate in this enterprise ... yet they can in no sense replace this specific science of the literary work. It is important to recognise that literary texts make a novel use of language and ideology ... by wresting them in a new direction and conscripting them into a project peculiar to them alone.[13]

Macherey goes on to say that '*autonomy must not be confused with independence*', which is certainly true. If what I understand as traditional criticism, in seeking to maintain a non-institutional (or de-institutionalized) understanding of literature, has perpetrated such a confusion or added to its currency then it certainly has done literature a disservice.[14] Nor do I have any problem with what Macherey goes on immediately to say: 'The work only establishes the difference which brings it into being, by establishing relations to that which it is not; otherwise it would have no reality and would actually be unreadable and invisible.'[15] Clearly a pattern of differences does help to distinguish literature in general from psychoanalysis, and *Confessions of Zeno* in particular from Freud. Clearly, too, if a work of literature were utterly independent from other forms of intellectual and moral discourse it would, as Macherey says, 'be unreadable and invisible'.

It is the conclusion Macherey comes to on the basis of these two statements, however, that is a contentious one from the point of view of this study:

> Thus the literary work must not be considered as a reality complete in itself, a thing apart, under the pretext of blocking all attempts at reduction; this would be to isolate it into incomprehensibility as the mythical product of some radical epiphany. *Even though the work is determined by its own rules, it possesses no internal principle of elaboration.* This notion of absolute independence generally characterises that mythical thinking which attests to entities already formed without explaining their origins and development.[16]

This is an *aut Caesar aut nihil* argument *par excellence*. Why, we might ask, does it follow that literature's possessing an 'internal principle of elaboration' implies that it is 'complete in itself'? A work of literature 'possesses no internal principle of elaboration'; yet apparently only 'in so far as it *is* self-elaborating' is that work 'a law unto itself' and 'an autonomous necessity'. It cannot be only a 'pretext' on the part of critics, then, that makes them resist 'all attempts of reduction'. If works of literature possess a principle of self-elaboration, that principle would surely tend to resist reduction. Macherey cannot have his cake and eat it, too. A poem is not independent; it does establish relations with that which it is not. But it does not follow that it therefore lacks the capacity for self-elaboration, nor does it follow that our wishing to block attempts at reduction on its behalf 'constitutes mythical thinking which attests to entities already formed without explaining their origins and development'. Macherey clearly understands that the 'wresting' and the 'conscripting' of things like language and ideology by literature are manifestations of literature's autonomy. Equally clearly, however, his position forbids him to accept that such acts of wresting and conscripting might themselves constitute principles of either elaboration or development where literature is concerned. Indeed, having committed himself to a reasonable position, Macherey soon abandons it, scuttling back to the safety of political dogma, in the first place, but also of literary–critical institutionalism. 'Through its relationship to the theoretical and ideological uses of language,' he goes on, apparently unaware of the extent to which he is contradicting his earlier conclusions, 'the text is also influenced by the formal function of the writer and by the problems of his individual existence; finally, specific literary works are determined by the history of literary production from which they receive the means of their own realisation.'[17]

But if Marxist aestheticians like Macherey have run into difficulty with the so-called 'relative autonomy' of works of art, and have retreated from it to concepts like 'formal functions' or 'the history of literary production', it does not necessarily follow that their bourgeois counterparts have had a more productive time of it. Harold Bloom mentions 'the autonomy of the aesthetic'; but it is not required for the reader to become deeply involved in that, or for me to present a philosophically rigorous account of the distinction between the moral (ethical) and the artistic (aesthetic) spheres of the kind Benedetto Croce and others have attempted to provide. The autonomy I am arguing for does not depend on such distinctions, however sophisticated. If it did it would be on shaky ground indeed. On the contrary, the implicit argument offered in this book as a whole is that essentialist accounts of such distinctions would be almost certainly bound to fail, in so far as they are intended to be accounts of literature. For they would be idealist accounts of a thing ultimately inexplicable in idealist terms, and Derrida is right to have rejected such terms at the outset. (Indeed, his doing so is what makes his account of literature a valuable one in my view.) It was no doubt the fear that he was drifting into a form of essentialism that prompted Macherey to drop his discussion of literary self-elaboration like the proverbial hot potato. Essentialism has become one of the intellectual bugaboos put up to warn off critics who stray from the institutional path. Whoever does not believe that literature is the product of random and contingent historical agencies, or the surreptitious marshalling of ideological oppression, or the enfeebled recipient of institutional largesse, or the pulverized victim of the hazardous play of dominations must – so the argument goes – regard it as a transcendental signified: con-substantial and co-eternal, so to speak.

There is no need for literary critics to submit to dilemmas of this kind. They need not do so because for them the notion of essential, ubiquitous, and abstract literary and aesthetic value is beside the point. The institutionalist dilemma presented in such terms only *is* a dilemma if the autonomy of literature were to be regarded as being based solely on abstract philosophical categories of the kind discussed by Croce. Works of literature are not individual expressions or variations of abstract qualities (sincerity, for example), the nature of which has been pre-established once and for all and which in turn guarantee the autonomy of literature. They are objects which, to borrow Macherey's words, wrest such abstractions in a new direction and conscript them into a project peculiar to them (the works) alone. Such works are, in terms of their origins and development, unique and unabstractable. Their autonomy is not to be found sheltered behind an iron curtain lowered between the aesthetic and the moral any more than it is to be found in some pre-existing sphere of copper-bottomed, quasi-Platonic moral essences and intrinsic properties. It is to be found in their very mode of existence, in their activity, which I am going to try to describe in the following chapters. What is presented here therefore is not intended to be a 'philosophical' account of literature, but a literary–critical one. That is why little use is made of analyses of literature coming from fields like aesthetics or the philosophy of mind.[18] To that extent this book, too, is or seeks to be non-idealist.

1.2

The evolution of Derrida's research topic is representative of an important element in modern criticism by virtue of the fact that, in his view, any attempt to begin a definition of literature leads necessarily to philosophy, science, politics, theology, and psychoanalysis, and to those transactions which take place between them and that 'strange institution', as he calls it, literature itself. Literature and criticism are always, in his view, liable to be contaminated by their sister-institutions and, to the extent that they are so contaminated, are unable to lay claim to ideality. Contamination, I hasten to add, is Derrida's word. Readers are bound to be struck by the negative connotations of the term when compared with, for example, 'influence'. Indeed, Derrida on one occasion allows his readers, albeit 'for the time being', to imagine the possible connotations of this 'essential disruption'. They are: 'internal division of the trait, impurity, corruption, contamination, decomposition, perversion, deformation, even cancerization, generous proliferation or degenerescence.'[19] The opposite of contamination is what Derrida calls 'the proper', which in turn has the French *propre* behind it, with all *its* connotations. Given this, it is hard for Derrida to persuade us that 'There is no more a "negative" contamination than there is a simple beyond or a simple inside of language, on the one side and the other of some border.'[20] The entire process implies the existence of threat and hostility among the institutions concerned, and readers might well ask why it is that if imaginative literature in works like *A Tale of Two Cities* and *Confessions of Zeno* proves itself so open to sister-institutions like Carlylean history and Freudian psychoanalysis, Derrida's vocabulary should be so insistently morbid and scatological in its implications.

The point is that in passages such as these Derrida is not *defending* the opposition of 'contamination' and 'the proper' as an intellectual structure, but ascribing it to a critical tradition bent on preserving the purity of literature: a tradition he wishes to deconstruct. (Such a tradition, as Derrida has it, returns ' "strategically," ideally, to an origin or to a "priority" held to be simple, intact, normal, pure, standard, self-identical, in order *then* to think in terms of derivation, complication, deterioration, accident, etc.') The critical tradition Derrida has in mind here is not confined to the art-for-art's-sake attitudes of Walter Pater, Oscar Wilde, and others. On the contrary, it extends throughout the twentieth century, from Croce and Jean-Pierre Richard to T.S. Eliot, the New Critics, and F.R. Leavis. This is the tradition Derrida had in mind, no doubt, when, asked whether 'the tradition of literary criticism has shown itself to be as governed by metaphysical presuppositions as philosophy, and more so than the literary texts it treats of', he responded: 'To give too sweeping a reply, I would say yes' ('TSI' 52). When, in his *Æsthetic*, Croce constructs a theory that seeks to protect the artistic 'intuition' from the philosophical 'concept'; when Wimsatt and Beardsley sweep aside 'the intentional fallacy', or concern themselves in the same discussion with the relation of Eliot's notes to Eliot's poetry in *The Waste Land*; or when F.R. Leavis speaks (in 'Reality and Sincerity') of one of Thomas Hardy's poems in terms of its being 'never anything other than self-communing', these critics are all regarding literature (or in Croce's case the arts generally) as a pure entity from which contaminatory influences should be diverted.[21] It is important that traditional criticism appreciate the force and the implications of Derrida's argument here.

But whereas traditional criticism has undoubtedly been 'governed by metaphysical presuppositions' to some extent, critics sympathetic to Derrida's analysis should be cautious of making generalizations too sweeping in their implications. 'A text', as Derrida points out, 'is never *totally* governed by "metaphysical assumptions"' ('TSI' 53; my italics). The belief that a literary–critical text might be so governed perhaps lies behind Derek Attridge's idea that traditional criticism has (at all times and in all places, as it were) taken for granted 'the rules of syllogistic reason, the ultimate priority of meaning over its mode of articulation, and such fundamental and absolute oppositions as the intelligible and the sensible, form and matter, subject and object, nature and culture, presence and absence'.[22] Some of the oppositions on this list, it is true, have escaped the attention of traditional criticism. Samuel Johnson probably did have a fairly settled view of the opposition of nature to culture. But to say that Coleridge felt the same about form and matter, or T.S. Eliot about presence and absence, or Dryden about the intelligible and the sensible, is absurd. The same belief, that a literary–critical text might be totally governed by metaphysical assumptions, leads Attridge to decide that the 'moral influence' of literature has been 'represented in the most generalized of terms' by traditional literary criticism,[23] which is demonstrably untrue. To use two words neither of which is remotely satisfactory (and which have been proved to be unsatisfactory by traditional literary criticism), it is the 'aesthetic' and the 'moral' curiosity and imaginativeness of traditional criticism that supplement – or, if we prefer Derrida's more melodramatic vocabulary, rupture and undermine – its leanings towards the 'metaphysical'. Precisely because no traditional literary criticism of value has ever been able to keep separate the aesthetic and the moral as philosophical categories, it has never fully subscribed to the metaphysical programme, whatever it may have thought it was doing or intended to do. 'What *is* purely literary criticism?' Leavis exasperatedly asked himself on one occasion.[24] In so far as traditional criticism seeks that peculiar closeness of response to the words on the page upon which it places so much value, then no doubt it runs the risk of falling victim to metaphysical assumptions about 'self-communing', self-presence, organicism, and related shibboleths – though there is plenty of traditionally-orientated criticism which avoids that risk, in my view. But such criticism is also able to recognize that the whole critical enterprise is 'contaminated' by issues which the indivisibility of its aesthetic and moral responses itself raises. That 'closeness of response' is a species of moral curiosity which is predicated on the recognition, not the denial, that the aesthetic realm is contaminated by forces from outside itself. So far is that realm contaminated, indeed, that the notion of a pure, 'proper', or 'poetic' aesthetic sphere, had it entered the heads of those traditional critics worth consulting, would not have stayed there long: the evidence for which conclusion being the very difficulties such critics have always had with a category like 'aesthetic'.

Nor does traditional literary criticism take steps to evade such difficulties. In fact it takes particular interest in attempting to describe and occasionally to sharpen them, because it has to respond to the contamination found in literary works themselves. No reader of *Hamlet*, or *Gulliver's Travels*, or *Persuasion*, or 'The Love Song of J. Alfred Prufrock' has ever been likely to subscribe, in anything other than a wish-fulfilling way, to a notion of the human subject as a Kantian transcendental signified. Quite the reverse. The capacity of traditional criticism to encounter problems relating to 'the intelligible and the sensible, form and matter, subject and object, nature and culture, presence and absence' lends it a degree of flexibility of which Derrida's vocabulary ('assumptions', 'presuppositions', etc.) takes little account. For every case where critics do fall back on purist assumptions, there are others where such critics' moral curiosity leads them to revise (or at least recognize) the assumptions they are working with, and which they feel their readers might share.[25] This may not involve a recognition of the radical dehiscence Derrida finds in the written syntagma; but neither does it necessarily involve an obsessive pursuit of 'purity' or a mindless parroting of metaphysics.

Derrida's idea that an opposition between contamination and the proper is a metaphysical assumption of traditional literary criticism has a degree of justification then, provided we remember that an equally strong current moves in a different direction. Nor is it the problem that Derrida has kept certain superstitions alive in order to legitimate the prospect of calling them into question, as Gerald Graff puts it.[26] Rather he has tended to present one half of the opposition (institutional contamination) as being more powerful an intellectual phenomenon than the other (resistance). Moreover, he has left this opposition lying around, so to speak, for use in hands far clumsier and less responsible than his own. (He himself ruefully mentions 'the global and massive effect to which books are unfortunately reduced once they have been closed and once they start being discussed'.)[27] What I have called institutional criticism depends upon a crudification of just such an opposition, to the effect that literature's autonomy ('the proper') is fatally compromised (or in fact revealed to be nothing but an ideological construction) by the very contaminatory forces from which traditional criticism seeks to protect it. What we have in such a doctrine is not a deconstruction of the 'metaphysical' opposition but merely an inversion of it, and only an apparent inversion at that. The worst forms of institutionalism are so besotted by this inversion that, paradoxically, they themselves end up defending a kind of weightlessly purist notion of literature, made up of catch-phrases like 'the play of the signifier' and 'nothing outside of the text' on the one hand, and ill-informed and morally unimaginative attacks on the individual subject and the referential function of language on the other. Derrida is by no means to be blamed for being the unwitting source of such crudifications; and in so far as his language permits, he opposes their circulation.

An important element in such crudifications is the idea that literature itself and the contaminatory influences to which it is open are beyond any conceivable reckoning. And we can see elements in Derrida's intellectual project which lend credence to such an idea. Thus Derrida's jump from the ideality of literature to Hegel's semiology may seem quite arbitrary or capricious, but Hegel's semiology (or rather, Derrida's deconstruction *of* it) is in fact only one of a possibly infinite series of perspectives on or instances of that principle of contamination Derrida describes. His writings have gone on to deal with many more 'according', as he puts it, 'to a rule of increasing complexity, generalization, or accumulation'.[28] After 1974, for example, he began to place particular and overtly institutional emphasis

> on rights and on what is proper, what is one's own, on the rights of property, on copyright, on the signature and the market, on the market for painting or, more generally, for culture and all its representations, on speculation and what is proper, one's own, on the name, on destination and restitution, on all the institutional borders and structures of discourses, on the whole machinery of publishing and on the media. ('TT' 48–9)

It is less the contents of the list that are symptomatic than its insatiably speculative tendency. It has an almost Miltonic zest for accumulation: for piling up and displaying the elements it seeks to encompass. The number of instances of institutional contamination Derrida might describe in this fashion, from Hegel's semiology to the signature, is to all intents and purposes infinite. There will never be any end to them nor will Derrida ever find himself having enumerated and evaluated their influence: first, because the putting of a limit to such influences will always appear to be arbitrary; and second, because it is impossible to say what further combinations they will form with *other* influences, enumerated or not.

This is not a cause for regret, Derrida's admirers believe. It is not the destination but the trip itself that counts. There are, I think, only two destinations it could arrive at. Either the number and influence of such institutional contaminations can in time be understood, leaving us with a kind of inalienable, uncontaminated rump or residue of which we must again ask 'what is literature?'; or (more likely) we will find that literature is nothing *but* the sum or the focus of its contaminations. Derrida himself prefers to keep permanently on the move.[29] Nor is it surprising that what we often find in his work is a highly self-conscious restlessness (about words, titles, the provenance of the piece concerned, and introductory argumentative terms and positions, for example) that finds vent in a display of hypertrophic, polysemic extemporization.[30] Such extemporizations always end somewhere, as extemporizations must. After twenty-five years of 'deconstructive questioning' ('TT' 42) Derrida did ultimately register, present, and defend the thesis the institutional standing of which had preoccupied him for so long. But institutional criticism generally speaking often depends on an alliance between Derrida's stress on the idealist, 'metaphysical' opposition of the proper and contamination, on the one hand, and this speculative, accumulative element in his writing and thought (going along with the principle of contamination), on the other. Rather than move *beyond* the idealist opposition, such criticism simply inherits the opposite term and bases itself in the opposite camp: if the traditionalist metaphysicians are purists, we shall aid and abet the contaminants. The net effect has been a view that the posited purity of literature and criticism is one bombarded by an absolutely unquantifiable number of contaminatory effects. Not only is criticism quite incapable of establishing rational grounds for itself in such a maelstrom (any attempt to do so being either nakedly or surreptitiously interventionist, so the argument runs), but literature itself is equally unable to evaluate, resist, convert, or otherwise regulate the influences to which it is subject.

There is an important issue raised here about the nature of Derrida's work and of his influence; and it might help explain the success and failure of deconstruction to look at it historically. As I began to suggest in the Introduction, Derrida's project was nothing much less than a hugely ambitious attack on Platonism and the Western philosophical tradition deriving from it – an attack inspired to some extent, of course, by his immediate intellectual predecessors, Nietzsche and Heidegger above all. It was Plato and people like him, Derrida argued in effect, who opposed the proper to contamination for their own intellectual purposes. He urged us to deconstruct the entire opposition and get beyond it, much as a critic of colonialism might urge his or her followers to get beyond the entire colonial set of oppositions between us and them, white and black, powerful and powerless, etc. But in the end it appears that while Derrida could see the promised land he could not get there, and certainly most of those influenced by him could not. Instead what he did as often as not (though he wriggled in the snare most piteously on occasion), and what those travelling alongside him did almost inevitably, was not to transcend the opposition at all but simply to join the other side: to seek common cause with those manifestations of any and every kind that the Platonic tradition tended to marginalize. So in most feminist literary theory, post-colonialist literary theory, orientalist literary theory, etc., we see the empire striking back, the repressed returning, the wretched of the earth and the insulted and injured asserting themselves against the centre. In due course deconstruction became a philosophical ally of traditional leftist thought, and got sucked into the very dialectic it sought to transcend. It offered sophisticated weapons of aggression and hermeneutics of suspicion to the intellectual forces who at last had a foot on the Platonic barricade. No wonder it was so enthusiastically taken up in the years immediately after 1968, when direct protest had its chance and failed, and when the

Solzhenitsyn affair finally despatched the Communist 'great experiment'. But no wonder it crumpled, too – for Derrida is, to put it crudely, an anarchist among socialists, a Bakunin among Marxists. He wanted to deconstruct the entire circus; those who took him up only wanted to change the ringmaster. In terms of literary criticism he wanted to get beyond the proper/contamination opposition to somewhere else where the nature of literature might truly be said to be; contemporary literary theory, overwhelmingly, from New Historicism and cultural studies to 'queer lit.' and all stations in between wants to preserve the opposition, attack the purist metaphysic (which is a straw man in any case), and set aside any aspect of literature which might tend to disrupt business as usual.

In the end, then, Derrida did not transcend the dialectic, or transcended it only intermittently by using a language of his own few could understand; he *expanded* the dialectic, almost infinitely in every direction ('speculation and what is proper, one's own, on the name, on destination and restitution, on all the institutional borders and structures of discourses, on the whole machinery of publishing and on the media', etc.). The fundamentally leftist intellectual movement that carried him to fame had an insatiable appetite for things of this kind; his attempts to get beyond them ('the linked series formed by the trace, *différance*, undecidables, dissemination, the supplement, the graft, the hymen, the parergon, etc.'), on the other hand, hardly interested that movement at all. We can see Derrida's crisis at work even in the work of his summarized in this chapter: he could point to the great opposition of the proper and the contaminated, and he could call for its deconstruction; but on those occasions when he came closest to carrying that deconstruction out he lost his readers in the murk, and the temptation to slip back into the endless and gratifying task of enumerating the sources of anti-purist contamination was ever-present. So, instead of a concentrated and meaningful attack on what is central in the Western tradition, and instead of the genuinely new theory of literature which he anticipated would be the result, what Derrida provided was an extended frittering-away of his project as he circled his Platonic other – he being gallantly supported by his admirers, of course, who always told him the margins were more important than the centre.

That is, I think, why there is a slippage in Derrida between the project announced and the amount actually achieved: between calling superstitions into question and keeping them alive. But just because writers fail to do what they want does not mean everything they get done is worthless – far from it. (F.R. Leavis is a strikingly similar case of an immense intellectual project that was ultimately thwarted or frittered away; but Leavis said many excellent things before he became terminally obsessed by the relative importance of T.S. Eliot and D.H. Lawrence.) Somewhere in Derrida, between the deconstructionist mountaineer lost in the fog and the routine genealogist of contamination, is a writer – again, much like Leavis, if I may say so – who knows that literature is something and who is trying by every power at his command to say what is is. So it is that any enterprise of genuinely deconstructive questioning depends upon there being a lively sense of the autonomy of literature: of just the kind, in fact, to which Derrida shows himself perfectly alive. His arriving at Hegel's semiology, or the rules of copyright, or the nature of the signature, all in fact, by his own account, depend on some pre-existent notion of literature. You cannot chart the orbits of contaminatory moons around a vacuum; such moons would fall into a vacuum and leave us with no institutions whatsoever: only an unimaginable, unintelligible chaos. Just as the ideality of literature is contaminated by psychoanalysis so, as Jacques Lacan would be the first to point out, the converse is true. The process is an entirely mutual one. We then either have to ask what is doing the contaminating in each case, or admit that we can never know and that what we have are not discrete institutions at all (or anything like them) but an endless reflexivity of contamination which renders Derrida's original series of questions (what takes place between psychoanalysis and literature, for example) meaningless.[31]

Framed in this way, my argument with Derrida, which is less with him than with those critics who, following his example, threaten to turn all literary debate into a debate about institutions, may seem to be taking an abstract turn. Nor do I want to suggest that the only alternative to such abstractions is some kind of Anglo-Saxon empiricism. On the contrary: in the chapters that follow I, too, will resort to the institutions of philosophy, psychoanalysis, and history, but in a different spirit. The point is that the resort to institutions cuts both ways. On the one hand, we are bound to recognize that the institution of literature *is* contaminated by its fellows, and in something like the radical, highly complex way Derrida has outlined. Literature is to that extent an institutionalized agency formed, moulded, and influenced by its own institutional existence as well by that of others. Indeed literature positively revels in such contaminations. On the other hand, we must also recognize the extent to which the institution of literature is capable of resisting such contaminations as well as submitting to them. There is a cynical definition of a pessimist (who finds his glass half empty) and an optimist (who finds it half full). I wish I could say that my argument with those critics who deny the ideality of literature and resort to institutions as a basis for doing so is a similarly indifferent matter of perception and mental attitude. But it is not. Derrida, Richard Rorty, Freud, and the New Historicists all see the glass as very much less than half empty; and I see it as very much more than half full.

I said earlier that most of Derrida's work suggests that the question 'what is literature?' is a question to be answered only in institutional terms. 'To what and to whom is this due?', as he himself put it. But there is at least one important exception to this rule: or rather, one piece in particular which implies that such a rule may have exceptions. In another of his writings about the institutions of tertiary education Derrida analyses what he calls 'a certain concrete actuality in the problems that assail us in the university'.[32] The concrete actuality he has in mind is the contaminatory threat to the independence of the university presented by 'multinational military–industrial complexes or techno-economic networks, or rather international technomilitary networks that are apparently multi- or trans-national in form' ('PR' 11). 'We have only to mention telecommunications and data processing', he goes on, 'to assess the extent of the phenomenon' – and there follows another of those lists the speculative nature of which I have already commented upon:

> the 'orientation' of research is limitless, everything in these areas proceeds 'in view' of technical and instrumental security. At the service of war, of national and international security, research programs have to encompass the entire field of information, the stock-piling of knowledge, the workings and thus also the essence of language and of all semiotic systems, translation, coding and decoding, the play of presence and absence, hermeneutics, semantics, structural and generative linguistics, pragmatics, rhetoric.

Should literature and literary criticism feel themselves removed from this set of contaminatory developments, they are wrong, for a similar use of 'literature, poetry, the arts and fiction in general' might be made in 'communications strategy, the theory of commands, [and] the most refined military pragmatics of jussive utterances' ('PR' 13). The distinction conventionally made (by 'metaphysicians') between applied and pure forms of academic research, or between practical and imaginative forms of writing are fictions. Nor is this a case of vulgar censorship on the part of the military–industrial complex; that complex now functions 'through multiple channels that are decentralized, [and] difficult to bring together into a system' ('PR' 13). The contamination is as invisible as it is insidious; moreover it has already, in Derrida's view, achieved 'the university's total subjection to the technologies of informatization' ('PR' 14).

That institutions like universities are liable to be permeated by contamination of this kind is unarguable. Nor is the case any different where 'literature, poetry, the arts and fiction in general' are concerned. At certain times and in certain instances literature has proved itself shockingly complicit with contaminatory forces emanating from the military–industrial complex. (Wordsworth's 'Thanksgiving Ode' of 1816 springs to mind.) But again, we are bound to feel that the bulk of Derrida's persuasive skill has been spent in enumerating the forces of contamination on the one hand, and their hapless victims among the university disciplines on the other. A text may never be 'totally governed' by metaphysical assumptions, but it would appear universities can be 'totally subjected' to the counterparts of those assumptions operating in the public sphere. So diverse are the multiple and decentralized channels of evil influence that the possibility of their being turned back seems slender indeed: more so if those who might recognize their existence are themselves totally subjected to that influence.

The implications for universities of such an argument are grim. But I doubt we need feel so oppressed with misgivings when we turn to literature. The case of Charles Dickens, for example, suggests that the scope, scale, and diversity of contaminatory emanations from institutions like the military–industrial complex, far from stifling, invalidating, or prohibiting our capacity to comprehend them, actually inspires certain authors to undertake exactly that task. Dickens' ability to encompass the vast and indissoluble forces of appropriation and corruption omnipresent in his society is testified by novel after novel, from *Oliver Twist* to *Our Mutual Friend*. It is the very challenge that inspired him. Nor is Dickens by any means a unique case: Jane Austen, Henry James, D.H. Lawrence, and James Joyce were all capable of achieving a similar understanding of contamination in their differing orbits of fictional interest, from *Pride and Prejudice* to *The Spoils of Poynton* and from *Women in Love* to *Ulysses*. For what are such novels if they are not, among other things, examinations of the contaminations and corruptions emanating from materialism, acquisitiveness, possessiveness, and colonial parochialism: examinations springing, not from some abstract, preconceived notion of human imperfectability, but from the experience of individuals in particular social situations?

Nor do we have to turn to classic literature for illustrations of this capacity. Martin Amis' highly Dickensian novel, *London Fields*, is explicitly concerned with the contaminatory effects of the military–industrial complex on human relations in general, on sexual relations in particular, and on authorial self-consciousness above all. It is not a success on the scale of *Our Mutual Friend* – a novel with which it has several striking affiliations. A promised nuclear catastrophe, for example, which Amis sees in highly dramatized terms, is finally transformed into nothing more momentous or life-threatening than a Guy Fawkes' Night fireworks display. But there is no need to regard this as evidence that contemporary fiction, like the contemporary university, is in a state of 'total subjection to the technologies of informatization'. On the contrary: whereas *London Fields* is in many ways a portentous treatment of the issue of nuclear war, it is also a robust, humorous, and wholly dramatic *mutation* of the language, grammar, and dialect of such technologies: any such mutation being also a kind of resistance. No one familiar with the British newspaper industry's coverage of international military tension could fail to recognize such acts of mutation at work in the novel. On one occasion the hero of the narrative has his indifference to 'the Crisis' challenged by his wife, and turns to his paper for support:

> Over the past month Keith had kept himself abreast of the Crisis by sometimes reading the filler that his tabloid sometimes ran at the foot of page fourteen. The little headline varied. YANKS: &@f*! or RED NYET or GRRSKI! Or, once, in unusually small type: TOWEL-HEAD DEADLOCK. Keith now turned to page fourteen with a flourish. There was an article by the Slimming Editor on the health of the President's wife. But no filler.[33]

This is a point of great importance. The very scope and scale of contaminatory influence at work in institutions provides inspiration for works of literature. Despite its 'radical precariousness and the radical form of its historicity'[34] – or of course because of these things – literature has proved itself an immensely resilient way of looking at the world. If a moral problem does arise in this area, it is the extent to which imaginative authors revel in the insidiousness of the coercive structures whose existence they have intimated. Jane Austen could be quite as unforgiving in deploying first impressions in her novels as

Lizzie Bennet is in life; Henry James was just as willing to wallow in the paraphernalia of 'good taste' as the heroine of *The Spoils of Poynton*; Dickens' *Barnaby Rudge* reveals an imagination nearly as violent in its attitude towards women as were the forces of bigotry that novel sought to analyse; and Lawrence could be at least as sexually prescriptive as the Edwardians whose sexual cant he detested. But this is not a moral problem for authors alone: it is a moral problem for all of us.

Of course Derrida, too, wishes to see the university and its fellow-institutions ('literature, poetry, the arts and fiction in general') resist the appropriations and reappropriations of its work by the military–industrial complex, and this makes 'The Principle of Reason' a horse of a different colour from 'The Time of a Thesis'. Above all, the former is an explicit attempt 'to define new responsibilites in the face of the university's total subjection to the technologies of informatization', and it is interesting to see what Derrida believes such responsibilities incur. First and foremost they involve 'a community of thought' which would – as we might expect – 'interrogate the essence of reason and the principle of reason'. Moreover:

> It is not certain that such thinking can bring together a community or found an institution in the traditional sense of these words. What is meant by community and institution must be rethought. This thinking must also unmask – an infinite task – all the ruses of end-orienting reason, the paths by which apparently disinterested research can find itself indirectly reappropriated, reinvested by pro-grams of all sorts. ('PR' 16)

What we have here, running alongside Derrida's habitual emphasis on the infinitude of institutional contamination (and another typical slide from deconstructing a proper/contamination opposition to an occupation of the opposite term), is a clear statement of principle: that resistance to such contamination involves the remoulding of the insti-tutions concerned themselves. The institution may be thoroughly con-taminated, but it can still be 'rethought' – which suggests it is not thoroughly contaminated at all. 'It is not a matter simply of questions that one *formulates* while submitting onself … to the principle of reason,' Derrida goes on, 'but also of preparing oneself thereby to *transform* the modes of writing, approaches to pedagogy, the procedures of academic exchange, the relation to languages, to other disciplines, to the institu-tion in general, to its inside and outside' ('PR' 17; my italics). It is pre-cisely this step, envisaging as it does (*pace* Bennington) not only an institution with an outside and an inside, but a transformation of 'modes of writing', of the individual's relationship to institutions, and of each by the other, that is insufficiently stressed in Derrida's other accounts of contamination, and often lacking altogether in other critics' approaches to the issue. It is a step leading directly to the conclusion that 'The decision of thought cannot be an intra-institutional event, an academic moment' ('PR' 19).

If imaginative literature has found itself able to engage with institutional influences without losing its autonomy, the same is true of criticism. A moment's reflection will suggest that this must be so. But the autonomy of literary criticism that finds its *raison d'être* in the autonomy of literature is not an absolute one either; nor does it depend on that view of intellectual activity described by Carlyle in his essay, 'On History', where 'Poetry, Divinity, Politics, Physics, have each their adherents and adversaries; each little guild supporting a defensive and offensive war for its own special domain'. Of all humanistic intellectual disciplines literary criticism is the most open to influence from outside itself. Critics are much more likely to make forays into philosophy, social history, and psychoanalysis, than philosophers, historians, and analysts are to make the return trip, as Derrida's remarks quoted at the beginning of this chapter show. Literary critics regularly find themselves writing about Victorian sexuality, for example, or the Tudor court, or Puritanism, or sincerity and authenticity. This is so for one good reason above all others: that literature *itself* and the individual novels, plays, and poems which comprise it, are so curious and so open to influence and to contamination even while preserving prerogatives of their own. Literature is that 'Free Emporium' Carlyle felt the historical past in its totality to be, and the fact that academic and institutional 'belligerents' do not 'peaceably meet and furnish themselves there' as Carlyle assumed they would, but in fact behave like bargain-hunters at Harrods' sale, only goes to prove the point. It is for this reason and no other that departments of literature do in actuality find themselves 'central' to the humanities in a way which departments of Sociology, Psychology, Philosophy, Anthropology, Political Science, and History can never be: not out of a spirit of blind imperialism or conceit, but because their object of study, while remaining peculiarly deaf to many aspects of human life, is the closest thing we have to an integrated view of it. It is because in literature all those social forces and manifestations which other disciplines study in isolation are encountered together and in the lives of individuals much like ourselves, that the institutions of literature and criticism are inevitably more contentious areas than are the other humanities. (So contentious in fact that some would like to replace departments of literature altogether with departments of cultural studies, or have already done so in everything but name.) There never has been a time in the history of critical reflection on literature, inside universities or outside them, when this has not been so.

I hope it will become clear that the principle of autonomy that is outlined in this study is in fact consonant with a great deal in Derrida's own position – or at least the position he points to or describes. If literature is a specialized form of thought, to an important extent self-explanatory and self-justifying, it is an exploratory and dramatic mode of communication which is involved less in communicating the edicts of 'metaphysics' and more in breaking them down: deconstructing them, if you like. In this sense literature really is concerned with disturbing the questions 'what is?' and 'what does it mean', and so what is said here does not (hopefully) constitute a return to what Derrida calls 'the "I-don't-understand-therefore-it's-irrational-non-analytic-magical-illogical-perverse-seductive-diabolical" that has always signed the triumph of the old obscurantism'.[35] In that respect, this study, too, is interested in 'saying otherwise'. I do, it is true, feel that Derrida's perennial tactic of maximizing the forces of institutional contamination and minimizing literature's capacity to cope with such forces, has led many critics to the belief that literature does not possess such a capacity at all. Were Derrida simply a philosopher with a literary–critical bent (like Richard Rorty or Alasdair MacIntyre) such reservations would be grave enough. But his, clearly, is not as simple a case as theirs, whereas his influence is a great deal wider. Whether his most constant interest is directed towards that writing which is called literary I am not sure; but certainly his interest in literature is more searching than Rorty's or MacIntyre's, and it is for precisely this reason that I wish not to reject his conclusions but to supplement them in this study by pursuing an interest from another point of the compass.

1.3

To speak of literature preserving its prerogatives is only half the story. I want now to turn away from the negative side of this study – the criticisms it makes of Derrida here; those it will make of Richard Rorty, Freud, and others in the chapters that follow; and, indeed, the negative definition of literature that is the result of such criticisms – to the more positive points this book will try to make.

The first thing to say is that however often I take issue with them, the philosophers, psychoanalysts, and theoreticians of history discussed in the chapters below make an irreplaceable contribution to the discussion, the study, and the understanding of literature. This study is quite curt with Richard Rorty; quite curt with Freud; very curt indeed, some might say, with the New Historicists. There really have been occasions, I think, on which self-evidently partial accounts of literature have been presented as primary, or revolutionary, or all-encompassing. Freud's attitude can be immensely hubristic, just as Rorty's can be smugly pluralistic, and the New Historicists' can be blindly 'scientific'. In each case there is a notable lack of real intellectual curiosity and flexibility, and that is a pronounced intellectual demerit where the study of literature is concerned. But I hope it is also made very clear that Freud, for example, presented issues no literary critic could have envisaged or can ignore now; that certain principles derived from Object Relations open up certain literary texts in a quite remarkable and sympathetic way; that Alasdair MacIntyre can speculate with great boldness and authority where classical tragedy is concerned; that Paul Ricoeur is on to something in his discussion of time in history and literature; and so on and so forth. This is not simply the tokenistic and passive stance of defending the right of people to say things you do not agree with. What is true of literature is or should be true of the criticism devoted to it: if literature's activity involves taking up and converting the institutional influences to which it is subject, then the same is true of criticism and there is no justification for it to be aloof or defensive in this respect. Literature is itself overwhelmingly an inclusive, all-engrossing, all-welcoming medium: and it would be an enormous and culpable misjudgement for me to encourage a 'hands off literature!' attitude.

So it should be clear from the outset: works of literature are necessarily in dialogue with the historical developments which surround them, the psychological occurrences which precede them, and the institutional structures which mould them. 'There is no creature whose inward being is so strong', as George Eliot points out at the close of *Middlemarch*, 'that it is not greatly determined by what lies outside it.' But the dialogue which provides literature with its autonomy, and in so doing provides literary critics with intellectual autonomy, too, is that dialogue the poem, play, or novel initiates and sustains with its writer and its readers about *itself*. And this is very much what I mean by the activity we find in literature: activity which helps establish its autonomy. This is not an argument for the ideality of literature but in fact for its contingency; for any work is contingent not just upon those structures, occurrences, and developments mentioned above, but also upon its own activity: the transformations it itself presents both to its author and its readers.

One reason for considering the proposition that literature might present a form of activity which transforms institutional contamination is that so many imaginative writers have themselves spoken of or intuited something similar in their own work. 'Things which I do half at Random', as Keats put it, 'are afterwards confirmed by my judgment in a dozen features of Propriety'.[36] Isaac Babel, too, in a cautious interview given before the Union of Soviet Writers in 1937, made the disquietingly formalist confession that 'When you put pen to paper, there's no telling where it may lead you or where the devil you may end up. You don't always fall in with the rhythm or with the expressions as they've taken shape in your mind.'[37] The widow of another writer murdered by Stalin, Osip Mandelstam, said something similar: 'The whole process of composition', she argued, 'is one of straining to catch and record something compounded of harmony and sense as it is relayed from an unknown source and gradually forms itself into words.'[38] 'Habent sua fata libelli', as Thomas Mann wrote about his initial, unambitious, plans for the books which became *Buddenbrooks, The Magic Mountain*, and *Joseph and his Brothers*, 'not only after their publication, but particularly during their genesis. The author knows little about them when he lays hands on them.'[39] 'When I think indeed of those of my many false measurements that have resulted, after much anguish, in decent symmetries,' Henry James wrote in the preface to *The Awkward Age*, 'I find the whole case, I profess, a theme for the philosopher.'

> The little ideas one wouldn't have treated save for the design of keeping them small, the developed situations that one would never with malice prepense have undertaken, the long stories that had thoroughly meant to be short, the short subjects that had underhandedly plotted to be long, the hypocrisy of modest beginnings, the audacity of misplaced middles, the triumph of intentions never entertained – with these patches, as I look about, I see my experience paved: an experience to which nothing is wanting save, I confess, some grasp of its final lesson.

Such testimony is not conclusive, of course. These writers might simply be deluded. But a great many authors do appear to experience something similar to what Keats, Babel, Mandelstam, Mann, and James between them describe. The South African-born novelist and critic,

Dan Jacobson, for example, gives us a particularly intense manifestation of the theme: not in himself but in a young and highly egocentric writer of fiction described in one of his novels, who reflects on an important development in his work:

> For the very first time since he'd begun work on this long story he'd felt it beginning to respond to him, like some living thing; it was showing its own motives, which he had to elicit, its own shape, which he had to follow. It was extraordinary, he said, the change that had taken place in his feeling about the work. A fortnight ago he'd felt like a man with a flat tire and a pump in his hand; he had simply been pumping away, almost mechanically. But now there was nothing mechanical about what he was doing: he had to be alert, cautious, obedient to the demands that he could feel the work wanted to make of him. For the first time he'd realized that this was the 'escape' which his work offered and which people talked about without knowing what they meant by it. Once escaped from oneself, one submitted oneself to an impersonal will. And it didn't matter that the will had originated in oneself. Once it had reached a certain degree of detachment its existence was as objective as any other – at least as objective as all the other wills whose reality people never questioned, but which were also projections of themselves: the will of the state, or the will of industry, or the will of God.[40]

This adds something important to the almost off-the-cuff remarks by Keats and the others. The young writer concerned has to submit himself, on occasion, 'to the demands that he could feel the work wanted to make of him'; he had to give way, on occasion, 'to an impersonal will'. But it should be noted that at no stage does Jacobson entertain the idea that words on the page are actively volitional. The will originated in the author, without doubt; only it manifested itself – at least in part – as something impersonal, something very much 'other', even though it was, in fact, a projection of himself. The experience matters, as Leavis would say, not because it is mine but because it is what it is.

Two alternative ways of explaining the effect Jacobson describes present themselves. His character's experience, we might say, is either one of poetic inspiration or of mere chance. Neither explanation seems to me to be very helpful – or is helpful only up to a point. No doubt some heightened sense of awareness and attention does visit authors; and no doubt chance plays an immensely important role in writing or in any other artistic activity. But actually I think that 'inspiration' is only the inflated and sentimentalized word we use to describe precisely what

Jacobson describes here in such lugubriously everyday terms ('A fortnight ago he'd felt like a man with a flat tire and a pump in his hand'). Equally, chance explains only a very little. It is chance that had Charlotte Brontë make a start on *Jane Eyre* while her father was recovering from an operation on his cataracts; it is chance that had the words 'Unreal City' start a paragraph in 'The Burial of the Dead' section of *The Waste Land*. But what chance blows in, chance will blow away: it is because something is already going on in works like these that Keats speaks of doing things only '*half* at Random', that eye-injuries become a major imaginative obsession in *Jane Eyre*, and that 'Unreal City' in Eliot's poem produces 'Under the brown fog of a winter dawn', which in turn produces 'I had not thought death had undone so many': the death-knell of the crowd flowing over London Bridge.[41] In each case the writer concerned had to be alert, cautious, and obedient to the demands that he could feel the work wanted to make of him or her. Left to themselves, chance items can only aggregate; it is because they present themselves to the author as the action of an impersonal will that they hatch and generate patterns of meaning in works of literature: patterns which the author (like the reader, in due course) feels compelled to follow. Moreover, if this process throws up opportunities it also imposes constraints: the author finds the same impersonal will prevents him doing what he might otherwise intend. If a poet finds he cannot do something, he must invent something else more appropriate, and if that something is successful it imposes further constraints as regards the rest of the poem, and so on and so forth. Every constraint presents itself as an opportunity, and vice versa. There is no need, I believe, to posit the existence of volitional agency to ink and paper in order to call this a kind of activity.

The examples given from Charlotte Brontë and T.S. Eliot are necessarily small in scale. Fuller illustrations will be given in Chapter 3, because this is an issue where we are dealing with writers' perceptions and the way in which they respond to them, so psychological aspects clearly come into play. But it is this phenomenon, this dialectic of prompting and recognition, inescapably associated with the text itself, that is the activity of literature this study stands for and seeks to illuminate. Many years after writing the passage quoted above, Dan Jacobson came at the issue once more, only from the critic's side of the fence rather than the artist's:

> It is not and never can be the ebb and flow of events outside a novel or poem (great historical events, little biographical events, 'movements', issues, trends, changes in sensibility, and all the rest) which

most searchingly examine the assertions and implications of any kind which it contains. All these matter less to it than the ebb and flow of the events in the story or poem itself. Its power lies in the fact that every element of which it is constituted, from the largest development of its plot or story to the tiniest inflection of its rhythm, is itself an 'event', which comments on every other and is in turn commented on by every other. Each draws something from, and expresses something of, all the warring ideas and ambitions of the writer: many of which he can acknowledge and repudiate in no form other than that given to him by his art. Ideally speaking, in a work of literature there are no privileged areas – even if the author himself tries to set them up – which are protected from the reciprocal or fluctuating processes just described, or which are entitled to special consideration by virtue of the topics they comprehend or the assertions they contain. Indeed, the greater the work, the less it will permit the assertions made within it, in any form, to stand free from itself; the more it will resist declarations of independence by any of its parts.[42]

It is by virtue of this element in literature that it is able to 'resist' and to transform not only those centrifugal forces which might allow parts of the work to stand free from the whole, as Jacobson suggests, but also those centripetal forces described by Derrida; not only the comparatively clumsy forces of historical or psychological causation but also the sophisticated, sequestered velleities of institutional contamination.

But here another very important issue presents itself: one which, like the last, must be treated in greater detail later in the study (in this case in Chapter 4). Writers may find their experience paved, as James put it, with patches of contrariness, but it is not only imaginative authors who find their experience paved in such a way. Discursive works of history or philosophy, but also the humblest private letters, have a strikingly similar capacity to surprise their authors and their readers by generating unexpected lines of reflection and arriving at unforeseen conclusions:

But the end of Mr Brooke's pen was a thinking organ, evolving sentences, especially of a benevolent kind, before the rest of his mind could well overtake them. It expressed regrets and proposed remedies, which, when Mr Brooke read them, seemed felicitously worded – suprisingly the right thing, and determined a sequel which he had never before thought of. In this case, his pen found it such a pity that young Ladislaw should not have come into the neighbourhood just at that time, in order that Mr Brooke might make his acquaintance more fully, and that they might go over the long-neglected Italian drawings together – it also felt such an interest in a young man who was starting in life with a stock of ideas – that by the end of the second page it had persuaded Mr Brooke to invite young Ladislaw, since he could not be received at Lowick, to come to Tipton Grange. Why not?[43]

Is literature different in degree or in kind from writings like Mr Brooke's? Clearly, Mr Brooke's letter is a central issue both for Derrida and myself; indeed for any critic concerned to assess the autonomy of literature. Earlier I translated into the terms of this study the idea that a person is autonomous to the degree that what he thinks and does cannot be explained without reference to his own activity of mind. And Derrida does quite explicitly recognize a form of what I am calling 'activity' within written texts. What I mean is the canonical Derridean principle of the 'dangerous supplement' and the capacity of texts to deconstruct themselves despite the intentions of their authors. (Some readers may regard these as highly paradoxical, indeed negative forms of 'activity': but they are very close to what I am trying to describe.) 'It is because writing is *inaugural*', he writes, ' ... that it is dangerous and anguishing. It does not know where it is going ... '.[44] What could be more true of Mr Brooke?

But Derrida's view of the inaugural is one this study must differ with in the end: directed as that view is by a limited and parsimonious understanding of what traditional criticism can do. '[T]he notion of an Idea or "interior design" as simply anterior to a work which would supposedly be the expression of it,' he writes, 'is a prejudice: a prejudice of the traditional criticism called *idealist*.'[45] What Derrida describes is a misconception, certainly, shared by many people in all walks of the literary life; but is it really true to say that traditional criticism has spent much of its time labouring under that misconception? What Derrida means by the inaugural, it turns out, is that 'the writer writes *in* a language and *in* a logic whose proper system, laws, and life his discourse by definition cannot dominate absolutely. He uses them only by letting himself, after a fashion and up to a point, be governed by the system.'[46] No wonder he calls it 'capricious only through cowardice'.[47] One more problem is that Derrida emphatically does not regard the dangerous supplement as a form of activity unique to literature. The language and the logic of literature may constitute a specialized variety of *différance* or textuality generally speaking; they may be different from other languages and other logics in degree, but not in kind. On the contrary, despite his initially working out the concept in relation to Rousseau, and despite the fact that literary texts have repeatedly offered him occasions on which to refine or extend the idea, and despite the slippage between 'writing' and 'literature' in an essay like 'Force and Signification', Derrida is just as likely to find the dangerous supplement at work in jurisprudential and constitutional documents, as his publications in such fields indicate.

It is Derrida's belief in so to speak *pre-existing* languages and logics that makes him, in my view, an institutionalist critic *par excellence*, for whom writers are 'after a fashion and up to a point ... *governed by the system*'. (Here once again, we might detect Derrida's habit of joining in the contaminatory process rather than deconstructing it.) That logics and languages exist within and help constitute the institution of literature is clear; I differ from Derrida only in suggesting that works of literature themselves govern and re-legislate the system, not just on occasion or with permission or by chance, but in order to be what they are. Every work of history, psychology, or philosophy involves, at some level or other, a critical reflection on what the institution is to which it belongs; and every such reflection is, 'after a fashion and up to a point', a re-legislation of that institution. Like other forms of discourse, a work of literature comes into being only by virtue of this kind of contestation; unlike them, it must preserve that state of affairs throughout. Works of literature have functions outside this struggle with the institution which gives them birth – they have relations of every kind, without which they would be meaningless – but none of these functions has seniority, and none can be carried out in an institutional context where a pre-existing language and logic governs their disposition or effect. For a work of literature continuously to privilege one of its 'relational' functions (telling the truth, for example, or providing pleasure, or communicating ideology, or issuing moral instruction) over its need to keep such elements in flux would destroy the context in which those functions can be carried out.

1.4

From the use I have made of 'The Time of a Thesis' to represent a certain trend in criticism, and from the scattered references to Richard Rorty, Sigmund Freud, and New Historicism, readers may suspect that this book aspires to membership of what is fast becoming a poisonous genre all its own: the 'anti-Theory' book. That is not its aim. Derrida is trying to do something new in the study of literature (whereas it is my argument with New Historicism, for example, that it is seeking to revive a mode of criticism that is not merely old but antiquated). To do something new is very difficult, and Derrida is to be respected, not pilloried, for making the attempt. It is true, though, that this book does make extensive criticisms of critical writers whose reputations are on the wax, as it were, and who also happen to have done their work in the United States or on the Continent. Among these are Derrida himself, Richard Rorty, Alasdair MacIntyre, Charles Taylor, Martha Nussbaum, Freud, Hayden White, Paul Ricoeur, and American New Historicists like Jerome McGann and Stephen Greenblatt. Conversely, it also depends a great deal on writers whose reputations are, if not on the wane, then much more obscure nowadays, and who also often happen to have done their work in Britain. Among these are Marion Milner, Hanna Segal, Michael Polanyi, R.G. Collingwood, Isaiah Berlin, Cardinal Newman, and even that panjandrum, behemoth, and *bête noire*, F.R. Leavis himself. Moreover, the book is amply provided with illustrative material that also helps me prove my case – material which is drawn from that literature institutionally-minded critics might regard as canonical: from Alexander Pope to James Joyce, Shakespeare to George Eliot, Dickens to Conrad, and Jane Austen to Vladimir Nabokov.

But it is not only to defend myself against the charge of being an Anglocentric and reactionary that I wish to make something of a brief critical raid here on an essay by a notorious reactionary Anglophile, T.S. Eliot. 'Tradition and the Individual Talent' (to which in a more general sense this study is greatly indebted, as the reader will see) helps illustrate three other much more important points: that the distinction between theory and practice which this book is bound on occasion to enforce is itself a theoretical position which literature tends to undermine; that partly for this very reason, and partly by virtue of its dialectic capacity to transform our expectations, literature is able not to resolve but to dramatize and intensify intellectual preoccupations of the theory/practice kind; and that for *this* very reason, every work of literature is itself an act of literary–critical thinking about what literature is: a piece of critical thinking about literature, that is to say, not arrived at *a priori* by the author, but implicit in and embodied in the work itself, uniquely.[48]

This last point has, I think, very important implications for those who, like Derrida, can find an answer to the question 'what is literature?' only in institutions. The institution of literary criticism, Derrida and others argue, 'is a very recent invention', 'installed at the same time as the modern European universities, from the beginning of the nineteenth century, thereabouts'.[49] There is a grain of truth in this, of course. What we think of as 'literary criticism' did become very much more formalized after the Schlegel brothers' lectures on literature of the early 1800s; after Coleridge's lectures and his *Biographia Literaria*; after Hazlitt's lectures and essays; and after Stendhal's *Racine et Shakespeare*. (Nor of course were any of those pieces of criticism institutionally pure and unalloyed: quite the contrary.) With Arnold, Taine, Sainte-Beuve, Saintsbury, Quiller-Couch, and I.A. Richards criticism became more formalized still. But even having granted him all this, Derrida would still have as hard a time convincing us there was no institution of literary criticism in eighteenth-century Britain (for example) as he does convincing us that feminist literary criticism, albeit as 'an identifiable institutional phenomenon', grew up alongside deconstruction at the end of the 1960s ('TSI' 57). For in eighteenth-century Britain we find – at the tip of the iceberg, so to speak – Pope's *Essay on Criticism* and his translations of Homer; Johnson's *English Dictionary* and his *Lives of the Poets*; Boswell's *Life of Johnson*; the editors and critics dicussed by Christopher Ricks in *Milton's Grand Style*; important editions of Shakespeare by Rowe, Pope, Theobald, Warburton, Johnson, Capell, Steevens, and Malone; as well as important studies of the same dramatist by Lord Kames and Maurice Morgann. Then there is the fact that, up to Leavis, almost every major critic in English – from Philip Sidney to T.S. Eliot – was himself a creative writer. Derrida articulates a view of institutions that is itself peculiarly institutional, in the sense that he tends to see the institution of literary criticism as something easily 'identifiable' in terms of its own self-consciousness, something distinct: something, indeed, with simply assignable limits.

This is not only a question of pointing out the literary critics who wrote before the Schlegels, from Aristotle to Dryden, and from Philip Sidney to Boileau, and who therefore pre-dated the institution of literary criticism. Either to accept Derrida's account of the institution of literary criticism *tout court*, or to revise it in such a way, would be to give him far too much ground. The institution of literary criticism, whether academic or not, is not the only place in which critical thinking about literature is carried out. Indeed such critical thinking is carried out at its highest level of intensity in literary works themselves.[50] I do not have in mind here Pope's discussion of 'what oft was thought but ne'er so well expressed' in the *Essay on Criticism*; or Jane Austen's discussion of the novel in *Northanger Abbey*. Nor do I have in mind that different class of instances: the mechanicals' scene from *A Midsummer Night's Dream*, for example; or the massive case of writer's block which impels Wordsworth to review the proper subjects for epic poetry in the first book of *The Prelude*; or Keats' literary–critical and ethical (aesthetic and moral) grilling at the hands of the priestess Moneta which prompts him to similar reflections in the second *Fall of Hyperion*; or Hamlet's speech to the players; or Stephen Dedalus' own speeches on *Hamlet* in the 'Scylla and Charybdis' episode of *Ulysses*. All these manifestations of the critical impulse, real and important as they are, are also dramatically subservient to and dependent upon those acts of critical thought about literature which the novels, poems, and plays concerned themselves embody in taking the form they do. Like them, too, these manifestations are not the author's, strictly speaking; it is not a question of Joyce or Shakespeare putting on his critical hat. Neither the explicit critical ideas which a few works of literature evince nor the implicit ones which every work of literature embodies belong *to* anybody; they belong *in* the individual novels, poems, or plays that fostered them. The presence and action of such implicit critical thinking in works of literature is one of the ways in which we can explain, for example, the widely differing dramatic modes of Shakespeare's four Roman plays; of *Silas Marner* and *Romola* among George Eliot's novels; of *Barnaby Rudge* and *Hard Times* among Dickens'; of *Kangaroo* and *Sons and Lovers* among Lawrence's; Keats' discovery of the ode form; and Byron's discovery of the ottava rima. As literary critics we may find it very difficult to extrapolate or isolate such critical thinking; similarly, other imaginative writers coming after Shakespeare, say, or Joyce, find it very difficult to recognize such thinking, and their responses to it, as *critical* thinking at all. Like most of us they think criticism is done only in institutions.

This does not mean that Shakespeare is the most influential literary critic in English literature. T.S. Eliot himself might lay claim to that distinction. But Shakespeare's critical thought about literature has had an immeasurable impact: less on English drama, perhaps, than on the novel and poetry. The best example I can give of the kind of critical thought Shakespeare carried out in his drama is not mine but S.L. Goldberg's. 'The difference between formalized writing and dramatic writing', Goldberg felt, 'can be seen in a tiny exchange in Shakespeare's *Richard III*, a good deal of which, like a good deal of his early work generally, is written in a mode he had the good luck and the good sense to grow out of'. Goldberg then quoted this passage:

> *Buckingham.*   Now my lord, what shall we do if we perceive
>   Lord Hastings will not yield to our complots?
> *Gloucester.*   Chop off his head ...

'In the question,' Goldberg continued, 'we are aware mainly of the rhetoric; in the reply, we are aware – very sharply aware – of a person.'[51] If what we see in Shakespeare here – feeling his way towards that flexible spoken idiom of his mature work – is not critical thinking about literature then it is hard to say what is. The important point being that Shakespeare did not arrive at this new idiom of Gloucester's by intellection, as it were; on the contrary he arrived at it by means of and in response to the very rhetorical stiffness we see in Buckingham. A fortnight ago, so to speak, he'd felt like a man with a flat tire and a pump in his hand...

Which brings me to 'Tradition and the Individual Talent'. Put simply, tradition occupies the first part of the essay, the individual talent part two, while the third part acts as a summary, a conclusion and, as Eliot himself admits, as a 'halt at the frontier of metaphysics or mysticism', into which part two was in danger of turning. Part one of Eliot's essay is the presentation of a series of iconoclastic paradoxes about tradition so familiar they hardly need repetition: that the critic's own idea of the tradition could not itself be described as being 'traditional'; that poets should be prized less for their individuality than for their dependence on other poets; that poetic expression thus involves surrender; that the poetic tradition is at one and the same time timeless and time-bound; that the 'existing monuments' of the tradition form an order modified by the new; that past and present achievements are each evaluative of each other; that novelty and originality are by these means inseparable from tradition and conformity; that what Eliot called 'the main current' may not necessarily flow 'through the most distinguished reputations'; and that Shakespeare got more 'essential history' from Plutarch than we unfortunates could hope to get from the entire British Museum. The whole performance is capped by the idea that 'The progress of an artist is continual self-sacrifice, a continual extinction of personality.'

Of course as Eliot sees it the individual talent is barely *individual* at all. The poet is not a personality but a medium: a place or site where 'special, or very varied, feelings are at liberty to enter into new combinations': where, let us say, Eliot's own morbid prudishness about sex, his urgent desire for moments of transfiguration, his reading of seventeenth-century English and nineteenth-century French poetry, and *Hamlet* all collide to make 'The Love Song of J. Alfred Prufrock'. Listing these ingredients of 'Prufrock' (and we could list similar ones of *The Waste Land*) is something Eliot would have resisted it to the bitter end. For him there were no personal elements in 'Prufrock'. For him the distinction between 'the man who suffers and the mind which creates' is absolute. The mind, he is at pains to emphasize, 'digest[s] and transmute[s] the passions which are its material.'

In seeking to evict personal elements or ingredients from poetry entirely, and by these means protect what he called its impersonality and we (by bending terms once more) might call its ideality, Eliot got into great difficulties with the essay. He makes particularly heavy weather of a distinction he draws between 'emotions' and 'feelings'. Our experience of art, he suggests, 'may be formed out of one emotion, or may be a combination of several; and various feelings, inhering for the writer in particular words or phrases or images, may be added to compose the final result.' 'Emotions' are sensed by both writer and reader in the whole scene or theme a poem presents; 'feelings' on the other hand, belong exclusively to the writer, and relate to the 'particular words or phrases or images' which he adds to the emotions and which communicate those emotions in turn.

If this all sounds rather uncertain and confused, it is so. In so far as Eliot's critical problems here can be traced to a single source, it is that he has now begun to see the whole process in terms anterior or exterior to poetry itself: before the process described by Dan Jacobson – the ebb and flow of the events in the poem itself – begins. It is only in the stage *before* poetry starts to happen (or after it is over, perhaps) that any distinctions can be made between 'the man who suffers and the mind which creates', between theme and expression, and between what he calls elsewhere in the essay 'structural' and 'art' emotions. While poetry is happening, so to speak, such distinctions disappear (for reader as well as writer), and so it is that the 'man who suffers', the personal elements, enter 'The Love Song of J. Alfred Prufrock' as naturally as do the allusions to *Hamlet* or the poetry of Laforgue.

That is to say, it is not the author's mind (as Eliot seems to think) that digests and transmutes the passions which are its material, so much as the poem itself. These acts of digestion and transmutation are the upshot and product of the activity and the dialectic which this study aims to describe. If it is not the mind, working in isolation, that achieves such transmutations, however, neither is it language. Language cannot play by itself – though poets will always be surprised by 'what words and syntactical conventions do to dictate thought and disguise or transmute basic intention, perception and apprehension', as Leavis put it.[52] Poets' use of language is constrained, as well as given scope, by the particular poetic task upon which they are engaged. In that respect, neither language nor the poet is free to 'play' in the quasi-Derridean sense. It is under the pressure of the poem as a whole, at whatever stage in its evolution it has reached, rather than as a result of whatever pressures arise from constituent parts of it, like the author's volition or the random sproutings of phonemic coincidence, that words must find their place.

That Eliot knew neither the mind nor language (acting together or in isolation) are sufficient, critically speaking, to explain what happens in poetry is indicated by what he says elsewhere in 'Tradition and Individual Talent': 'it is not', he writes, 'the "greatness", the intensity, of the emotions, the components, but the intensity of the artistic process, the pressure, so to speak, under which the fusion takes place, that counts.' It is under the burden or the pressure of the poem that the poet's 'individuality' truly does begin to disappear, and the poet really does become servant, not master, medium, not personality.[53] And then all the paradoxical things Eliot says about tradition in the first part of his essay begin to make sense, too: not merely intellectually, as an iconoclastic critical argument addressed to the status quo, but descriptively where poetry is concerned. Under the pressure of the poem the poet does experience all the past poets existing simultaneously; then those poets do 'assert their immortality most vigorously'; then there is, for both poet and reader, a true 'sense of the timeless as well as the temporal and of the timeless and the temporal together'; then the old and the new really are in flux, adjusting and revising their relations to each other continually; then there really is individuality and conformity at one and the same moment; and then, finally, the poet really does discover the nature of his or her debts, which may not be to 'distinguished reputations' at all, but to poets and poetry previously neglected.

This is what Eliot means, surely, when he refers to the poet's 'passive attending upon the event'. It turns out that what he has to say about both tradition and the 'extinction of personality' relate more to a degree of essential passivity in the poetic process than they do to the inadequate distinctions he makes (for his own reasons possibly, given his desire to distance himself from the powerful emotions with which his poetry so often dealt) between the poet's mind on the one hand and his sufferings as an individual on the other. It is a notion of passivity, too, which sheds light on his idea that 'Impressions and experiences which are important for the man may take no place in the poetry, and those which become important in the poetry may play quite a negligible part in the man, the personality.' With this idea in mind, Eliot seeks to improve on Wordsworth's famous definition of poetry as 'emotion recollected in tranquillity'. Poetry, Eliot insists, is not emotion alone; nor is it entirely an act of recollection; least of all does it always require tranquillity. It is at least in part 'a passive attending upon the event', as I have said, and the power of that notion for Eliot is suggested by the countless occasions on which it surfaces not only in his explicitly critical writing but in his poetry: most strikingly, perhaps, in a passage from among the drafts of *The Waste Land* – which, for the purposes of this study, is as good an answer to the question 'what is literature?' as any other, and as vivid an illustration of literature's autonomy:

> I am the Resurrection and the Life
> I am the things that stay, and those that flow.
> I am the husband and the wife
> And the victim and the sacrificial knife
> I am the fire, and the butter also.[54]

It is by no means a new discovery that in 'Tradition and the Individual Talent' Eliot (like Derrida, in my view) over-emphasizes one half of the critical equation. Certainly his notion of authorial passivity implicitly recognizes the active, transformative element in literature that Derrida tends to see as being lost in contamination. But this same notion of impersonality neglects the fact that poets are as active on some occasions as they are passive on others. Poets, novelists, and playwrights do not work (to borrow a phrase from *In Memoriam*) 'without a conscience or an aim': rather they find such things become transformed in finding expression. Works of literature, like their authors, are sometimes the victim, and sometimes the sacrificial knife. We shall not have begun to understand them until we recognize this state of affairs.

2
'A New Spin on the Old Words': Criticism and Philosophy*

Rumours of the death of literature may be exaggerated but they continue to circulate.[1] The writing of books may not be dead; neither may the study of them be. But, as I began to suggest in the Introduction, the form that study has traditionally taken has undergone a great deal of change in the last fifty years. Not only are the traditional lines of distinction drawn between the humanities since the end of the nineteenth century in a state of flux and dissolution, but the areas of human life and culture that they are expected to explore are expanding and overlapping at an unprecedented pace.

Criticism's current sense of inadequacy – more urgent, I think, than any felt by contemporary psychologists, historians, and philosophers – perhaps has its root in two suspicions lying close beside each other in critics' minds. First, that philosophy, which is as abstract a field of study as literary criticism, is for all that a more important one because (even in the post-structuralist era) it seeks systematically to enquire into the nature and conditions of thought in a way quite beyond the scope of the poet or the novelist, let alone the critic. Second, that what Sir Philip Sidney called the 'tougher knowledges' – history, psychology, sociology, anthropology, political science, and the rest – are concerned with important phenomena, events, and developments that are by no means abstract (though it may be they are rendered so by those investigating them). Literary criticism has been notoriously dismissive of psychology and sociology, in particular; in making up for this a degree of overcompensation may be said to have crept into its recent re-alignments. Much of the sense of crisis that currently afflicts the study of literature results from a search it has repeatedly embarked upon for the epistemological rigour associated with the other disciplines I have mentioned. This is not to say that none of those fields of study have ever encountered any degree of epistemological doubt or self-consciousness. On the contrary, their existence depends on their doing just that. Philosophy depends almost completely on philosophical self-consciousness, and psychoanalysis and history, too, have often been riven with sectarian debate and fracture. Even under these conditions, however, these disciplines have comparatively rarely looked outside themselves for intellectual justification, no matter how large the gulfs that divided a Freud from a Jung, or a Michelet from a Ranke. In literary criticism the case is different. Despite the best efforts of some of its most influential practitioners – T.S. Eliot, say, or I.A. Richards, or William Empson, or Northrop Frye, or some of the New Critics – literary criticism in English has remained stubbornly resistant to the kind of methodologies that psychology and history in particular, but philosophy also, have discovered for themselves.

In its present situation, then, criticism is not looking within itself in the hope of finding an active methodological tradition. On the contrary, where it finds such a thing it tends to repudiate it. Instead when criticism seeks to answer the question, 'what is literature?', it looks to philosophy, history, psychoanalysis, and other disciplines besides. But it is a function of criticism's weak claim to methodological consistency that the more it scoops up from intellectual systems with higher pretensions in this respect, the more vacuous it feels on its own account. The more it takes the more it gives away.

Of course, the situation is a good deal more complex than this summary might lead us to believe. Natural science itself has elevated uncertainty from an experimental distortion to an operational principle, and psychology, history, and philosophy have all to a greater or lesser extent distanced themselves from the quasi-scientific ambitions some of their leading exponents have occasionally set for them as forms of rational enquiry. We no longer feel that the truth is out there waiting for us if we could only find it, and literary criticism has responded to this shift in our perceptions in much the same way as other disciplines have done. With a great deal less self-confidence, however, as the titles of those books and articles cited above make clear. In the fourth of the discourses making up *The Idea of a University* Cardinal Newman suggested that 'if you drop any science out of the circle of knowledge, you cannot keep its place vacant for it; that science is forgotten; the other sciences close up'; and this, without being melodramatic, is a possibility facing traditional literary criticism today. Certainly that possibility is one the critics I have mentioned seem to anticipate, some with sadness, many with glee. High Victorian that he was, Newman went on to say that in closing up like this, the other sciences 'exceed their proper bounds, and intrude where they have no right'. It is precisely that question that this book seeks to re-open. Is it true that 'the subject-matter' of criticism 'would be the prey of a dozen various sciences' – psychology, history, philosophy, cultural studies, etc. – if criticism itself were 'put out of possession'? Is it true that in such a case these sciences 'would be sure to teach wrongly, where they had no mission to teach at all'? Is it true, in short, that what traditional criticism unjustly forfeits, others unjustly seize?

This study does not suggest for one moment that literary critics should stop reading philosophy, history, psychology, sociology, and the rest forthwith, nor that scholars in those disciplines should stop reading literature. That would be a travesty of the argument it offers. Literary criticism has always come to involve itself with culture as a whole, and it was a part of the argument broached in the previous chapter that criticism's subject matter, literature, itself ensures that it does so. '[T]o be seriously interested in literary criticism', F.R. Leavis wrote, 'is inevitably to be led into other fields of interest'.[2] There is nothing wrong with literary critics taking an interest in other modes of cultural analysis. But if those modes of analysis come to have more importance for them than the imaginative literature they have studied, they forego not merely a specialized yet flexible and durable intellectual pursuit (itself, in the hands of Plato and Aristotle, permanently associated with philosophical and cultural issues of every kind) but also the very grounds on which they are able to make genuine contributions to the further refinement and extension of the disciplines they wish to emulate. Literary critics' value and interest for philosophers, psychoanalysts, and historians will sometimes seem disappointingly small; but it is by virtue of their being literary critics that they have any interest at all.

It is not the aim of this study to show the comparative theoretical poverty of literary criticism in a more revealing light than it stands in already, nor to re-circumscribe a discipline impinged upon from outside and exploding from within. Neither will I attempt a defence of old methods and old certainties in the study of literature, nor attempt to argue for the existence of so-called 'literary values'. I want to take a different course: examining not the approaches critics have made to history, or philosophy, or psychology, but the opposite: in this chapter, the approaches some philosophers have made to literature.

2.1 Richard Rorty

As in every good fairy story, just as the princess – the literary critic – is utterly languishing in her tower, so over the hill comes the knight on his white charger. Only in this case the knight is not another critic at all but a philosopher: Richard Rorty. That Rorty should make extravagant claims on behalf of literature is surprising enough in today's intellectual atmosphere. It is a long time, after all, since anybody spoke of poets being 'humanity's hero[es]',[3] or of their representing 'the vanguard of the species' (*CIS* 20). Even more encouragingly, for some at least, he speaks of 'The final victory of poetry in its ancient quarrel with philosophy' (*CIS* 40). The novel, Rorty suggests, 'is the characteristic genre of democracy, the genre most closely associated with the struggle for freedom and equality' (*H&O* 68). To a hypothetical group of inheritors of Western culture given the choice, he recommends the preservation of Dickens' novels rather than Heidegger's philosophy (*H&O* 68): advice which will sound more rash to some literary critics than it might to some philosophers.

It is not simply literature that Rorty wants to defend, however, but even that most outmoded, parasitic, and self-deprecating pursuit: literary criticism itself. Literary criticism is, he assures us, 'the presiding intellectual discipline' (*CIS* 83), whose 'rise … to preeminence within the high culture of the democracies' involves its 'gradual … assumption of the cultural role once claimed (successively) by religion, science, and philosophy' (*CIS* 82). In the 1920s and '30s, apparently, 'everyone from H.G. Wells to John Dewey was telling us that life and politics would become better if only we could adopt the attitude and habits of the natural scientist. We are now being told the same sort of thing about the attitude and habits of the literary critic' (*H&O* 129).

All this, needless to say, will be news to quite a few literary critics. When a writer makes such grandiose claims for an intellectual discipline outside his own we are bound to be a little wary. Especially so when the discipline concerned is, according to its own practitioners, feeling so down in the mouth. How can Rorty be so optimistic about literature and criticism? Is he mad?

To answer these questions I must summarize Rorty's general position. For Rorty as for so many philosophers the world is split into two. On his side are people he calls 'liberal ironists': 'liberal' because they place their faith in the bourgeois, democratic freedoms at present enjoyed in the West, while remaining aware of the fragility of those freedoms at home and abroad; 'ironists' because they believe everything in human thought and experience, from the tiniest personal neurosis to the grandest philosophical or political tradition (including liberalism), is the result of what Rorty calls contingency – which might be defined in Darwinian terms as a combination of chance and time. Both the behaviour of individuals and the behaviour of institutions emerge in evolutionary fashion out of a kind of primal soup: random, arbitrary, and without aim. Abstractions like 'Truth', 'God', 'Reason', and 'the Nature of Man' are the result of contingent human thought and should be treated as such. In this process of intellectual contingency and random historical change, words and language play an essential role. Like chromosomes and genes in natural evolution they are both triggers and records; they are powers for change but they are also ossifications, clichés, old practices, conformities.

On the other side from the liberal ironists are the 'metaphysicians': people who point to what Rorty calls 'the canonical Plato-Kant sequence' and who define philosophy as 'an attempt to know about certain things – quite general and important things' (*CIS* 76), like logic, or rationality, or ethics. For the metaphysician, philosophy is the study of the essential nature of man seen in abstract terms: a course of study which was developing quite normally until, in the eyes of those who follow it, it went off the rails with Hegel, Nietzsche, Heidegger, and Derrida.

I do not want to spend too much time on the metaphysicians. As my summary of their nature has perhaps suggested, they are the straw men in Rorty's argument: indispensable for dialectical reasons, it is hard to believe many of them exist in the simple form he describes. For Rorty, of course, the canonical sequence in Western analytical philosophy from Plato to Kant is one more contingency, one more chance arrangement, one more 'accidental coincidence of a private obsession with a public need' (*CIS* 37), as he puts it, with no stronger truth-claim than any other, only a longer history of intellectual utility.

With the ironists and the metaphysicians in mind, however, we can return to Rorty's Shelleyan hyperboles about heroic poets being the vanguard of the race and decode them with much the same sense of disappointment we feel when we decode Shelley's own *Defence of Poetry*. We find that it is not a question of poets being unacknowledged legislators of mankind, but a question of the legislators being unacknowledged poets, which is not at all the same thing. Poetic moments occur 'when things are not going well, when a new generation is dissatisfied' and, when they happen, 'people begin to toss around old words in new senses' (*H&O* 88). To toss words around in this way is to offer 'redescriptions' of the world. Of the thousands such redescriptions offered, only the tiniest handful are taken up or catch on in the societies where they are hatched. The metaphor becomes literalized, and the man or the woman who offered it up becomes, 'in the generic sense of the maker of new words', a poet (*CIS* 20). Thus it is that, according to Rorty, the metaphysician 'thinks of the high culture of liberalism centring around theory', whereas the liberal ironist 'thinks of it as centring around literature' (*CIS* 93), where literature – 'in the generic sense', presumably – is seen to embody precisely this capacity to generate new words and vocabularies.

If this were all there was to Rorty's defence of literature we could end our discussion here. He uses the term 'poet' and the term 'literature' much as Shelley did in his *Defence of Poetry* and we must make the best of it. Though the knight has given the princess a cheery wave from the fields below he has no intention of saving her, and that is that. (He has given us, for example, no explanation *why* certain metaphoric redescriptions become literalized while others fall by the wayside – and if he cannot explain this, what can he do?) But Rorty is not interested only in literature. He is interested in criticism. 'Literary criticism', he writes, 'does for [liberal] ironists what the search for universal moral principles is supposed to do for metaphysicians' (*CIS* 80). To make the situation plain: something literary critics do has the same centrality for a philosophical ironist like Rorty as those ideas of logic, rationality, and ethics had for Kant and Aristotle. It is an astonishing development; or an astonishing reversal. The point of it lies in Rorty's wanting us to give up the investigation of 'metaphysical' problems like Truth and Rationality, and replace them with redescriptions, new words, and new vocabularies. It is the literary critic's practice of comparison and analysis that Rorty finds so valuable in this respect. 'Since there is nothing beyond vocabularies which serves as a criterion of choice between them,' he writes, 'criticism is a matter of looking on this picture and on that, not of comparing both pictures with the original.' '[O]ur doubts about our own characters or our own culture', he goes on, 'can be resolved or assuaged only by enlarging our acquaintance. The easiest way of doing that is to read books.' Concerned that they will become stuck in their forebears' vocabularies, liberal ironists try to become acquainted with what Rorty calls 'strange people', like Alcibiades and Julien Sorel, or 'strange families' like the Karamazovs and the Casaubons. 'Ironists', he writes, 'read literary critics, and take them as moral advisers, simply because such critics have an exceptionally large range of acquaintance' (*CIS* 80). Because of the number of books they read, critics are less in danger than the rest of us of getting stuck in old vocabularies or in what I have called genetic ossifications.

The Karamazovs and Julien Sorel are figures from novels by Dostoevsky and Stendhal, but literary criticism extends much further than that. It has, Rorty suggests, 'been stretched further and further in the course of our century. ...to cover whatever the literary critics criticize' (*CIS* 81), just as literature 'now covers just about every sort of book which might conceivably have moral relevance' (*CIS* 82). The culturally literate person of today, Rorty expects, will have read *The Gulag Archipelago*, *Philosophical Investigations*, and *The Order of Things* as well as *Lolita* and *The Book of Laughter and Forgetting*. (This list is a revealing one in the sense that despite Rorty's urging our acceptance of cultural and intellectual pluralism there is nothing the least bit surprising on it. All these books are by white European men.) The end of this sort of argument is easy to predict. There is not 'much occasion' any more, Rorty suggests, 'to use the distinction...between philosophy and literature' (*CIS* 83). There is 'less and less point in calling it *literary* criticism'; less and less point in 'pretending to pursue academic specialties' (*CIS* 81). We should all 'work ourselves out of our jobs by conscientiously blurring the literature–philosophy distinction and promoting the idea of a seamless, undifferentiated "general text"' (*H&O* 86–7). All literature, imaginative or not ('Pythagoras, Plato, Milton, Newton, Goethe, Kant, Kierkegaard, Baudelaire, Darwin and Freud') is, Rorty writes, 'grist to be put through the same dialectical mill' (*CIS* 76). So much for literature.

Many literary critics, philosophers, and others nowadays incline towards a seamless, undifferentiated general text. What is odd about Rorty's particular version of the idea is that he puts it alongside others with quite different implications. We should, he says at one point, 'turn away from [the] dreams and ideal types' beloved by metaphysicians 'to narratives which trace the history of genres' (*H&O* 99). We should 'turn against theory and toward narrative' (*CIS* xvi). Rorty values novelists over theorists because the former are 'good at details' (*H&O* 81). But when Rorty himself becomes involved with literature, when he turns away from dreams and ideal types and towards those novelists he admires to unearth the details he regards so highly, then his grasp of detail, and his understanding of 'the history of genres' is revealed to be an unreflective and sketchy one. The mood of complacency, unreflectiveness, and cosy plurality originates, I am sure, in the feeble idea Rorty has of moral psychology, and that in turn originates in his unrealistic and dismissive attitude to the idea of truth in human activity ('there is nothing beyond vocabularies which serves as a criterion of choice between them').[4] No wonder he thinks books are the *easiest* way to enlarge your acquaintance. But these subjects are too large and too complex to discuss here. Instead, I would like to take three literary topics in turn, each dealt with by Rorty, and illustrate them where I can, as he does, by looking at individual writers.

Philosophical habits are hard to break, and Rorty draws many distinctions and differentiations across his 'seamless, undifferentiated "general text" '. The shallowest of these is the one he makes between 'books which supply novel stimuli to action' and 'those which simply offer relaxation'. Amongst the former he places *The Prelude*, *Middlemarch*, Nietzsche's *Genealogy of Morals*, and *King Lear*; amongst the latter *Murder on the Orient Express*, *Thunderball*, *Carry on Jeeves!*, and *Old Possum's Book of Practical Cats* (*CIS* 143). The distinction seems fair enough: we read *Thunderball* on the beach or on the train; we expect something a bit more profound from the *Genealogy of Morals*. But can we really believe that *Middlemarch* has nothing to offer in the way of relaxation, or that either it or *King Lear* provide 'novel stimuli to action'? As another example, what kind of 'stimuli to action' is offered by *The Waste Land*, and yet how much relaxation, paradoxically enough (given some of his subject matter), do we draw from Eliot's sinuous and undulatory use of rhythm? Rorty says that poems like Eliot's demand that we change our lives 'in some major or minor respect' (*CIS* 143), but what kind of changes, what kind of suggestions, what kind of stimuli to action are provided by *The Waste Land*? Become less sexually, emotionally, and spiritually sterile? Read *The Golden Bough*? Avoid tarot card readers? Leave your dull job at the bank? Get a more sympathetic boyfriend?

A second distinction Rorty draws is between books 'whose success can be judged on the basis of familiar criteria and those which cannot.' 'The latter class', he continues, 'contains only a fraction of all books, but it also contains the most important ones – those which make the greatest differences in the long run' (*CIS* 143). 'The more original a book or a kind of writing is,' Rorty writes, 'the more unprecedented, the less likely we are to have criteria in hand, and the less point there is in trying to assign it to a genre.' 'Only metaphysicians', he adds, 'think that our present genres and criteria exhaust the realm of possibility. Ironists continue to expand that realm' (*CIS* 135). An idea similar to this – that books like *Tristram Shandy*, *Ulysses*, *Remembrance of Things Past*, *The Naked Lunch*, and the *nouveau roman* generally speaking, each constitute some kind of massive fictional discovery superseding and demolishing the traditional novel – has been aired many times. The belief seems to be that somewhere below the cloudy peaks of James Joyce and William Burroughs lie murky plains where parochial and intellectually incurious minds like Jane Austen's, Henry James', and D.H. Lawrence's work, eyeless in Gaza at the mill with slaves, mindlessly dashing off novels on the old blueprint. 'Proust wrote a new kind of book', Rorty tells us enthusiastically; 'nobody had ever *thought* of something like *Remembrance of Things Past*' (*CIS* 136).

Rorty's faith in the talismanic qualities of certain novels is to a large extent underwritten by his view of philosophical history. The philosophers he is most interested in – Hegel, Nietzsche, Heidegger, and Derrida – each exist, he feels, in successively more intense states of Bloomian belatedness. Each philosopher has strenuously sought at once to subvert their predecessors' intellectual claims and to convert those claims to their own use, without themselves becoming ensnared in this process of gainsaying. Each philosopher in the now-canonical Hegel–Derrida sequence in turn announces the end of the Western metaphysical tradition only to find himself stuck, like Brer Rabbit, to the tar baby he wants to throw away.

The applicability or otherwise of Harold Bloom's ideas to philosophy or to literature itself is not the point at issue here. The idea that writers are original only in relation to their predecessors is more or less a truism. Where Rorty does a disservice to the novelists he mentions (and also, I imagine, to the philosophers) is in seeing this process in terms at once too dramatic and too solidified; too programmatic and too arbitrary. At any particular point – even at hinges of literary and artistic history like the Romantic and Modern eras – the tradition is a more fringed, more lipped, and more dispersed entity than Rorty imagines. He believes few criteria 'in hand' could apply to works of such originality as *Ulysses* or *Remembrance of Things Past*, but it is hard to say whether Joyce or Proust would have agreed. For very far from having their eyes fixed on horizons of boundless novelty, both writers were inextricably involved with their artistic predecessors. Proust's novel exists in the closest possible relation to the literary culture of nineteenth-century France, and Joyce exists like a vampire bat on the body of European fiction.[5] His use of symbolism in *Ulysses* has an intrusiveness more reminiscent of his much-admired Ibsen and the *fin-de-siècle* generally, than anything else. He spends one chapter of the same novel painstakingly satirizing a literary form as blatant and as self-serving as the women's magazine love story; another laboriously pastiching every style in the *Oxford Book of English Prose*. Whether this was a waste of his talents or a vindication of them is arguable. Rorty is right to say that no one had thought of including material of this kind in a serious novel before. The point is whether the experiments were worth making in this case, given the context (*Ulysses* as a whole) in which they were carried out. Even in the terms of Harold Bloom's arguments, such experiments hardly seem the mark of a fearless literary innovator – or an oedipally driven one come to that.

Originality can take many different forms. It is not restricted to the kind of innovations we associate with Proust and Joyce. 'Jane Austen,' as Leavis economically puts it, 'in her indebtedness to others, provides an exceptionally illuminating study of the nature of orginality'.[6] Few English novelists are more original and more conscious of criteria than Austen, in whose novels we find people living less by the normative moral codes to which her predecessors, Gothic and otherwise, paid homage, and more in accordance with the emotional imperatives of their own lives. The Gothic novel will always appear more original and more mutinous in its attitude to rules but in fact most Gothic characters only make a big noise in a little room, whereas Austen's apparently quiescent heroines lead lives of far greater emotional stress, of far greater moral involvement, and of far greater intensity – all of which are felt the more deeply for being to some degree suppressed or diverted by the social situations in which they find themselves. Every novel has criteria, and these can neither be inherited nor disowned *en bloc*.[7] In *Mansfield Park*, in *The Rainbow*, and in *Ulysses* they emerge in the same way: in a dialectic between what novelists have seen done by others and what they discover (in the act of writing) they are doing themselves.

The last of Rorty's differentiations I want to look at is one he makes between books aimed at 'serving human liberty' (the liberal half of the equation) and those which involve the search for what he calls 'private perfection' (the ironist half). In the first group he puts books by Dickens, Orwell, and Jürgen Habermas; in the second, ones by Proust, Nabokov, and Heidegger. This distinction sounds reasonable enough, especially when based on these examples. But if we take someone like Dickens we see how quickly it falls apart. Rorty places Dickens uncompromisingly within what he calls 'the novel of moral protest' (*H&O* 68). Novels of this kind, he feels, arouse in the reader an 'ability to envisage, and a desire to prevent, the actual and possible humiliation of others' (*CIS* 93); they 'sensitize one to the pain of those who do not speak our language' (*CIS* 94) – in the case of Dickens, the Victorian poor above all. Rorty believes that Dickens wanted his readers 'to notice and understand the people they passed on the street'. He wanted us to consider 'how we can arrange things so as to be comfortable with one another, how institutions can be changed so that everyone's right to be understood has a better chance of being gratified'. With 'no higher goal than comfortableness of human association,' Rorty argues, 'Dickens did an enormous amount for equality and freedom'.[8]

Again, this seems a reasonable summary, especially of Dickens' attitudes to institutions like the Circumlocution Office in *Little Dorrit*, or Chancery in *Bleak House*. But this 'comfortableness of human association', though clearly something of an ideal for Rorty himself, is nothing like all that Dickens wanted. The search for 'private perfection', far from having no attraction or interest for him, was an overriding impulse, impossible for him to quell. The idea of general human 'comfortableness' Rorty finds in Dickens is based almost entirely on Dickens' own quite personal nostalgia for a thing he never himself experienced but always sought, in and out of his fictions: an ideal family life. In fact one of the ways in which we can make sense of Dickens' manifest cruelties to his own wife and children may be in terms of his whole-hearted idolization of the family. His pages teem with neglected children, and it is impossible to say where the search for private perfection Dickens undertook on their behalf changes into a desire to serve human liberty. In Dickens' view, that which the Victorian poor lacked above all, and that which would crown their happiness could it be achieved, was exactly that domestic idyll that he himself pursued with such helpless, steely, patriarchal rigour.[9]

But for Rorty, the Dickensian utopia (his word) is 'a crowd of eccentrics rejoicing in each other's idiosyncrasies, *curious for novelty rather than nostalgic for primordiality*. The bigger, more varied, and more boisterous the crowd the better' (*H&O* 75; my italics). This sounds more like *Oliver!* than *Oliver Twist*; more like 'Food, Glorious Food' than Oliver's straightforward and pitiful request, 'Please Sir, I want some more'. We only have to think for a moment of those neglected children I mentioned to realize that they are far from rejoicing in the idiosyncrasies of Mr Dombey, Mr Murdstone, William Dorritt, Miss Havisham, Mrs Jellyby, Daniel Quilp, Fagin, and the rest. Behind Oliver's asking for more there lies the quintessentially primordial, familial scene of food bought with a father's wages and cooked by a mother's hand – and cooked for Oliver alone, not 300 other workhouse orphans rejoicing in one another's idiosyncrasies. No amount of man-hours spent by Dickens in the service of human liberty could put that shattered vision of Oliver's together again (or together for the first time), as Dickens well knew. Of course Dickens' novels had a huge social influence in revealing to the Victorians the conditions in which so many of their compatriots lived. But to say that Dickens' novels are solely or even only primarily interested in serving up such reminders is evidently untrue; just as untrue as to say that the utility of those novels extends only to the power and social influence of the reminders they unquestionably do offer.

To take the cases of novelists like Proust and Nabokov is a little more difficult. It will always be easier, perhaps, to find a seeker after 'private perfection' lurking inside a server of human liberty, than to find in Proust and Nabokov a quest for human liberty lying behind the pursuit of what Nabokov calls 'aesthetic bliss'.[10] Except that for Rorty the achievement of private perfection always *involves* the achievement of liberty. That is to say, he places great stress on what he calls 'self-creation' (*CIS* 84) and on the individual's freeing his or her self from the vocabularies and the outlooks of others. The importance of Sigmund Freud in Rorty's intellectual pantheon is the suggestion Rorty believes Freud makes, that 'only if we catch hold of some crucial idiosyncratic contingencies in our past shall we be able to make something worthwhile of ourselves, to create present selves whom we can respect' (*CIS* 33). The idea that the self can stand outside the self to create itself anew and award merit points for a job well done would, I think, have sounded as psychologically implausible to Freud or Proust as it does to us. It is no surprise to find that Rorty is unwilling to examine this idea critically, belonging as it does by rights to the domain of popular psychology. But even if we admit this to be a summary of *Remembrance of Things Past* (as Rorty suggests we should), we see that Proust's desire for personal moral liberty and private perfection is at the same time a call for general moral emancipation, too. One of the reasons Proust's novel is so reminiscent of the *Divine Comedy* is that the moral achievement it dramatizes is not merely a selfish one, laid on for Marcel alone. 'Men who produce works of genius', Proust argued,[11] 'have had the power, ceasing suddenly to live only for themselves, *to transform their personality into a sort of mirror*' – and that mirror is for us all to see ourselves in, not simply for Marcel to create a present self he can respect.

In turning to Nabokov, Rorty has another argument to offer: that Nabokov illustrates and warns against the dangers of too obsessively pursuing the goal of private perfection. In *Lolita*, Humbert Humbert's nympholeptic single-mindedness utterly blinds him to the cruelty with which he plots against, undermines, and finally destroys Lolita's childhood innocence. His search for aesthetic bliss renders him unaware of the humiliation and the pain he is inflicting. But even as he argues this part of his case (once more at first sight such a reasonable one) Rorty himself seems blind to any other implications in this particular novel of Nabokov's and, given Rorty's oft-repeated axiom that for a liberal 'cruelty is the worst thing we do', his impercipience on this point is surprising. He points out that the average reader of *Lolita* is likely to pass over some slight but telling references in the narrative to the deaths of various people who play no active role in the plot. The barber in Kasbeam, for example, had a son (dead for thirty years) whose sporting exploits he recounts to Humbert. Humbert scarcely notices this family tragedy and neither do we. For us as for Humbert the barber is a bore. In similar fashion, both we and Humbert forget that Lolita once had a baby brother 'who died at two when she was four'. 'This', Rorty suggests, 'is exactly the sort of thing Nabokov expects his ideal readers – the people whom he calls "a lot of little Nabokovs" – to notice. But, ruefully and contemptuously aware that most of his readers will fall short, he tells us in his Afterword [i.e. 'On a Book Entitled *Lolita*'] what we have missed' (*CIS* 162–3).

The question Rorty does not ask is *why* it should be that readers, in common with Humbert Humbert, fail to notice these things? What reason can we offer for our inadvertence? Only one: we, like Nabokov himself, are complicit in Humbert's pursuit of his nymphet: wholly, intently, excitedly. If we were not, the novel could hold little interest for us. On collecting Lolita from her summer camp, and with her virtually within his clutches, Humbert makes a sudden resolution to pull back:

> to give this wan-looking though sun-coloured little orphan *aux yeux battus* ... a sound education, a healthy and happy childhood, a clean home, nice girl-friends of her age among whom (if the fates deigned to repay me) I might find, perhaps, a pretty little *mägdlein* for Herr Doktor Humbert alone. But 'in a wink', as the Germans say, the angelic line of conduct was erased, and I overtook my prey (time moves ahead of our fancies!), and she was my Lolita again ...[12]

We can recognize how disappointed we should be as readers if Humbert obeyed this momentary instinct, abandoned his plot on Lolita's innocence, and transformed himself into a model father. We would surely accuse the novelist of arousing expectations he has no intention of satisfying. And in feeling this – in feeling that to let Lolita go now would be a complete anti-climax – we have (and not only momentarily) joined the circle of paedophilic child-abusers for whom this novel offers pornographic stimulation. For we can be sure that passages from *Lolita* are indeed read, gloatingly, in paedophile circles; and any claim of Nabokov's, of the kind made in 'On a Novel Entitled *Lolita*', that this (in effect) could not happen because the book is so well written is not admissible; 'fine writing' is no guarantee that misuse will not occur.[13] It is more than likely, in fact, that paedophiles take particular pleasure in reminding themselves that what they are reading is 'high' literature of the highest kind; nor do Nabokov's declared intentions delimit the effect of what he has written. In this respect we must face the fact that the novel actually encourages the kind of cruelty Rorty deplores.

It might be said that arguments of this kind cannot be made against *Lolita*; that the evidence of persons unknown and their reactions cannot be introduced in this way. But in fact we do not have to rely upon such evidence. We are a lot of little Nabokovs after all; we know well enough from our own natures how inflammable such perversions are and we recognize how easily the latent can become manifest. More pertinently still, we can draw the same sort of conclusion not from our own necessarily confused and inchoate feelings on this subject but from *Lolita* itself. For as a rule we also overlook something else in reading the novel, as did Rorty: that Humbert's expressions of shame, horror, and remorse, and his presentation of the moments that gave rise to these feelings, are all gathered together towards the end of the book.[14] Why should this be? After all, everything in Humbert's story is recollected, and most of it is recollected in sequence, except these moments in particular. They could have been given to us in the ordinary course of the story, as and when they actually occurred. Except that had they appeared in this way, the effect on the novel would have been catastrophic. The fun and therefore the gravity of the enterprise would have evaporated entirely; that complicity described above, on our own and Nabokov's part, would have been impossible to sustain, punctuated as it would have been by Humbert's admissions, hesitations, and mortifications. So these are shuffled off to the end, where they could do no harm to the paedophile fantasy, while at the same time, equally safely, they could satisfy Nabokov's, Rorty's, and our own imperative need for an improving, anti-cruelty message to be drawn from it all. As Nabokov suggests, there is 'no moral in tow' after *Lolita*.[15] There is the fact of our complicity, so powerfully evoked by the novel, make of it what we can – the kind of complicity which is widespread in literature, and which we can see registered, rather exquisitely as it happens, by Henry James in the preface to *The Wings of the Dove*. 'The case prescribed for its central figure a sick young woman,' James wrote: 'at the whole course of whose disintegration and the whole ordeal of whose consciousness one would have quite honestly to assist.' There is no point in bemoaning this aspect of literature, and there is a great deal of harm in pretending it does not exist. The moral power of literature lies not in messages more or less well hidden in the text but in the fact of our engagement with it – with all of it, paedophilia too. One of its functions is precisely to air impulses generally forbidden the reader in the real world; for better and for worse.

2.2   Alasdair MacIntyre and Charles Taylor

It would be going too far to say of Richard Rorty that, in Cardinal Newman's words, he has taught badly where he had no mission to teach at all. His theory of literature is patently limited in my view; but he has an inalienable right to put it forward. Moreover, other philosophers coming from the same neck of the woods as Rorty have approached literature in a more thoughtful way. In *After Virtue*, for example, Alasdair MacIntyre draws a profound distinction between the moral universes of classical Greece and its epigones on the one hand (represented by Plato, Aristotle, and Aquinas), and modern liberalism on the other (represented by Max Weber and Isaiah Berlin). For the first, 'there exists a cosmic order which dictates the place of each virtue in a total harmonious scheme of human life'; for the second, 'the variety and heterogeneity of human goods is such that their pursuit cannot be reconciled in any single moral order': any attempt to do so resulting in totalitarianism.[16] 'The interest of Sophocles', MacIntyre concludes, 'lies in his presentation of a view equally difficult for a Platonist or a Weberian to accept.' In the tragedies of Sophocles both these moral systems hold sway. That is what makes them tragedies:

> There *is* an objective moral order, but our perceptions of it are such that we cannot bring rival moral truths into complete harmony with each other and yet the acknowledgment of the moral order and of moral truth makes the kind of choice which a Weber or a Berlin urges upon us out of the question. For to choose does not exempt me from the authority of the claim which I choose to go against. (*AV* 143)

As attempts to understand Greek tragedy go, this seems to me a thoughtful and thought-provoking one, that only a philosopher could provide. Sophoclean tragedy, MacIntyre suggests, 'leaves unbridged the gap between the acknowledgment of authority, of a cosmic order and of the claims to truth involved in the recognition of the virtues on the one hand and our particular perceptions and judgements in particular situations on the other' (*AV* 143). In the same way, Charlotte Brontë's

Jane Eyre evokes but leaves unresolved the conflict of social morality and law (in and under which bigamy is forbidden) on the one hand, with the heroine's and Rochester's own irresistible emotional needs on the other. That literature is less interested in resolving conflicts of this kind than in exploring them is an important recognition for both philosophers and literary critics.

Nor do I have a problem with what MacIntyre goes on to propose, which is the existence of a philosophical position not only in Sophocles – who 'systematically explores rival allegiances to incompatible goods ... in a way that raises a key and complex set of questions about the virtues' (*AV* 142) – but in his tragedies also. For MacIntyre, the Sophoclean dramas 'present a view': in this instance they occupy and expound a third position relative to the Platonic and Weberian ones MacIntyre outlines. No doubt they do, in an important way; and it is appropriate for a philosopher to remind us of the fact.

But they also do something more, or something different. Sophocles occupied a philosophical position of some kind or other; but is the situation so straightforward where his dramas are concerned? Is it not the case that they question the holding of such positions and others like them? For dramas like Sophocles' tragedies are in part about what qualities count *as* virtues (pragmatism, for example, or obstinacy), and whether 'the virtues' can ever be said to exist out there, somewhere, as a class. Does *Antigone*, for example – talking of pragmatism and obstinacy – take up a carefully defined and perennially relevant philosophical position *vis-à-vis* an equally perennial philosophical problem? To some extent yes it does: 'Wherever the strength of a man's intellect, or moral sense, or affection brings him into opposition with the rules which society has sanctioned', as George Eliot wrote in 'The *Antigone* and Its Moral', '*there* is renewed the conflict between Antigone and Creon'. But the play also does something more than that, something which is not finally reducible to a philosophical discussion, and which in fact allows and impels imaginative writers to experiment with the very applicability of generalized philosophical positions to predicaments like the heroine's own. Does the struggle between Creon and Antigone present nothing more than a treatment of a philosophical disagreement of the Platonist vs Weberian kind which we can dispassionately adjudicate, or between the parties to which we can insert yet another position, once the affective superficies are removed? Is it not the fact, rather, that it is because the play does *not* rest content with such philosophical allowances or adjustments that we are compelled to see the conflict between Creon and Antigone as a genuine tragedy? MacIntyre draws no distinction between 'the Sophoclean view' or the Sophoclean 'account of the virtues' and the plays in which elements of these may appear; indeed what he goes on to say suggests that he does not see much need for any such distinction. 'Plato', he writes, 'has to expel the dramatic poets from the *Republic* because in part of the rivalry between their view and his' (*AV* 143–4). But might it not be that Plato expelled the poets because they had no view; because their work represented 'a divine release of the soul from the yoke of custom and convention' that was, Plato suggested in the *Phaedrus*, a kind of madness; because whereas they shed light on philosophical issues and problems in a way Plato could not help but recognize, they did not do so in the dialectical mode of philosophers and therefore could not be confuted? If that was the source of his anxiety then Plato, despite his notoriously testy attitude towards the poets, may have possessed a livelier understanding of them than do philosophers like Rorty and MacIntyre.

My argument that only by acts of intellectual misrepresentation or inadvertence can works of literature like *Antigone* can be absorbed within a seamless and undifferentiated general text – in which everything takes up or embodies a 'position' of some kind or another – may be pursued by way of more momentous example from MacIntyre's work. This time the current is flowing in the other direction. So far we have seen MacIntyre trying to adopt (or cashier) an imaginative author as a philosopher on the basis that he provides an 'account of the virtues' to set alongside Aquinas and Isaiah Berlin. This time the boot is on the other foot. The question of virtue and vice is normally taken to be a moral–philosophical one; but MacIntyre imaginatively argues that moral agency cannot be adequately assessed in abstract terms but must be seen in the context of the lives led by individuals. In particular he places emphasis on the moral agent as 'not only an actor, but an *author*' (*AV* 213; my italics). Man, he writes, 'is in his actions and practice, as well as in his fictions, *essentially a story-telling animal*' (*AV* 216; my italics). 'It is because we all live out narratives in our lives and because we understand our own lives in terms of the narratives that we live out', he argues, 'that the form of narrative is appropriate for understanding the actions of others. Stories are lived before they are told – except in the case of fiction' (*AV* 212). Thus mankind's narrative habit, which reaches its apogee in imaginative literature, is itself seen as a core moral issue with which philosophy must come to terms.

This idea is by no means unique to Alasdair MacIntyre. Indeed it is to be found quite commonly among the group of philosophers with which this chapter is particularly concerned. (The Rortyan philosophical attitude, Rorty says, 'makes conscience, like passion, one more set of human beliefs and desires – another story about how the world is, another Weltanschauung'; *H&O* 151.) Charles Taylor, for example, regards it as 'a basic condition of making sense of ourselves, that we grasp our lives as *narrative*'.[17] He goes on to argue that

> because we cannot but orient ourselves to the good, and thus determine our place relative to it and hence determine the direction of our lives, we must inescapably understand our lives in narrative form, as a 'quest'. But one could perhaps start from another point: because we have to determine our place in relation to the good, therefore we cannot be without an orientation to it, and hence must see our lives in story. From whichever direction, I see these conditions as connected facets of the same reality, inescapable structural requirements of human agency.[18]

Such narratives can take many forms:

> Typical modern forms of narrativity include stories of linear development, progress stories in history, or stories of continuous gain through individual lives and across generations, rags-to-riches stories, which have no ending point. And they include construals of life as growth, not just through childhood and adolescence, but through the later phases as well. Rather than seeing life in terms of predefined phases, making a whole whose shape is understood by unchanging tradition, we tell it as a story of growth towards often unprecedented ends. This is to mention only widely familiar forms, and not the most imaginative innovations of our times, such as the kind of unity through narration which Proust created for his life, which has struck such a deep chord in contemporary imagination. And of course there is the spiral picture of history, from innocence to strife and then to a higher harmony, borrowed from Christian divine history and the millenial movements but secularized by Marxism and a host of other theories, and immensely powerful in its hold on modern thought and feeling.[19]

This idea of life-as-narrative appears highly sympathetic to literature and literary criticism. It places a cardinal concern of literary thinking at the centre of moral discussion. The idea that man is a story-telling animal is the equivalent of Richard Rorty telling us that literary criticism is 'the presiding intellectual discipline', pre-eminent 'within the high culture of the democracies', and so forth. 'At last', critics might mutter to themselves, 'moral philosophy has recognized how abstract is the concept of life with which it has until now concerned itself. It has recognized that it must confront the world of moral reality – the lives actually led by Madame Bovary and people like her – as opposed to the Kantian-cum-utilitiarian vocabulary of actions, obligations, rights, and so on.' Talk about the death of literature is surely premature under such unexpectedly favourable circumstances.

Perhaps. 'The meaning of real human lives', Hayden White argues, 'is the meaning of the plots, quasi-plots, paraplots, or failed plots by which the events that those lives comprise are endowed with the aspect of stories having a discernible beginning, middle, and end.'[20] A beginning, a middle, and an end were all that Aristotle, with tragedy in mind, demanded of a story: but Charles Taylor does not restrict himself to bare bones like these, and certainly he does not seem to be thinking of tragedy. Quests, 'linear development', 'progress', 'continuous gain', 'rags-to-riches', 'growth', 'unity through narration', and 'the spiral picture ... from innocence to strife and then to a higher harmony': these are his expressions. The list of possible narratives Taylor holds out to us seems enough to reflect the variety of human existence, until we recognize the peculiarly anodyne yet optimistic tone of the narrative types presented in such passages: story-lines more reminiscent of Horatio Alger and Samuel Smiles than, say, *Hamlet*, or *Persuasion*, or *Middlemarch*.

The emphasis on growth, understanding, and moral prosperity we find in Taylor's discussion of this issue betrays, I think, a failure of imagination on his part. There is, for example, an implicit belief that life is a linear development, that it can be grasped, that there is continuous gain (or perhaps continuous loss): in any event, that its pattern or configuration is revealed in the light of such developments – indeed that that is what 'developments' *are*. 'If', writes MacIntyre,

> a human life is understood as a progress through harms and dangers, moral and physical, which someone may encounter and overcome in better and worse ways and with a greater or lesser measure of success, the virtues will find their place as those qualities the possession and exercise of which generally tend to success in this enterprise and the vices likewise as qualities which likewise tend to failure. Each human life will then embody a story whose shape and form will depend upon what is counted as a harm and danger and upon how success and failure, progress and its opposite, are understood and evaluated. To answer these questions will also explicitly and implicitly be to answer the question as to what the virtues and vices are. (*AV* 144)

This is a careful passage. MacIntyre speaks of better and worse ways, greater and lesser measures of success. But he also – in a manoeuvre that reminds us of Rorty's cheerfully pragmatic yet utopian view of moral psychology – simply equates what counts as virtue and vice with personal success or personal failure. For Taylor the virtues are those qualities which advance the individual's 'progress through harms and dangers, moral and physical', whereas the vices are those qualities which retard it. If you overcome a moral or physical danger it was virtue that helped you do it; if you succumb, you were tripped up by a vice. No wonder each human life will then take the form of a *story*, the shape or form of which will depend on what counts as a harm and danger and how success and failure are to be assessed. What else could the individual life amount to, after all, under such conditions? It sounds terrific: we can make something worthwhile of ourselves, as Rorty would say, or create present selves whom we can respect, more or less at the drop of a hat. But it also sounds unrealistic, evasive, and mean: for if you can justify yourself simply by telling (or changing) a story, why should we care about virtue and vice, and why should we come to regard one person as being any better than another? And if stories are *that* easy to change, why should we care about them, either?

The interest literature takes in the moral issues arising from the framing of such narratives is a central one, to say the least. Two issues in particular present themselves consistently. First, when we reflect upon our own lives, or the lives laid out for us in a novel like *Middlemarch*, we cannot help feeling that a great deal of such lives are made up of shuttling back and forth over insoluble problems, of 'progress' meeting frustrations which themselves put desired goals into a new light, and of responsibilities and obligations which are neither strictly inherited nor strictly dispensable; that ideas like unity, harmony, continuous gain, and endowment are either distant or ambiguous goods; and that growth, understanding, grasping, and the rest are either precarious (witness Dorothea Brooke), or postponed for certain positive reasons (witness Dr Lydgate), or arrive too late (witness Mr Casaubon), or never arrive at all (witness Mr Brooke), or arrive only for the undeserving (witness Fred Vincy). None of these facts is a reason to stop trying to make sense of our lives; but taken together they do present good reasons for philosophers to be a little more curious about the variety of shapes narrative can take – or their simple lack of shape, come to that.

The second point is also illustrated by *Middlemarch*. The banker Bulstrode has certainly achieved 'unity through narration'. He has told himself a story about his life and allowed this story to gain credence with his fellow townsfolk: a 'spiral picture', if you like, 'from innocence to strife and then to a higher harmony'; a story which mitigates and suppresses a shameful episode from his own past. The telling of this story has saved him from a great deal of harms and dangers, moral and physical: poverty, for example, and shame. Moreover, it has been the necessary accompaniment to a great deal of 'progress' and 'success' for him in Middlemarch – including the founding and endowment of a fever hospital administered along enlightened medical and philanthropic lines. But it is a lie, which crushes him in the end and which cannot be retold so as to make it anything else. Are expressions like 'better and worse ways' and 'greater or lesser measure of success' adequate for anyone, including Bulstrode himself, to understand his life? How do we begin the labelling of virtues and vices in such a case? Why, for example, has Bulstrode become involved in charitable exercises? Is it genuinely virtuous behaviour on his part, or an attempt to re-invent himself and cover his tracks, Rorty-style?

The moral costs attached to achieving unity through narration are no less high in the case of man who is unambiguously good. Dr Lydgate also tells himself the story of his life: the brilliant young medical man; the scientist and good Samaritan, whose brief and intense entanglement with a French actress has, as it were, cauterized the emotional vulnerability of youth and left him 'experienced' without cynicism, and philanthropic without sentimentality. This is not a morally bad story, any more than Bulstrode's is. But it, too, involves the mitigation or suppression of certain elements in Lydgate's character that eventually must have their way: his emotional vulnerability certainly, but also his paternalism, his uxoriousness, and his sexuality. As it turns out Lydgate dies aged fifty, a successful practitioner in London and a Continental resort, and the author of a book on gout. As for Lydgate and Bulstrode, so for the rest of us story-telling animals: those narratives we construct for ourselves and impose on others do not involve elements of fantasy and self-delusion accidentally and marginally. The incorporation of such elements is the reason for the narratives being framed in the first place. No conceivable story by a human being could avoid such contamination. On the contrary, the contamination is the point.

George Eliot probably would not have gone so far as to say that, morally conventional person that she was in certain areas. But Emily Brontë is a different kettle of fish altogether, and a most unremitting enquirer into those narrative delusions we visit upon ourselves and our significant others. It is a commonplace in the criticism devoted to *Wuthering Heights* that Mr Lockwood, who is the primary narrator of the book, and who transcribes the novel from his own testimony and that of the secondary narrator, Nelly Dean, is less an authorial figure than a witness, an auditor, and above all perhaps something of an idealized reader. A nondescript member of the leisured classes with no visible emotional ties, he is an apparently objective and neutral personality. Moreover, he has time on his hands. He is bored and needs stimulation. That stimulation is provided by his first visit to the Heights and the peculiar domestic arrangements he encounters there; by the jottings and scribblings Cathy Earnshaw has left in her books; and by the horrific dream he experiences while staying overnight. He very soon shows signs of illness. After his visit and his four-hour trudge through the snow back to Thrushcross Grange he develops all the symptoms of a fullblown fever: 'my head felt hot', he tells us, 'and the rest of me chill: moreover, I was excited almost to the pitch of foolishness through my nerves and brain. This caused me to feel, not uncomfortable, but rather fearful, as I am still, of serious effects from the incidents of today and yesterday.'[21]

'Excited to the pitch of foolishness' but 'not uncomfortable'. It is hardly a fanciful suggestion to say that this is our state of mind, too, with regard to what we have encountered so far at Lockwood's side. Like Lockwood we are feverish; not with a real temperature but with a longing to know more about the Heights and its mysterious occupants. Like Lockwood, too, we are stuck where we are: he by illness, we by choice; both by curiosity. Indeed, Lockwood remains ill throughout the telling of the story. Only with the end of Nelly's narration does his strength recover and then, significantly, he at once decides to leave the neighbourhood and the story, and go back to London. Only by accident does he ever come back north to hear the conclusion of the novel. He resumes his narration with the date, 1802, and within a few pages he is sitting by the fireside with Nelly once again: 'but, sit down,' she says, to us as well as him, 'and let me take your hat, and I'll tell you all about it' (*WH* 340).

If Lockwood is something of an idealized reader, encouraging us to persevere with this singularly idiosyncratic and enigmatic story, then Nelly is something of an idealized writer, whose nature reflects on Emily Brontë's contribution to the novel just as Lockwood's reflects on ours. Two things in particular mark her as such. First, she takes a profound interest in other people's lives. Although Nelly knows it does not fall in her 'province' to arrange a romance between Lockwood and young Catherine, she drops pregnant hints all the same (*WH* 329). She is also madly inquisitive. 'Tell my why you are so queer, Mr Heathcliff?' Nelly asks in the novel's last chapter; 'Where were you last night? I'm not putting the question through idle curiosity, but –'. Of course that is exactly what motivates her, as Heathcliff himself says: 'And now you'd better go', he tells her: 'You'll neither see nor hear anything to frighten you, if you refrain from prying' (*WH* 358). To refrain from prying is beyond Nelly, as Heathcliff should have known by this stage. A few hours later, Nelly says, 'I deemed it proper, though unsummoned, to carry a candle, and his supper' to him, if only to find out what he is up to now. Related to this aspect of her personality is her profoundly novelistic habit of forcing other people to speculate on turns their lives might take in the future. 'Suppose for a minute,' she asks the thirteen year-old Catherine, 'that master and I were dead, and you were by yourself in the world – how would you feel then?' (*WH* 257.)

The second feature of Nelly which proves her a born story-teller but also a morally dubious human being is her habit of embroidering the truth, or suppressing its existence, or simply telling lies. ('Telling tales' is the English expression.) When the doctor comes to see Heathcliff in the novel's final chapter Nelly conceals the fact that he has eaten nothing for four days, 'fearing', as she says, 'it might lead to trouble' (*WH* 365). Throughout the book, and especially where Cathy's secret reception of Heathcliff after her marriage and Catherine's secret relationship with Linton are concerned, Nelly plays a double game, keeping secrets on people's behalf while being fearful of the consequences should the truth come out. On other occasions, she receives confidences only to betray them. 'You'll not tell, will you?' Catherine says after revealing her secret visits to Linton; 'It will be very heartless if you do' (*WH* 286). In response, Nelly walks straight to Edgar, 'relating the whole story', as she says – with a few omissions. At the climax of the novel, when Catherine is forced to marry Linton while Nelly is imprisoned at the Heights, she has the chance to reflect on her role in the whole sorry affair:

> I seated myself in a chair, and rocked, to and fro, passing harsh judgment on my many derelictions of duty; from which, it struck me then, all the misfortunes of all my employers sprang. It was not the case, in reality, I am aware; but it was, in my imagination, that dismal night, and I thought Heathcliff himself less guilty than I. (*WH* 308)

Even after her release from the Heights, the report of events Nelly gives to the dying Edgar is a selective one: 'I said Heathcliff forced me to go in,' she recalls, 'which was not quite true' (*WH* 314).

To qualify as readers, it would appear, we must be in a state of heightened awareness combined with lethargy; forgetful of ourselves, of others, and the outside world as a whole; and intent on the narrative to the exclusion of everything else: cocooned, in short, in our armchairs. It is a state Emily Brontë deliberately associates with Lockwood's continuing illness: a fact from which we can draw our own conclusions. As for Lockwood's objectivity and neutrality as ideal reader, these are revealed to be what they are: a combination of prudish, pseudo-genteel, and stiflingly bourgeois superiority on the one hand, combined with a subtle and flickering self-interest on the other, especially as regards his putative flirtation with young Catherine – which he is too callow to initiate but which he holds before himself as a flattering confirmation of the very social and emotional refinement that removes him so completely from her consideration. As for Nelly: she, in telling the story, cannot help but reveal that she, too, is and has been a partial witness and a partial narrator. We know by her own admission that she has played fast and loose with the truth under the pressure of events. We know, too, that she is eager to excuse herself for doing so and that she feels guilty of actually being complicit with Heathcliff, whether by design or not.

At this stage an important caveat must be registered. Whereas it is true that Lockwood is a 'reader-figure' and Nelly a 'writer-figure' it by no means follows that the former is simply a reader-surrogate and the latter a writer-surrogate. We are neither asked to identify with Lockwood, nor manoeuvered into doing so; quite the contrary. 'A capital fellow!', Lockwood calls Heathcliff after his first visit to the Heights: to which all we can say is that Brontë's novel is of the kind that absolutely and resolutely forbids our resting content with the moral outlook of a Lockwood. (Indeed the inadequacy of that outlook is one of the things *Wuthering Heights* is about.) The same is true of Brontë's relationship to Nelly Dean. This is not a matter of seeing through Lockwood and Nelly Dean but of seeing them as what they are. The exercise would have remained a morally self-serving one, however, if the novel did not suggest that there is indeed more than a little of Lockwood in us on our side of the net, and more than a little of Nelly Dean in Emily Brontë on hers.

It seems that *Wuthering Heights* (like *Middlemarch*) raises some significant moral problems about the telling of tales. To be a reader is to indulge our sense of curiosity; to neglect the real world and its affairs; wilfully to place ourselves in a condition Emily Brontë compares with illness. To be a writer is to indulge our curiosity, too, but in an even more intrusive and meddling way: suppressing the truth to some extent and, on occasion, telling downright lies.

But even Emily Brontë draws the line somewhere. So intent is she on tale-telling as a moral habit, irremediably a part of life itself, that she avoids confusing the issue by alluding directly to her own role as author of *Wuthering Heights*. Jane Austen has no such reticence. In chapter seven of *Pride and Prejudice* we are supposed to disapprove most strongly of Mrs Bennet's crass opportunism in sending her eldest daughter Jane to Mr Bingley's house on horseback with the aim of forcing her to stay the night and thus further her relationship with that young man; disapprove even more strongly when Jane catches a cold that requires her stay to be extended. But what are we supposed to feel when Jane Austen herself sends Elizabeth Bennet off the following day to tend her sister, and by these means furthers Elizabeth's own relationship with Darcy? ('Every thing that is charming!' Mrs Bennet says at the end of the novel: 'Three daughters married!' Might not the author herself complacently say the same thing?) Charles Dickens, too, was quite happy to put himself, Hitchcock-like, in the picture. *Barnaby Rudge* is one of the most infuriatingly obscure of all his mystery-plots, which makes the following passage (on the early rumblings of anti-Catholicism which eventually became the Gordon riots) a noteworthy piece of authorial revelation:

> To surround anything, however monstrous or ridiculous, with an air of mystery, is to invest it with a secret charm, and power of attraction which to the crowd is irresistible. False priests, false prophets, false doctors, false patriots, false prodigies of every kind, veiling their proceedings in mystery, have always addressed themselves at an immense advantage to the popular credulity, and have been, perhaps, more indebted to that resource in gaining and keeping for a time the upper hand of Truth and Common Sense, than to any half-dozen items in the whole catalogue of imposture. Curiosity is, and has been from the creation of the world, a master-passion. To awaken it, to gratify it by slight degrees, and yet leave something always in suspense, is to establish the surest hold that can be had, in wrong, on the *unthinking* portion of mankind.[22]

Brontë, Austen, and Dickens have this much to say about the stories we make up: the ones we tell ourselves (or others) about our lives. There are also the ones we inherit and use as primary material for narratives of our own: so that the Heights becomes Gingerbread Cottage, Heathcliff the foundling baby, Catherine Sleeping Beauty at Thrushcross Grange, Jane Eyre and Rochester Beauty and the Beast, Fanny Price

Cinderella, Quilp Rumpelstiltskin, and so on. 'We enter human society', Alasdair MacIntyre writes,

> with one or more imputed characters – roles into which we have been drafted – and we have to learn what they are in order to be able to understand how others respond to us and how our responses to them are apt to be construed. It is through hearing stories about wicked step-mothers, lost children, good but misguided kings, wolves that suckle twin boys, youngest sons who receive no inheritance but must make their own way in the world and eldest sons who waste their inheritance on riotous living and go into exile to live with the swine, that children learn or mis-learn both what a child and what a parent is, what the cast of characters may be in the drama into which they have been born and what the ways of the world are. Deprive children of stories and you leave them unscripted, anxious stutterers in their actions as in their words. Hence there is no way to give us an understanding of any society, including our own, except through the stock of stories which constitute its initial dramatic resources. (*AV* 216)

Many things present themselves for comment in this passage: most immediately the things it takes for granted. Maybe, after all, there are those who do not *want* to learn 'what the ways of the world are'. Some of us might want to change the ways of the world – encouraged to do so, sometimes, by works of literature. Feminists, for example, might find MacIntyre's comment about children 'mis-learning' their gender-roles both disingenuous and tardy, given the fact that he mentions only one female role-model and that a negative one: the wicked step-mother. More important even than this, however, is the quality of MacIntyre's discussion of those 'imputed characters', 'roles' and dramas into which we are born. The vocabulary seems full of promise, were it not that MacIntyre sees the entire process in such inert and passive terms: characters are imputed, we are drafted into roles or told stories, at best we might pick and choose from a pre-determined stock of narratives, and so on.

The avowed destination of such a discussion is that the behaviour of story-telling animals is to be understood above all in terms of literature: characters, roles, narratives, etc. Here again we have literary criticism 'doing for ironists what the search for universal moral principles is supposed to do for metaphysicians'. In fact, what MacIntyre says amounts to only a partial understanding of literature's educative and moral influence. (Welcome, surely; but also incomplete.) He begins by saying that man is a story-telling animal; he ends up, like Rorty, sacking literature as grist for the dialectical mill. It is the final outcome of a way of reading literature that sees Plato and the poets as simply having divergent 'views', or Sophocles' dramas expounding a 'position' relative to classical Greek thought and modern liberalism: that tends to see philosophy and literature as undifferentiated approaches to the world. To some extent they are: *The Portrait of a Lady* surely is, among other things, a member of 'a long tradition of moral commentary, earlier members of which are Diderot's *Le Neveu de Rameau* and Kierkegaard's *Enten-Eller'* (*AV* 25). But is that the *most* important thing to say about James' novel? especially when we bear in mind the fact that the conversion of the moral agent into something part-author, part-character – a story-telling animal who by means of proleptic and retrospective narration ends up playing fast and loose with the virtues and vices according to his success in the world – is something about which literature itself expresses grave reservations?

Intimately connected to and arising from this understanding of literature's moral activity is the vacuous quality of that 'stock of stories' which MacIntyre says makes up a culture's 'initial dramatic resources'. It is because he does not take account of the kinds of moral problem presented by *Wuthering Heights*, and dramatized with such reflexive subtlety through the voices of its narrators, that MacIntyre is able to see this whole process of acculturation by means of narrative in such meliorative, passive, and teleological terms. In fact this teleogical perspective on culture's 'initial dramatic resources' is one he and a feminist criticism of him might share, despite arriving at diametrically opposite conclusions: where he sees such a process of acculturation as desirable, necessary, and beneficent, feminists would regard the same process as an act of patriarchal conspiracy. What *Wuthering Heights* suggests is that the processes of incorporating traditional stories (on the one hand) and of telling our own stories (on the other), are not as morally cut-and-dried as either MacIntyre or his feminist critics might imagine.

For if we come into the world with what MacIntyre calls 'an imputed character', it is possible for us swiftly to develop a moral outlook which may not be in harmony with either that character or with the attitudes, events, and outcomes encountered in the stories we are told. Not that readers' attitudes to stories and their writers are always to be thought of as resistant. But they are neither as pasteurized and innocuous as MacIntyre would have us believe, or as collusive and insidious as his feminist critics might argue. At one stage in *Wuthering Heights*, Nelly makes an extensive comparison between Hindley Earnshaw and Edgar Linton as fathers, husbands, and men. 'But you'll not want to hear my moralizing,' she tells Lockwood (and us); 'you'll judge as well as I can, all these things; at least, you'll think you will, and that's the same' (*WH* 220). The story-teller's reserving to herself a privileged moral viewpoint is answered by the reader's insistence on doing something very similar. The two of them would be in a state of mutual incomprehension – 'unscripted, anxious stutterers', if you like – were it not for the essential moral fluidity or lability of the whole enterprise: in this case *Wuthering Heights* itself. This fluidity or lability makes Emily Brontë's novel one of the most sceptical perspectives on 'story-telling animals' in the language; it prevents the processes described by MacIntyre being seen as either self-evidently remedial or self-evidently coercive; it makes the writing and reading of literature an engrossing but also an educative experience. This moral fluidity also goes some way towards demonstrating how intractable literature can be to the sort of philosophical treatment meted out to it by Rorty, MacIntyre, and Taylor. In doing so it reveals the 'seamless, undifferentiated "general text"' Rorty gushes about so enthusiastically to be a chimera.

It does not follow that we can choose to lapse into what Charles Taylor calls 'inarticulacy'. It is true that humans make sense of their lives by means of converting them into narratives, though I think it is a more intermittent activity than the philosophers discussed here believe, and one very much less likely to issue in the kind of 'onward and upward' vocabulary Taylor employs, with its emphasis on growth, understanding, and the rest. ('A place for everything, and everything in its place', as Samuel Smiles himself said.) Such moral activity takes place; therefore the interest moral philosophers take in it is welcome. If I am less sanguine than the philosophers about the outcomes of this ingrained moral habit, it is not because I have read more literature than them, or because I have read it better, but because I have read it in a different way.

Charles Taylor, it is true, recognizes a morally questionable element in the entire narrativizing process he describes:

we can readily see why some people distrust articulation as a source of delusion or fear it as a profanation. … It is not mainly because there are so many dead formulations, so many trite imitations, although this is one of the reasons why one may prefer silence. … What is worse is that the whole thing may be counterfeited. This is not to say that words of power themselves may be counterfeit. But the act by which their pronouncing releases force can be rhetorically imitated, either to feed our self-conceit or for even more sinister purposes, such as the defence of a discreditable status quo. Trite formulae may combine with the historical sham to weave a cocoon of moral assurance around us which actually insulates us from the energy of true moral sources. And there is worse: the release of power can be hideously caricatured to enhance the energy of evil, as at Nuremburg. As for the narrative constructions of our lives, there is no need to speak at length about the possibilities of delusion which attend us here.[23]

Where Cathy and Heathcliff, or Nelly and Lockwood, or the Charles Dickens who wrote *David Copperfield* fit among these delusions I will leave the reader to decide. As I say, it is not a question of arresting such a moral habit, even if we could; only of suggesting to those philosophers who find the word 'narrative' either essential or convenient just how complex the activity is and to what unexpected, possibly dubious, purposes it may be put. Stories like those Lydgate and Bulstrode tell themselves and allow others to understand are evidence in particular of our capacity to delude ourselves and others and to rationalize our doing so. Story-telling animals may be habitual tellers of fibs, like Nelly Dean. But despite that fact we still possess an equally powerful emotional need for other things besides delusions: for absolutes like justice and truth; for something better than what Charles Taylor calls the BA, or 'best account' principle.

Despite what Nelly Dean would have us believe, there are occasions on which the BA principle or the retrospective re-quantifying of virtue and vice in terms of success and failure will not do, and literature is very interested in such occasions. It is no use interrupting King Lear and suggesting that he make do with a best account of his relationship with his daughters, and through them with natural justice; no point in telling him that there is nothing beyond vocabularies to serve as a criterion of choice between them. (Least of all is it any use advising him not to throw in the cards and lapse into inarticulacy!) Nor do I think that Lear is a special case, and that the stress he encounters is of a different order from the rest of us. It would be equally useless to issue similar advice to Lydgate in his miserable marriage, or to Bulstrode after his exposure. The only thing special about Lear is that he is articulate (or at least not completely inarticulate) at moments when the rest of us really would be lost for words. For most of us the falling apart of our tenderly fostered narratives does indeed reduce us to inarticulacy, let the philosophers say what they like. When the catastrophe finally strikes Bulstrode, and he is left alone with his grieving wife, what Taylor calls inarticulacy becomes his natural defence:

> Some time, perhaps – when he was dying – he would tell her all: in the deep shadow of that time, when she held his hand in the gathering darkness, she might listen without recoiling from his touch. Perhaps: but concealment had been the habit of his life, and the impulse to confession had no power against the dread of a deeper humiliation.[24]

Maybe it would have been better not to have confected the stories in the first place. Maybe it is true that the desire to avoid certain harms, and the ability to do so by putting some narratives about, only lures us into deeper water – before, as it were, 'human voices wake us, and we drown'. In fact the telling of stories is an activity which in and of itself reminds those involved, narrators and listeners alike, of the risks involved.

2.3 Martha Nussbaum

Before we leave the subject I want to turn to one last philosopher. Of all the recent North American studies in moral and ethical philosophy which seek to incorporate literature into the accounts they offer – and which are welcome for doing so – Martha Nussbaum's *Love's Knowledge* is the most extensive and ambitious, and also the most concentrated in literary–critical terms. It appears to be a highly specialized study, limited as it is to Proust, *David Copperfield*, Samuel Beckett's trilogy, and (above all and in particular) mid-to-late Henry James. In part this is a claim for limited liability on Nussbaum's behalf. 'I have', she writes, 'confined myself to only one small part of one literary tradition; but in doing so I do not mean to imply that there are not other traditions, other perspectives, whose inclusion would be important for the full completion of this enquiry.'[25] Nussbaum's work on Dickens, however, encourages her to spread her net, 'from a defense of James to the more general defense of the novel' (*LK* 364), which defence is her real subject. The moral–philosophical objective of her enquiry, after all, is an answer to the ancient question 'how to live?', and so even if her choice of texts is limited that choice is clearly an important one with representative implications in the Western tradition at least.

For Nussbaum, as for Richard Rorty, 'social democracy and the art of the novel are allies' (*LK* 391); novels are 'enquiries into the human good' (*LK* 390); novels are a principle means of 'puzzling out, in times of great moral difficulty, what might be, for us, the best way to live' (*LK* 170); novels create a reading community 'in which each person's imagining and thinking and feeling are respected as morally valuable' (*LK* 48). In particular, for Nussbaum the novel is a moral enquiry of a specific kind: such enquiries 'show us the worth and richness of plural qualitative thinking and engender in their reader a richly qualitative kind of seeing' (*LK* 36); they 'suggest that to see any single feature of a situation appropriately it is usually essential to see it in its relations of connectedness to many other features of its complex and concrete context' (*LK* 38); they involve 'the recognition of plural incommensurable goods' (*LK* 63), as opposed to that unified and transcendent system leading to ultimate idealities described by Plato and others; and they involve recognition flowing on from this, of 'the richness and diversity of the positive commitments of a good person living in a world of uncontrolled happening' (*LK* 64). Thus novels of the kind Nussbaum admires 'are written in a style that gives sufficient attention to particularity and emotion' and 'involve their readers in relevant activities of searching and feeling' (*LK* 46): 'in the activity of literary imagining we are led to imagine and describe with greater precision, focusing our attention on each word, feeling each event more keenly – whereas much of actual life goes by without that heightened awareness, and is thus, in a certain sense, not fully lived' (*LK* 47).

The unexamined life is not worth living; and despite this fleeting allusion to Plato, Nussbaum's approach – in particular, her emphasis on social democracy, personhood, and pluralism, on 'searching and feeling' where self and others are concerned, and on the importance of the moral context to decisions and judgements – is basically an Aristotelian one, however liberalized. In being so her approach is also distinctly Rortyan, Tayloresque, MacIntyrish. These four philosophers taken as a group not only constitute a highly influential group in contemporary moral and social philosophy, with a pronounced interest in literature, but are representative *Aristotelians*, ethically speaking. Their emphasis on moral realism and on the plurality and multifariousness of the world is quintessentially Aristotelian, as is their dedication to *phronesis* as a way of making sense of that world. They share an Aristotelian suspicion of moral or categorical absolutes, and they are as a rule dedicated (as Aristotle was) to the pursuit of the ethical and social mean – the balance, the medium – between the vices of excess and the vices of defect. Like Aristotle, they are less interested in what virtue is, in Platonic and essential terms, than in the practical discovery of how we should or can become good; and their desired aim, like his, is human happiness: *eudaimonia*, 'flourishing'. Thus we have Rorty's emphasis on vocabularies, for example; or MacIntyre and Taylor's emphasis on lives-as-narrative. The first two chapters of David Daiches' undergraduate classic, *Critical Approaches to Literature*, are called 'The Platonic Dilemma' and 'The Aristotelian Solution': and in this group of philosophers the solution to the challenge left by Plato in general and the *Republic* in particular is meliorist, pragmatic, reformist, balanced: just as it was for Aristotle himself.[26]

There is nothing wrong with that. The world is a plural and multifarious place, and all of us could do with more practical wisdom with which to make sense of it. And which one of us would not like a little more *eudaimonia* in our lives when all is said and done? Literature has never stopped insisting upon the multifariousness of the world, and has often yearned for *eudaimonia* more than anything else. I am going to mention Tolstoy in a moment, and no writer pursued a sense of human flourishing more intently than he did, in the sections of *Anna Karenina* devoted to Levin and his family, above all, but also in story after story elsewhere. But then no writer recorded more mournfully – but also, somehow, more zestfully – the speed with which that sense of flourishing can disappear: when the archetypyal Tolstoyan landowner catches sight of a pretty peasant, for example, in the short story of his called, simply, 'The Devil'.

If literature just said to us that Aristotelian flourishing is unattainable, or impossible to sustain due to its fragility, that would be one thing; and it would not necessarily stop us from aiming to achieve it. But literature often says more than this – something that philosophers like Plato, or Rousseau, or Nietzsche might concur with, too: that a sense of human flourishing that is built upon the notion of an ethical middle way (valuable as that idea must always be for us), and which banishes not simply the vices of defect but the vices of excess, involves the suppression of essential human qualities. Grace, for example, or wit, or charm, or genius, or the almost spiritual desire for unquestioning belief, or the urge on our part to demand and supply comprehensive accounts of the world, multifarious though it may be, and so on. It may be an excellent thing for us to remember, generally speaking, the richness and diversity of our positive commitments in a world of uncontrolled happening; but it may also be an excellent thing for us to forget exactly those things once in a while.

What Martha Nussbaum would make of *Moby-Dick* I am not sure. But that novel does provide an excellent instance of what I mean. In chapter twenty-three, as the *Pequod* 'thrust her vindictive bows into the cold malicious waves' outside Nantucket harbour, the narrator addresses the helmsman, struggling along the leeward shore onto which the wind would drive them if it could. 'The port would fain give succor', Melville writes; 'the port is pitiful; in the port is safety, comfort, hearthstone, supper, warm blankets, friends, all that's kind to our mortalities. But in that gale, the port, the land, is that ship's direst jeopardy; she must fly all hospitality; one touch of land, though it but graze the keel, would make her shudder through and through.' And the moral follows accordingly:

> Know ye, now, Bulkington? Glimpses do ye seem to see of that mortally intolerable truth; that all deep, earnest thinking is but the intrepid effort of the soul to keep the open independence of her sea; while the wildest winds of heaven and earth conspire to cast her on the treacherous, slavish shore?
>
> But as in landlessness alone resides the highest truth, shoreless, indefinite as God – so, better is it to perish in that howling infinite, than be ingloriously dashed upon the lee, even if that were safety! For worm-like, then, oh! who would craven crawl to land! Terrors of the terrible! is all this agony so vain? Take heart, take heart, O Bulkington! Bear thee grimly, demigod! Up from the spray of thy ocean-perishing – straight up, leaps thy apotheosis!

Well: Most books that live, live in spite of the author's laying it on thick, as D.H. Lawrence would say. And there is a kind of wilful proto-Nietzscheanism about much of *Moby-Dick*. Nor am I saying that we ought to spend more time with the tigers of wrath than the horses of instruction: quite the contrary. But there is something in *Moby-Dick* that writers quite different from Melville – good, balanced Aristotelians like Pope, Samuel Johnson, and even Jane Austen – have testified to also. Whether or not we would want to embark on three years' whaling with the *Pequod*, we have to acknowledge that Ahab possesses some human qualities we would be loth to lose: energy, courage, dynamism, 'vision', passion. ('All visible objects', Ahab says, 'are but as pasteboard masks' – and he is right, surely, if only up to a point. Sometimes that is just how things appear to us, and it is not necessarily evidence that we have 'fallen out of life' when we see them as such. The white whale, for example, remains a remarkably innocent creature; but it is something *behind* the whale's pasteboard mask that Ahab pursues: and he throws up a lot of sparks in the chase.) We see those qualities (or others like them) in named individuals like Ahab, King Lear, and Henry Crawford (from *Mansfield Park*); but we also see them in those anti-Augustan vices of excess Pope, Swift, and Johnson are simplistically taken to oppose *tout court*. The fact is that Pope, Swift, and Johnson have much more appetite for excess (Dullness, Yahoos, Vanity) than their Augustan training would suggest they should have.

So it is that what Nussbaum calls the Aristotelian enquiry in *Love's Knowledge* – concerned as she puts it 'to state the opening question in a general and inclusive way, excluding at the start no major story about the good life for human beings' – is one which in fact does involve some wholesale acts of exclusion: doubly so when she goes on to say that such an enquiry 'asks…what it is for a human being to live well' and what will contribute to human betterment in two ways in particular, 'by promoting individual clarification and self-understanding, and by moving individuals towards communal attunement' (*LK* 173). (Roll on Richard Rorty, with his private perfection and his human liberty.) Nussbaum cannot see, for example, that to ask the question 'what is it for a human being to live well' is already a drastic limitation on 'the good life for human beings'. (In short, that the question *how* to live is not the same question as how to *live*.)[27] Neither can she see that individual clarification and communal attunement may be ideals for some but not for others. ('The novel takes its stand with Aristotle', she believes, 'that human beings are fundamentally social; I believe this, and it is one of the origins of my own interest in the novel'; *LK* 166.) How much communal attunement does Hamlet display, or Julien Sorel, or Madame Bovary (or Nietzsche or Kafka or Wittgenstein or Mandelstam)? Given the nature of his community, would it have been a good thing if Hamlet had displayed more? ('Good Hamlet, cast thy nighted colour off,/And let thine eye look like a friend on Denmark.') So when Nussbaum says that 'It is…the human good that we are seeking, and not the good of some other being' (*LK* 66), and when she says (with these words of Aristotle's ringing in her ears) that 'After reading Derrida…I feel a certain hunger for blood' – not for his blood, that is to say, but for 'writing about literature that talks of human lives and choices as if they matter to us all' (*LK* 171) – a part of us wonders what species in fact she has in mind that she should regard it with so much moral loftiness; and how much blood we actually get from *her*; and whether she herself is able to talk about human lives and choices not merely as pabulum for the Aristotelian project but as if they really matter.

Nor is it surprising that the Jamesian idea of the novel as record of moral negotiation should be of special importance to the 'Aristotelian nontranscendent enquiry' upon which Nussbaum has launched herself – and which she believes to be 'an ally, rather than the enemy of literature' (*LK* 389). We can see that James fits the project and the project fits James: and that makes us worry about both of them. The Aristotelian principle of moral noncommensurability, for example, says:

> Look and see how rich and diverse the ultimate values in the world are. Do not fail to investigate each moral item, cherishing it for its own specific nature and not reducing it to something else. These injunctions lead in the direction of a long and open-ended list... (*LK* 82)

The capacity to see the richness and diversity of the world, to recognize that they reflect incommensurate, ultimate values, and to cherish the results of your moral investigations without engaging in reductionism, is what we would normally call maturity; and according to Nussbaum the author of *The Golden Bowl* represents such an Aristotelian capacity to the full. 'We might describe the new ideal this way' Nussbaum writes:

> See clearly and with high intelligence. Respond with the vibrant sympathy of a vividly active imagination. If there are conflicts, face them squarely and with keen perception. Choose as well as you can for overt action, but at every moment remember the more comprehensive duties of the imagination and emotions. If love of your husband requires hurting and lying to Charlotte [in *The Golden Bowl*], then do these cruel things, making the better choice. But never cease, all the while, to be richly conscious of Charlotte's pain and to bear, in imagination and feeling, the full burden of your guilt as the cause of that pain. If life is a tragedy, see that; respond to that fact with pity for others and fear for yourself. Never for a moment close your eyes or dull your feelings. (*LK* 134–5)

It is easy to make fun of this long and open-ended list. Why not add, like Tolstoy, '*Must not read novels*', or 'Only play cards in emergencies', or 'Keep away from women'? Tolstoy filled his diary with instructions of this kind only to record the next morning, as often as not, 'Spent the day badly; went to the gipsies.' ('It's easier', he wrote on 17 March 1847, 'to write ten volumes of philosophy than to put one single principle into practice.') But putting the mischievous impulse to one side – not to mention the issue of what relation all this actually has to Aristotle – what does it mean to be richly conscious, Rorty-style, of someone else's pain: what exactly is that? How much interest should you take in someone else's pain? Interest of what kind? And then again, if your life is a tragedy, is not your inability to see it in those terms one of the things that makes it tragic? The worst is not, after all, if we can say 'this is the worst'.

But however hard it may be for the rest of us to imagine becoming more vibrant and vividly active at the drop of a hat, for Nussbaum the things of this kind she sees in *The Golden Bowl* add up to a kind of moral dispensation: for us to be 'finely aware and richly responsible', as James rather featly puts it in the the the preface to *The Princess Casamassima*. Reading a novel of James' is like 'a Socratic working-through of the interlocutor's or reader's own moral intuitions that will leave this person clearer about his or her own moral aims'. The 'moral assessment process' entered into in this way involves so much 'exploration and unraveling', so much 'actively seeing and caring for all the parties concerned', that the reader (or in the case of Maggie Verver, the character) is bound to be 'safely right in the perfection of his or her attention' (*LK* 142–3). So it is that 'the person of practical wisdom' reveals himself to be 'surprisingly close to the artist and/or the perceiver of art' (*LK* 84), and the artist and the perceiver together really do rise, arm-in-arm, to pre-eminence within the high culture of the democracies, as Rorty would say.

This is an ideal, of course; and Nussbaum can see that this is not all that James had to contribute to the Aristotelian view. The noncommensurability principle and the fine awareness and rich responsibility went only so far, after all: you cannot give equal attention to everything. 'The demands of the new ideal of seeing', for example, 'are not always compatible with an adequate fulfillment of each of our commitments, for some loves are exclusive and demand a blindness in other quarters' (*LK* 136) – an expression well worth saving up for the divorce court. Human beings, it seems, like Humbert Humbert, 'are inclined to miss things': 'to pass over things, to leave out certain interpretative possiblities while pursuing others' (*LK* 144), which is something of a puzzle when you remember that the principle of noncommensurability more or less insured against any such thing. (After all, if there are so many ultimate goods, why pass over any one of them? Is one more ultimate than the others?) 'The effort to see and really to represent', Nussbaum quotes James as saying, 'is no idle business in face of the constant force that makes for muddlement.'

> So Henry James on the task of the moral imagination. We live amid bewildering complexities. Obtuseness and refusal of vision are our besetting vices. Responsible lucidity can be wrested from that darkness only by painful, vigilant effort, the intense scrutiny of particulars. Our highest and hardest task is to make ourselves people 'on whom nothing is lost.' (*LK* 148)

'Every age', Dan Jacobson suggests, 'has its own particular forms of philistinism, which it finds almost impossible to recognize as such. How difficult it is in our own case to believe that a critical approach which apparently does literature so much honour, which treats literary works as the nearest thing we have to scriptures and oracles, can itself be philistine: indifferent to art, even hostile to it.'[28] This will seem a harsh criticism to bring alongside a book like *Love's Knowledge*; yet I cannot help doing so. It is bound to seem churlish to say that obtuseness of vision can on many occasions be saving graces of humanity rather than besetting vices; that 'the complicated delicacies of the human heart' may indeed 'keep us from the excessive crudeness of hope' (*LK* 213) but be no more welcome or more useful as a result; and that while 'Life…is a tough, complex business, requiring, at its best, much refinement of feeling and much clarity of thought' (*LK* 188), it also requires something quite different from those things: something not very welcome, maybe, in the Aristotelian nontranscendent enquiry, but important and business-like in itself.

It is hard to say what that 'something' is; perhaps it is best to say that as life is a tough and complex business it sometimes requires a little less refinement of feeling and clarity of thought, and a little more force and decisiveness – things more conducive, it may be, to 'individual clarification' than to 'communal attunement'. Nobody would be particularly surprised I imagine, on the basis of the summary of *Love's Knowledge* offered here, to learn that D.H. Lawrence rates only one mention in the book (and that in regard to an essay of Wayne Booth's about him). But here are two passages from letters Lawrence wrote to the same friend (a Buddhist, it so happens: Earl Brewster), the first in 1921:

> No, I don't understand a bit what you mean about rightness and about relationships and about the world. Damn the world, anyhow. And I hate 'understanding' people, and I hate more still to be understood. Damn understanding more than anything;

the second in 1926:

> All truth – and real living is the only truth – has in it the elements of battle and repudiation. *Nothing is wholesale.* The problem of truth is: How can we most deeply *live?* – And the answer is different in every case.[29]

This is not a question of making a choice in some crude way, clearly: though I think the differences between Lawrence and James on these issues are very profound, with large implications for the fiction they produced and the lives they led. The answer to the question how can we most deeply live is different in every case, as Lawrence points out: different for him, different for Earl Brewster, different for Melville and Henry James. But these small examples do suggest that literature may not necessarily 'take its stand' with Aristotle and the social, any more than the human race as a whole does.

Nussbaum can see that 'books may also promote self-absorption and hinder mutuality' (*LK* 240); that reading a lot of Henry James and Proust (or any other novelist you care to name) might be regarded by some (Plato, say) as 'a preparation for a life that is lived at one remove from life, a life that gains fineness and clarity by warding off certain risks and dangers.' She can ask, as a result, 'Is this good, or is it bad?' (*LK* 188). She can see that she could be accused of 'lacking in general rule-guided toughness' (*LK* 198), but not that there might be other varieties of moral 'toughness' than philosophically-oriented, rule-guided ones. She can see that literature poses the question 'How should one live?' in a way unfamiliar to, say, Kantians and utilitarians; she can also see that literature has, on occasion, the potential to show us 'the limits of that ethical question itself', to show us things that 'lead us outside of the ethical attitude altogether, outside of the quest for balanced vision and perfect rightness.' But for her the space outside that quest is a kind of twilight zone almost by definition. The novel 'can include, or at least indicate *the silence into which its own responsive prose has no entry*' (*LK* 190; my italics): but why should we assume that the extra-Aristotelian, mutuality-hindering zone of moral and intellectual idealism is a silent one? Is Ahab silent? (Or D.H. Lawrence?!)

What Nussbaum cannot see is that humanity in general and writers in particular very much want to have their moral cake and eat it, too; and that their urge to have both causes harm but also good. That urge is essential for works of literature to be brought into being in the first place, but that is only one of its minor functions. Nussbaum suggests that we 'reject as incoherent'

> the aspiration to leave behind altogether the constitutive conditions of our humanity, and to seek for a life that is really the life of another sort of human being. ... [Her argument] asks us to bound our aspirations by recalling that there are some very general conditions of human existence that are also necessary conditions for the values that we know, love, and appropriately pursue. (*LK* 379)

But the aspiration she would have us leave behind is not only a constitutive condition of humanity: it is a constitutive condition of her entire enquiry. In so far as her work is a moralistic philosophy that describes how we should live, as opposed to a moral philosophy that describes how we actually do, of course she wishes to alter the 'conditions' of humanity (without leaving them behind altogether). And every one of us, in so far as we are reflective creatures at all, entertains aspirations of the same kind, more or less continuously. Inevitably such aspirations are, in some degree or other, transcendent – if only in the sense of changing conditions and leaving them behind that way – and their being so is one of the constitutive conditions of humanity. The general conditions of human existence are ones we accept at best only provisionally, as and when they do not interfere with what we want to do. We do not want our aspirations to be bounded in the least. And as for 'the values that we know, love, and appropriately pursue', these have been like red rags to a bull on more occasions than Nussbaum has had hot dinners:

> *Queen.*   Good Hamlet, cast thy nighted colour off,
> And let thine eye look like a friend on Denmark.
> Do not for ever with thy veilèd lids
> Seek for thy noble father in the dust:
> Though know'st 'tis common; all that live must die,
> Passing through nature to eternity.

> *Hamlet.*   Ay, madam, it is common.
> *Queen.*   If it be,
> Why seems it so particular with thee?
>   (I. ii. 68–76)

The appropriateness of such values is the last thing we voluntarily surrender to the sphere of given human conditions – in works of literature least of all. The conditions and the values we do not know and which we seek out all the same, have the capacity to motivate us at least as powerfully as our perception that 'given' values (loyalty to dead husbands in Gertrude's case – and loyalty to dead fathers in Hamlet's) are being abused.

The same point can be put another way. We may indeed live amid a huge panoply of incommensurable goods – the kind of wandering rocks Richard Rorty calls 'lots of cultural options but no privileged central discipline or practice'; and such a panoply may demand Aristotelian practical wisdom for us to negotiate it. But we also have an ineradicable belief that one of the ways to make the negotiation – the best way, whether it is hard or easy, brings you the admiration of your fellows or earns you only loneliness and ostracism – is to affirm an entirely contrary principle, in which the rival goods *can* be set in order and the whole *be* twisted into some final significance, be that final significance Platonic, Christian, Kantian, utilitarian, Marxist, feminist, post-modernist, 'humanist', or whatever. (The belief that the incommensurables must be reconciled motivates Hamlet during the first half of his drama and brings him to level such shattering accusations at his mother in the closet scene; the unwilling recognition that they cannot leads him to say that there is a special providence in the fall of a sparrow.)

It is easy to see why a moral philosopher might want to get us off that infernal aspirational mechanism (as Karl Popper sought to do in thinking about the open society and its enemies: hopeless and cruel idealists like Plato and Marx), and might want to find some field of moral endeavour that offers just such an escape: novels, for example. It is easy to imagine why such a philosopher might say that 'As readers of stories we are deeply immersed in the messy impure world of human particularity; and we learn, as readers, to ascribe a high importance to events that befall our particular heroes and heroines as they move through the world of contingency' (*LK* 386). (Roll on Alasdair MacIntyre and Charles Taylor.) But this is not an escape at all. The more deeply immersed we are in the messy impure world of human particularity, the more urgently we wish to get out of it and to have the thing come to some sort of 'commensurable' conclusion: a death, or a marriage, or a conclusion that says there is no significance, *à la* Samuel Beckett, but which is just as commensurable and 'Platonic' an ending for saying so. We want heroes and heroines to get *beyond* the world of uncontrolled happening we find them experiencing. There is nothing in works of literature to suggest that they have found a way to circumvent that pattern; they could not, any more than we can. Our urge to accept runs alongside our urge to deny; our urge to commit runs alongside our urge to transcend; our urge to gather together (and to domesticate) runs alongside our urge to be free – and our urge to make final, definitive sense of the 'bewildering complexities' among which we live runs alongside our Aristotelian capacity to acknowledge that we cannot. Those who live the life of pure and seamless commensurability – or think they do – 'have no interest in or understanding of literary works of the familiar sort', granted (*LK* 124). But who lives that life? Certainly Plato did not; his was in fact a lively interest in and understanding of literature, however limited: he understood that it was morally dubious, which it is, and that he should condemn it, which he did. But what form did his condemnation take? A literary form! We may live the life of incommensurability and of a plurality of goods, but we commonly refuse to recognize the fact, and act accordingly.

Nussbaum's belief is that literary theory will and must eventually return to 'a concern with the practical – to the ethical and social questions that give literature its high importance in our lives' (*LK* 168). So the question asked about reading – 'Is this good, or is it bad?' – is one she answers by re-situating it, to offer what she calls 'perceptive equilibrium' as a kind of social value. She calls for a 'revolution' in our attitudes: 'that, in public and in private, we create our lives with one another with as much subtlety, responsiveness, delicacy, and imagination as are involved in the creation of a work of literary art, dismantling our anger, fostering our gentleness' (*LK* 216).

In fact Nussbaum herself does not call for this revolution, though she clearly seconds it enthusiastically: one novel in particular does. When I say that the novel concerned is *The Princess Casamassima* we would have to acknowledge that this would be a revolution indeed, if it could convert the pitifully pulverized Hyacinth Robinson into a harbinger of itself. It would be the turning of an apparent failure into a success: in fact an excellent example of how writers like James and Nussbaum try to get beyond the 'constitutive conditions' of Western politics. As is this:

> Some major choices affecting our lives – say, Supreme Court decisions – [are] made in effect by one or two complex reflective processes

in the minds of one or two reading, thinking, feeling beings. An eloquent piece of writing ... might possibly alter the course of that reflection. Do we know such things before attempting? (*LK* 193)

Copies of *The Princess Casamassima* could be mailed to the President; but if they are, the senders must hold one belief about literature very close to their hearts indeed, as to all intents and purposes a political creed:

> Novels like this one create that revolution as a record, and also generate it, as an act, in the hearts of its readers, who exemplify for some brief hours the record and who may come to feel, thereafter, a marked discontent with the crudeness of everyday discourse and action and feeling, a marked desire for the finer, the more truly compassionate thing. (*LK* 217)

In fact Wordsworth sent a copy of *Lyrical Ballads* to Charles James Fox; and the politician read the poems and sent an appreciative letter to the author – which is more or less as far as it went.

I hope that the foregoing discussion (all of it, Rorty, MacIntyre, and Taylor included) suggests to the reader how vulnerable these loosely Aristotelian accounts of literature can be, particularly when *phronesis* comes to be seen as a state of mind equated with liberal pluralism, and 'the positive commitments of a good person living in a world of uncontrolled happening' are seen as a kind of moral ideal. It is fatally easy to add a Jamesian fine awareness and rich responsibility to this mixture and produce something almost indestructably naïve. (The reader or the character 'safely right in the perfection of his or her attention', and so on.) There could be no more disturbing case of naïvete in any novelist than that scene in *The Ambassadors* (Book 5, Chapter 2) where Lambert Strether, the dessicated New Englander suddenly swamped by the moral and experiential fleshpots of Paris, grasps little Billham like the Ancient Mariner and, amid conditions of almost no conscious authorial irony whatsoever, urges him at inordinate length to 'Live all you can; it's a mistake not to.' (I say inordinate length because little Billham does not seem the type given to feeling either marked discontent with crudeness or marked desire for the finer thing. Indeed Strether's speech seems like water off a duck's back. So much for the reader or listener exemplifying the Jamesian record.) 'Don't at any rate miss things out of stupidity', Strether pleads:

> Of course I don't take you for a fool, or I shouldn't be addressing you thus awfully. Do what you like so long as you don't make my mistake. For it was a mistake. Live!

Nor is that scene in Paris a marginal or secondary one: James' notebooks prove that it was the inspiration and core of the novel. In his entry recording the germ of *The Ambassadors* he decided 'I can't make him [Strether] a novelist. ... But I want him "intellectual," I want him *fine*, clever, literary almost: it deepens the irony, the tragedy.'[30] To which what can you say, but how blind can even the very greatest writers be? For the irony here is at Strether's expense, certainly, as James intended; but it is at James' expense at least as much as Strether's. The tragedy is his. In Strether's pitiful and misdirected jeremiad we have the author talking about himself, desperately trying to set things right and acknowledge past mistakes. 'We must know as much as possible, in our beautiful art ... what we are talking about', James wrote to Hugh Walpole in 1913, 'and the only way to know is to have lived and loved and cursed and floundered and enjoyed and suffered. I think I don't regret a single "excess" of my responsive youth – I only regret, in chilled age, certain occasions and possibilities I *didn't* embrace.'[31]

So much for the Aristotelian non-transcendent enquiry and for 'individual clarification'. So much for seeing clearly and with high intelligence, for responding with the vibrant sympathy of a vividly active imagination, for facing conflicts squarely and with keen perception; so much for seeing your life as a tragedy if that is what it is. Why should we ask of James here in *The Ambassadors* what we could never do ourselves: 'Never for a moment close your eyes or dull your feelings'? Why should Henry James not close his eyes occasionally, like Bulstrode, Lydgate, and the rest of us? Simply because he is a *novelist*? Does being a novelist protect him from the constant force that makes for muddlement, or from entertaining attitudes far from finely aware and richly responsible – about his own life, for example, but also about 'a Jewry that had burst all bounds' in his native city?

> That it has burst all bounds in New York, almost any combination of figures or of objects taken at hazard sufficiently proclaims; but I remember how the rising waters, on this summer night, rose, to the imagination, even above the housetops and seemed to sound their murmur to the pale distant stars. It was as if we had been thus,

in the crowded, hustled roadway, where multiplication, multiplication of everything, was the dominant note, at the bottom of some vast sallow aquarium in which innumerable fish, of over-developed proboscis, were to bump together, for ever, amid heaped spoils of the sea.[32]

In his early days as a critic, and with *Our Mutual Friend* in mind, James assured his readers that 'A story based upon those elementary passions in which alone we seek the true and final manifestation of character must be told in a spirit of intellectual superiority to those passions. That is, the author must understand what he is talking about.'[33] According to the preface to *The Princess Casamassima* characters, too, must be 'intense *perceivers*' as their creator should be; of interest to us 'only in proportion as they feel their respective situations'. There are those who are finely aware and richly responsible, and

It is those moved in this latter fashion who 'get most' out of all that happens to them and who in so doing enable us ... also to get most. Their being finely aware – as Hamlet and Lear, say, are finely aware – *makes* absolutely the intensity of their adventure, gives the maximum of sense to what befalls them. We care, our curiosity and our sympathy care, comparatively little for what happens to the stupid, the coarse and the blind ...[34]

These matters will always be subject to debate: but are either Hamlet or King Lear 'finely aware and richly responsible'? The men who, never mind their other failings, treated Ophelia and Cordelia as they did? *Finally* aware both of them may be, up to a point – but finely, hardly at all, unless you mean in narcissistic terms. Talking of street life: who would have thought, for example, that Daniel Defoe could be more finely aware and richly responsible than Henry James? Yet he is, in his way, without poor, stupid, coarse, blind Moll Flanders having the least idea about what her 'respective situation' is:

I Went out now by Day-light, and wandred about I knew not whither, and in search of I knew not what, when the Devil put a Snare in my way of a dreadful Nature indeed, and such a one as I have never had before or since; going thro' *Aldersgate-street* there was a pretty little Child had been at a Dancing-school, and was going home, all alone, and my Prompter, like a true Devil, set me upon this innocent Creature; I talk'd to it, and it prattl'd to me again, and I took it by the Hand and led it a long till I came to a pav'd Alley that goes into *Bartholomew Close*, and I led it in there; the Child said that was not its way home; I said, yes, my Dear it is, I'll show you the way home; the Child had a little Necklace on of Gold Beads, and I had my Eye upon that, and in the dark of the Alley I stoop'd, pretending to mend the Child's Clog that was loose, and took off her Necklace and the Child never felt it, and so led the Child on again: Here, I say, the Devil put me upon killing the Child in the dark Alley, that it might not Cry; but the very thought frighted me so that I was ready to drop down, but I turn'd the Child about and bad it go back again, for that was not its way home; the Child said so she would, and I went thro' into *Bartholomew Close*, and then turn'd round to another Passage that goes into *Long-lane*, so away into *Charterhouse-Yard* and out into *St. John's-street*, then crossing into *Smithfield*, went down *Chick-lane* and into *Field-lane* to *Holbourn-bridge*, when mixing with the Crowd of People usually passing there, it was not possible to have been found out; and thus I enterpriz'd my second Sally into the World.[35]

Needless to say, this confession of Moll's is not the end of it. Having told her tale and recorded her statement she immediately wants to change it; wants us to see the events in a different light, wants to exculpate herself, blame somebody else, blame anybody but herself. The story she has told is true (no one could make up one like this), but it is not a Best Account; so she quickly revises it. The parents were neglectful ('poor little Lamb ... it would teach them to take more Care of it another time'); the mother was vain ('to have her Child look Fine at the Dancing School'); the maid was irresponsible ('careless Jade ... taken up perhaps with some Fellow that had met her by the way'): 'However, I did the Child no harm, I did not so much as fright it ... and did nothing but what, as I may say, meer Necessity drove me to.'

What should we, can we, say to Moll Flanders, 'intellectually superior' to her passions as we believe ourselves to be? Congratulate her for behaving so well as a story-telling animal but so badly as a human being, telling her story and then revising it, 'from innocence to strife and then to a higher harmony'? Or condemn her for 'obtuseness and refusal of vision', for insufficient individual clarification and communal attunement? And once we have made those decisions what shall we go on to say about the book in which she appears? Decide whether her confession promotes human liberty or private perfection, when it evidently promotes neither? Decide whether what we have here is a stimulus or a relaxant, when it is evidently something more than either of those things? Decide whether or not it falls under the 'familiar criteria' (moral or aesthetic) of the early eighteenth-century novel-cum-biography, when it evidently both does and does not? The questions are worth asking and the issues are worth raising, under certain circumstances, no doubt: but are they the *most* important issues and questions raised by what Moll reveals about herself, or Nelly Dean, or Humbert Humbert, or Lambert Strether, or Henry James? In thinking that these and others like them *are* the most important questions, is it not true that certain philosophers have abandoned the rigour associated with their own science without inheriting the rigour of their neighbours'?

3

'These Shafts Can Conquer Troy, These Shafts Alone': Criticism and Psychoanalysis*

There is no doubt that psychoanalysis today is a more sophisticated and humane discipline than it was under Freud and his 'inner circle' of fellow-analysts. The ambitiousness of its aims psychoanalysis has always appreciated; the difficulty of achieving them is now in a clearer perspective. We are more sceptical than another child of Freud's time, Thomas Mann, who praised what he called 'the practical and constructive zeal of experts who erected a structure of more general investigation round the psychiatric and medical core' of psychoanalysis.[1] A great deal of the stridency, the bombast, and the intellectual self-satisfaction of the pioneers has leached away, to be replaced with a genuine degree of intellectual humility.

But developments of this kind have only gone so far. There remains even in this most self-lacerating and contentious science a foundational set of beliefs that is protected and transmitted in many ways. Analysts are notoriously shy of criticizing Freud himself, certainly; but it is also true the intellectual discipline most interested in the family and in the tangle of relationships existing between parents and children is itself predominantly clannish and dynastic. Thus the basic set of principles is transmitted, more or less intact, from generation to generation. But the very value and centrality of this inheritance has made keeping faith with it an issue with great potential for factiousness and dissension, often with a distinct flavour of Oedipal rivalry. Freud's intellectual couplings and uncouplings with Breuer, Fliess, Adler, Stekel, Rank, and Jung are well-enough known; but then there are Anna Freud's disagreements with Melanie Klein (the euphemistically titled 'Controversial Discussions' of 1943–44), Melanie Klein's with her daughter Melitta Schmideberg, and Jacques-Alain Miller's controversial editorship of his father-in-law Jacques Lacan's posthumous papers. In France the Paris

Psychoanalytical Society was followed by the French Psychoanalytical Society which was followed by the *École Freudienne de Paris* which was followed by the so-called 'Fourth Group'. All these mutations and schisms involved the enigmatic Lacan.

So it is that interested outsiders may be in a better position to question what Thomas Mann called the 'core' of Freudian belief, or at least to describe and comment upon the organizing principles upon which it rests. The outsider whose approach I would like to consider briefly here, before turning to some psychoanalysts themselves, is the British philosopher R.G. Collingwood.

It was Collingwood's belief that certain problems long developing within Western culture reached their climax in the First World War. 'The War', he wrote, 'was an unprecedented triumph for natural science'; but it was also 'an unprecedented disgrace to the human intellect.' Collingwood was involved, as he himself tells us, in the preparations for the Versailles peace conference of 1919, a conference from which he drew a salutary conclusion:

> The contrast between the success of modern European minds in controlling almost any situation in which the elements are physical bodies and the forces physical ones, and their inability to control situations in which the elements are human beings and the forces mental forces, left an indelible mark on the memory of every one who was concerned in it.[2]

It was this moral dilemma which, according to Collingwood, assisted at the birth of psychology as a generalized 'science of the mind'. It was not only Freud who had ambitious ideas about what psychology could achieve, but post-war European intellectual culture as a whole. For some, psychology emerged as the science of the mind which was to balance the massive potential, for evil as well as good, in natural science – 'a humanism of the future', to quote Thomas Mann again. That it proved unable to provide any such balance of knowledge is not Freud's fault, though perhaps Freud and his followers might have dissociated themselves more decisively from unrealistic intellectual aspirations of this kind. This they could have done, Collingwood argues, had psychology stuck to its remit: 'to study that which is neither mind in the proper traditional sense (consciousness, reason, will) nor yet body, but ψυχή [psyche] or such functions as sensation and appetite'.[3] Instead, Freud convinced himself that logic and ethics were a kind of humanist façade, that large areas of philosophy had given way to psychology in the progress of the sciences, and that moral philosophy in particular had been made redundant by his discoveries.[4] For Freudian psycho-analysis, as Collingwood puts it, 'reason and will were only concretions of sense and appetite'. 'If that was so,' he went on, 'it followed that logic and ethics could disappear, and that their functions could be taken over by psychology. For there was no such thing as "mind"; what had been so called was only "psyche".' Thus when he came to read Freud's writings, Collingwood found 'that they reached a very high scientific level when dealing with problems in psychotherapy, but sank beneath contempt when they treated of ethics, politics, religion, or social structure.'[5]

It is on the basis of something like the criticism of Freud offered by Collingwood that one particular re-evaluation of psychoanalysis has already begun to take place. The intellectual preponderance of psychology as a 'science of the mind' over moral philosophy has already come to an end.[6] Psychoanalysis surely wastes its energies if it sees reason and will merely as 'concretions of sense and appetite', whereas philosophy abdicates its responsibilities if it allows psychoanalysis to labour under misapprehensions of that kind. What I want to pursue here, however (from a literary–critical rather than a philosophical point of view), is not intellectual rivalry but intellectual co-operation. The discussions of some aspects of psychoanalysis that follow have their basis in Collingwood's more sweeping criticisms, certainly; but they also try to indicate the kind of positive contribution psychoanalysis has made and can make to our understanding of literature.[7]

The first section of the chapter is not intended to be a general survey of Freud's work, though that is the form it may often seem to take. It is notoriously difficult to study any one aspect of Freud in isolation, and so I am bound to stray into considerations of what Lionel Trilling calls Freud's 'whole conception of the mind', and his conception of the unconscious in particular. The issues are as follows. First, what is it that Freud had to say, implicitly as well as explicitly, about literature? and second, does his account of the mind amount to a clarification or a distortion of the elements and forces at work in literary creativity? Only by answering this second question can we decide whether the institutional claim psychoanalysis makes on the autonomy of literature is justified. But this section goes a little further than that. Where I have found Freud's account insufficient, and therefore suggestive, I have taken the opportunity to advance in positive terms the idea of literature with which this book as a whole is concerned. Freud's theory of dreams is one such case; another is the discussion of discontinuity in consciousness which brings the section to a close.

3.1   Freud

Freud's genius was both heuristic and systematic: that is his strength and that is his weakness. What we often find in him are brilliant indeed almost inspirational pieces of guesswork which quickly become embedded in a system of intellectual belief itself dependent on a series of more or less valuable insights from other occasions. There is nothing unscientific about Freud's procedure in this respect. Every scientist (every thinker in any field) works in much the same way: the value of heuristic insights are gauged by the extent to which they fit a theory that is to a large extent predetermined. The problem lies not so much with Freud's method, as with the relation of that method to its perceived subject-matter. On the basis of his own exploration and description of the mechanism of repression, Freud went some way to denying the validity of those explorations and descriptions of other areas of mental life offered by other analysts. He clearly felt, for example, that his new science could explain not merely unconscious instincts but also those mental activities defined by him as deriving *from* those instincts: thought, art, science, literature, religion, and the rest. Where possible, rival accounts of the mind were ostracized and their influence stifled by means of the professional structures and personal loyalties that Freud commanded. But in other no less important cases, Freud converted rival accounts (whether their provenance was psychoanalytical or not) to square with his own.

'The creative writer cannot evade the psychiatrist nor the psychiatrist the creative writer' (*PFL* xiv. 69). There are two reasons in particular for the length and intimacy of this connection. 'Whoever wants to make out the ways of reasoning upon which the analytic method rests', writes Emile Benveniste, 'is brought to a remarkable observation. From the moment a disturbance is observed until its cure, it looks as though nothing material were in operation. Nothing is done which lends itself to an objective observation.' 'The principal difference' between psychoanalysis and other scientific disciplines, in Benveniste's view, is that 'the analyst operates on what the subject *says* to him':

> He considers him in the discourses which he holds with him and examines him in his locutory or 'fabulatory' behavior, and through the patient's discourses another discourse slowly takes shape for the analyst, one which he will endeavor to explain: that of the complex buried in the unconscious. The success of the cure depends on bringing this complex to light, and this in turn testifies to the

correctness of the induction. Thus, from patient to analyst, and from analyst to patient, the entire process operates through language.[8]

Given the situation as Benveniste describes it, it is easy to see how fixated psychoanalysis might become with that set of relationships which binds narrators to auditors, and writers to readers. It is also easy to see how fixated literary criticism might become with the slowly evolving 'latent' discourses they might assume to be hidden beneath the 'manifest' ones presented by works of literature.

The second reason for the close cohabitation of psychoanalysis and literature is more self-evident. Freud was interested in anthropology, and found a great deal of (rather dubious) support for his theories there. He was also interested, for the purpose of drawing analogies, in economics, mechanics, and archaeology. But his interest in literature was an overriding one because literature was not only a source of psychological insight from which Freud could draw endlessly: it was a *rival* source of psychological insight: varied, boundless, and nearly as old as the human race itself. Literature appeared to provide Freud with irrefutable evidence of the existence of the unconscious, in authors and fictional characters alike. No wonder Freud in 1906 pounced gleefully on a novel by an obscure German playwright and wrote 'Delusions and Dreams in Jensen's *Gradiva*' the following year, triumphantly exhibiting the book's congruence with his own theories. No wonder he forsook any such demonstrations in the future, realizing that they suggested the insights of psychoanalysis to be of the kind found in second-rate literature.

Nor were the results much happier when Freud turned his attention to a work of literature that is by no means second-rate: Shakespeare's *Hamlet*, for example. 'The conflict in *Hamlet* is so effectively concealed', he wrote, 'that it was left to me to unearth it' (*PFL* xiv. 126). In 'The Moses of Michelangelo' he is no less strident: 'it was not until the material of the tragedy had been traced back by psychoanalysis to the Oedipus theme', Freud suggested, 'that the mystery of its effect was at last explained'; 'before this was done, what a mass of differing and contradictory interpretative attempts, what a variety of opinions about the hero's character and the dramatist's intentions!' (*PFL* xiv. 255). So much for the blossoming ineptitudes of literary critics. But neither Shakespeare himself nor his audience come off much better. As for the former, 'it can of course only be the poet's own mind which confronts us in Hamlet',[9] which makes Shakespeare seem a very incomplete dramatist. Where the audience is concerned, the spectator seeing *Hamlet*, according to Freud, 'is in the grip of his emotions instead of taking stock of what is happening' (*PFL* xiv. 126), whereas most spectators might feel that they are in the grip of their emotions *because* they are taking stock of what is happening.

Nothing much in the way of literary criticism could be expected from someone holding such views.[10] The connections Freud makes between critic and text, dramatist and character, and audience and play, are too unimaginative. (This is the subtle purveyor of half-truths who equated catharsis with 'blowing off steam' (*PFL* xiv. 121).) Stephen Dedalus' discussion of *Hamlet* in the 'Scylla and Charybdis' episode of *Ulysses*, it could be argued, presents a flattened critical argument concerning Shakespeare's feelings about paternity similar to Freud's own discussion of the play in *The Interpretation of Dreams*. And so it does: in a particular dramatic context where paternity and sonship are essential issues, the existence of which distinguish what Stephen has to say from what Freud arrived at when wearing his literary–critical hat.

As Lionel Trilling suggests, then: what Freud might contribute to our understanding of literature 'lies in no specific statement that he makes about art, but is, rather, implicit in his whole conception of the mind'.[11] 'If we consider the bulk of criticism that has been written under the influence of psychoanalysis', Richard Wollheim writes,

> we can see that it deliberately models itself upon those parts of psychoanalysis which are concerned with the discovery of a hidden or latent content inside a public or manifest content: and the parts of psychoanalysis I have in mind are, of course, the analysis of symptoms, the theory of parapraxes (errors, etc.), and, supremely, the interpretation of dreams.[12]

Critical work based on Freud, that is to say, in seeking the latent behind the manifest, is in turn based on his idea of the unconscious, and it is to the unconscious that we must now turn – twice in fact, because whereas Freud's official doctrine relating to the unconscious must be considered, so, too, must a less highly elaborated notion of it which Freud registered but seems to have regarded as of little importance.

In rendering explicit Freud's implicit contribution to literary criticism many writers have turned to analogies between the imaginative work of literature and the dream. The connection Freud makes between the two is both emphatic and cautious, preserving all the while a degree of what politicians call 'deniability'. 'We are perfectly aware', he wrote in 'Creative Writers and Day-Dreaming', 'that very many imaginative writings are far removed from the model of the naive day-dream; and yet I cannot suppress the suspicion that even the most extreme deviations from that model could be linked with it through an uninterrupted series of transitional cases' (*PFL* xiv. 138). In a word, this is Freud's theory of literature: a theory which has a germ of truth in it, certainly; but which has also introduced a host of misconceptions of what literature is, and what the criticism of it involves. A 'piece of creative writing', Freud went on, 'like a day-dream, is a continuation of, and a substitute for, what was once the play of childhood' (*PFL* xiv. 139).

> The writer softens the character of his egoistic day-dreams by altering and disguising it, and he bribes us by the purely formal – that is, aesthetic – yield of pleasure which he offers us in the presentation of his phantasies. (*PFL* xiv. 141)

For Freud both the play of children and the fantasies of adults are outlets of the drive that pre-dates all its later derivatives: wish-fulfilment. 'A child's play', he wrote, 'is determined by wishes' (*PFL* xiv. 133), and adult fantasies are merely internalized and therefore socially amenable forms of play. 'The motive force of phantasies are unsatisfied wishes, and every single phantasy is the fulfilment of a wish, a correction of unsatisfying reality' (*PFL* xiv. 134). Like dreams, play, and fantasy, literature is the individual's response to the drive towards wish-fulfilment: 'a correction of unsatisfying reality' or a response or correction rendered acceptable to others by being larded over with an 'aesthetic' coating. Once the coating is removed the work of literature is revealed as what it truly is.

Critics coming after Freud have rendered his original argument more sophisticated in some respects, but they have also extended it, shifting the analogy from 'the model of the naive day-dream' to dreams proper, quite outside the individual's control. In doing so, of course, they have availed themselves of the Freudian concept of the unconscious in its totality. Literature, according to one such critic,

> contains elements of the repressed unconscious – the 'primaeval wishes' of childhood that are later repressed; the literary work, like a dream, represents the fulfillment of such forbidden wishes, but in a way that disguises their true nature so that both the repressing

tendency and the wish are satisfied. It is through its appeal to such repressed interests still active in the unconscious that the work engages our emotions. The formal, moral, and philosophical aspects of literature are deeply rooted in unconscious material and are worked out in conjunction with it.[13]

The two arguments presented here are the *sine qua non* of the Freudian approach. First, literature engages the reader's emotions by appealing to the unconscious, whether it be the writer's, the reader's, or a set of primeval wishes that are assumed to be common to both. Second, certain manifest aspects of a work of literature (formal or moral, for example) are 'worked out' in conjunction with and 'deeply rooted in' its latent aspects. The first thing to say about such arguments is that they have some truth in them. But they also amount to a distortion, not only of literature's relation to its readers, but also of the much more important unconscious element that is at work in the writing and reading of literature, and which I shall try to describe in what follows. That element is not a question of literature's manifest elements being 'rooted' in the unconscious, nor of their being 'worked out', like a sum or a blocked drain. Above all, however, it is psychoanalytic critics' assimilation of literature with the 'primaeval' wishes of childhood and with the 'correction of unsatisfying reality' which such wishes strive to bring about, that I wish to consider here. This is not to say that no such elements as these contribute to literature. But the core assumption that such repressed interests are the sole or primary motive force of literature, or that literature itself can play no role in 'correcting' *them*, indeed, has proved an obstacle to fuller understanding of the psychology of creativity in this area.

For Freud, dreams are the result of a system at once dynamic and closed. The dynamic tensions of infant and childhood psychological experience, and only of that experience, are repressed until some later experience, acting as a catalyst, allows one such tension, or a group of them, to pass over into consciousness in disguise: 'a dream is a (disguised) fulfilment of a (suppressed or repressed) wish' (*PFL* iv. 244). That these wishes derive inevitably from infancy and childhood is a belief that Freud emphasizes time and time again in *The Interpretation of Dreams*. With the passing of the Oedipal phase a lid is lowered over the unconscious. Nothing can be added, nothing can be taken away: 'it is a prominent feature of unconscious processes that they are indestructible. In the unconscious nothing can be brought to an end, nothing is past or forgotten' (*PFL* iv. 733).

It will be immediately obvious why both Freud's admirers and his critics are made uneasy by his use of the word 'unconscious' as a noun rather than an adjective. Almost inevitably, it suggests a hydraulic or hydrostatic system in which pressure built up in one chamber is released into others. 'We may suppose', Freud writes, illustrating this tendency in his thought, 'that the repressed exercises a continuous pressure in the direction of the conscious, so that this pressure must be balanced by an unceasing counter-pressure.'[14] The corollary of this hydrostatic system is what David Archard calls 'the constancy principle': a desirable balance between 'an accumulation of tension as pain, and a reduction of tension, or discharge, as pleasure'.[15]

Most critics have jumped directly from this model of the unconscious to Freud's four famous classes of dream-work, which act as the valves and the conduits of the hydrostatic system: condensation, displacement, consideration for representability and secondary revision. Dream-work, Freud says, 'carries out no other function than the translation of dream-thoughts in accordance with the four conditions to which it is subject' (*PFL* iv. 576), and many critics have been tempted to see literature as an expressive mode operating along almost identical lines. But Freud provides a number of other observations and rules of thumb relating to dreams which are at least as significant for literature as those four. That 'one component of the content of the dream is a repetition of a recent impression of the previous day' (*PFL* iv. 267); that 'Dreams are the guardians of sleep and not its disturbers' (*PFL* iv. 330); that in dreams 'propinquity in time' suggests 'connection in subject matter' (*PFL* iv. 346), are conclusions that are really neither here nor there where literature is concerned. We also readily grant to the Freudian unconscious the corollary that 'Dreams are completely egoistic' (*PFL* iv. 434), whereas we know that nothing like this could be said of literature, even in its most introspective and confessional, or exultant and self-celebrating modes.

'Dreams are brief, meagre and laconic in comparison with the range and wealth of the dream-thoughts' (*PFL* iv. 383). If such a principle were extended to cover not merely authors' own mental lives, but their intellectual milieux and historical contexts, it could be argued that works of literature are 'brief, meagre and laconic' in a similar way: that *Antony and Cleopatra* or *Great Expectations* are only meagre reflections of all the things Shakespeare or Dickens may be imagined to have thought about and experienced, and of all the intellectual, moral, social, and political structures and developments of their different eras. But an argument along these lines would amount to a misunderstanding of the ways in which literature works. Unlike the dreams described by Freud, works of literature are not the result of an internalized set of pre-occupations, only tangentially affected by the outside world, of which the author is a kind of passive conduit or duct. Neither does their success with readers depend on the extent to which they dramatize or disguise archaic or infantile experiences so widespread that, like the Oedipus complex, they amount to a collective unconscious (by any other name).

But this does not mean that the kinds of transformations authors make on such material are at all times and in all places conscious transformations. To say that Freud has not got the unconscious element in literature quite right is not to say that no such element exists. What S.L. Goldberg called 'obscurer qualities and choices' underlying and shaping from below our 'conscious ideals and decisions' do indeed make their presence felt in literature.[16] Such qualities and choices emerge, however, not spontaneously in the author's mind but out of the author's relationship to what he or she is writing. It is for this reason that Lionel Trilling is wrong to suggest that 'the difference between, on the one hand, the dream and the neurosis, and, on the other hand, art' is that 'the poet is in command of his fantasy, while it is exactly the mark of the neurotic that he is possessed by his fantasy.'[17] If authors had the degree of command over their creative impulses Trilling imputes to them, then novels, poems, and plays really would be shallow forms of entertainment and intellection, and nothing more. It is precisely to the extent that authors do not have this command over their material that they are able to uncover and explore that part of the world (internal and external) which presents itself to them in and through the work they undertake. In this process, the author's thoughts and wishes, conscious or unconscious, and the intellectual and political contexts mentioned above (including the tastes and desires of the readership, collective or individual) are all at once partners, contributors, and ingredients in the drama or the structure of the work of literature they serve to vivify and revivify. This being the case, a work of literature is in one respect at least the reverse of a dream: it is not the enigmatic and fugitive representative of shadowy and titanic forces whose nature we can only guess at, but in fact an avenue by means of which such forces can be explored and transformed.

But Freud could never see literature in these terms. For him, what dreams, fantasies, play, and literature had in common was that all were articulations of psychological structures and tensions to which the writer can only add a kind of veneer or supplement: what, to quote a particularly shameful example, he called 'the impressive thoughts' in *Hamlet*, and the 'splendour of its language' (*PFL* xiv. 255). Processes and mental states such as these are the writer's primary material; until they are dealt with he has dealt with nothing; they are the causeway by means of which he reaches his audience and awakens its sympathies. In Freud, this aspect of psychoanalytic belief inevitably returns us to the same spot: 'what he [the writer] aims at is to awaken in us the same emotional attitude, the same mental constellation as that which in him produced the impetus to create' (*PFL* xiv. 254). The author wishes, aims, and intends – albeit unconsciously – to re-create in us that same 'mental constellation' that impelled him to write in the first place. Only then can his particular version of the talking cure begin to operate.

There is some truth in this, as I say. Indeed, Freud's remarks may remind the reader of some strikingly similar comments on poetry by one of its greatest English practitioners. In the preface to *Lyrical Ballads* Wordsworth defined poetry as 'the spontaneous overflow of powerful feelings', having 'its origin from emotion recollected in tranquillity':

> the emotion is contemplated till by a species of reaction the tranquillity disappears, and an emotion, kindred to that which was before the subject of contemplation, is gradually produced, and does itself actually exist in the mind. In this mood successful composition generally begins…

If we allow that contemplation may take an unconscious form and that an 'emotion' might, by a later generation, be called an 'impulse', Wordsworth's account appears to give a great deal of support to Freud's emphasis on the reader's gaining access to the 'mental constellation' of the author, Oedipal conflicts and all. That which existed in the poet's mind is recovered and communicated in turn. We have only to recall the high proportion of autobiographical material in Wordsworth's own poetry to gather support for such a view.

Except that Wordsworth is careful to point out that 'successful composition generally *begins*' in such a fashion. How it goes on is a separate issue: 'In this mood successful composition generally begins, and in a mood similar to this it is carried on; but the emotion, of whatever kind and in whatever degree, from various causes is qualified by various pleasures…'. From this point Wordsworth drifts away, distracted perhaps by the notion of pleasure and its function in poetry, which he discusses in a rather mechanical fashion. But in fact the word 'pleasures' is as good as any to describe the forces which waylay those emotions Wordsworth speaks of and those aims and intentions to which Freud alludes. Psychoanalytical writers and critics since Freud, however, have had great difficulty in taking account of what Wordsworth was trying to describe here. They find it hard either to deviate from the idea that there is something in the author's unconscious mind which passes the censor in the process of writing and which is then received and unpacked in the reader's unconscious, or to admit that there could be any other basis for literature's appeal than this.

Something along the lines of what Wordsworth describes surely does take place in the writing of literature. There is, however, another uniquely important element in play, more or less ignored by Freud. That element is not the writer's unconscious alone, nor the reader's, nor any imaginable combination of the two, but the unconscious relationship the writer has with what he writes (and reads), and reader has with what he can only read. As they progress, works of literature lay down and build upon dramatic structures and assumptions relating to what is permitted and plausible, not all of which will be understood by the author or the reader at the time. Such structures form something like an unconscious in the sense that they reveal themselves as the narrative progresses in the same bewildering number of forms as the Freudian unconscious reveals itself: intermittently, unexpectedly, paradoxically, suddenly. It is in this way and to this extent that the work itself is able to make its contribution to that whole gamut of unconscious and conscious perceptions and motivations (in reader as well as writer) of which the novel, poem, or play is constituted. All such acts take place within that dialectic between the author and his work with which this study as a whole is concerned: 'the internal action or plot of the story or poem, in all its manifestations, contains, reveals, and indeed in large part *is* the drama of the writer's relationship to his unfolding conception.'[18] In particular, what is recorded, and not what lay behind its coming to be so, acquires an existence outside the interaction of conscious and unconscious motives that may initially have compelled the writer to seek to put it there. It undergoes qualification, to adapt Wordsworth's phrase, by various (and other) pleasures. The writer is bound to continue, not on the basis of aims previously entertained but in response to what he finds in front of him and which has its own claims to assert.

Some of Freud's observations relating to dreams amount to vivid examples of the principle I have just tried to describe. To start with something basic: 'the most general and most striking psychological characteristic of the process of dreaming', he suggests, is that 'a thought, and as a rule a thought of something that is wished, is objectified in the dream, is represented as a scene, or, as it seems to us, is experienced' (*PFL* iv. 682). This will sound like a very simple, not to say naïve, observation. But when we think of the uses made of Freud by Surrealist artists like Dali, Magritte, and de Chirico, and compare them with (for example) the dramatic dreamscape found in the 'Circe' episode of Joyce's *Ulysses*, Freud's emphasis on our experiencing the dream by means of its 'scenic qualities' reveals its importance. What we have in many Surrealist paintings are not scenes but collections of props, however portentous. It is because Freud understood dreams to be more than collections of props that he, with what amounts to a literary–critical interest, tried to describe their dramatic construction.

Only rarely in literature do we experience those fluxes and refluxes of emotional participation and dissociation that dreams evoke with such disturbing power: what Joseph Conrad called 'that commingling of absurdity, surprise, and bewilderment in a tremor of struggling revolt, that notion of being captured by the incredible which is of the very essence of dreams'.[19] This is so presumably because, first, we know that dreams are involuntary experiences even as we experience them, and second, because we know at the same time that only *we* can appreciate, if not always understand, the momentousness of the events depicted. Reading and writing, by contrast, are actions of choice on our part. In addition they are actions taken in the knowledge that a host of other distinct centres of consciousness (some of which are the kinds of dramatized attitudes we meet in poetry, some fictional characters, and some putative readers like ourselves) are established in relation with each other at least partly as a result of our predispositions and judgements concerning them. Would that knowledge of this kind was available in dreams! In them we have no such distinct centres of consciousness to whom we can appeal in interpreting what we experience. Dreamers are not to dreams as writers and readers are to books: the dreamer is both agent and witness, hero and supernumerary, character and reader. But dreams and dramatic narratives both depend utterly on dramatic relationships being established – stealthily and appositely in literature; with astonishing speed and varying degrees of inconsequentiality in dreams – between protagonists or between protagonists and objects.[20] If there is any radical connection between dreaming and imaginative writing, and between both activities and our notions of selfhood, it surely lies here.

In seeing dreams as scenes rather than collections of symbolic props, Freud could hardly help shedding light on the relationship just sketched between the wholly involuntary narratives found in them and the more or less voluntary ones found in literature. In doing so he was able to make observations about dreams which have at least as much importance for our understanding of literature as do those classes of dreamwork listed above. For example: 'We could go so far as to say that the dream-work makes use, for the purpose of giving a visual representation of the dream-thoughts, of any method within its reach, whether waking criticism regards them as legitimate or illegitimate' (*PFL* iv. 537). In much the same way writers convert any material, however apparently inappropriate, for use in their narratives as and when those narratives require it. In works of imaginative literature, historical events can be distorted out of recognition, social barriers dissolved, generic expectations disappointed, and canons of plausibility reshaped. (Metaphor itself is a reshaping of our everyday canons of plausibility.) The shamelessness with which writers cannibalize their own and other people's works and lives is readily comparable to the frankness with which dreams lay hands on people and events in order to make their points.

But what forces dictate such literary cannibalizations? In the Freudian system, dream-thoughts travel between the polarities of consciousness and its opposite: 'regression, wherever it may occur, is an effect of a resistance opposing the progress of a thought into consciousness along the normal path, and of a simultaneous attraction exercised upon the thought by the presence of memories possessing great sensory force' (*PFL* iv. 698). Such thoughts are 'pushed from the one side (by the censorship of the *Cs.*) and pulled from the other (by the *Ucs.*), in the same kind of way in which people are conveyed to the top of the Great Pyramid' (*PFL* iv. 698 n.), and only in dreams, in symptoms, or under analysis can they be released. In the hydrostatic system there is a dialectic at work between expression and censorship, or between constraint and opportunity. A similar dialectic is to be found at work in the writing of literature. Nor are the terms of the dialectic, or the roles they predicate, fixed in imaginative writing. At any one moment either the author or the text can be seen to behave like the id (germinating ideas, suggesting arrangements, coining metaphors, coming upon rhymes, raising moral questions *ad infinitum*) or the ego (organizing, selecting, curtailing, dispensing with, or resolving all of these). The work in progress, to borrow some lines from Pope's Epistle to Burlington,

> Calls in the Country, catches opening glades,
> Joins willing woods, and varies shades from shades,

Now breaks or now directs, th' intending Lines;
Paints as you plant, and, as you work, designs.

The conditions of writing being what they are, the writer and the work under construction appear to take and swap the roles of 'creative unconscious' and 'censoring ego' continuously. Indeed, the moment the one recognizes the other in one of those roles, it seems to supplant its rival. The text concerned is not a mind or a consciousness of course, as these remarks might suggest. As Michael Riffaterre suggests, 'there is an unconscious of the text that *works like* the human unconscious' without being an unconscious itself.[21] It is not so much a question of the work of literature having volitions of this kind as of authors imputing such volitions to it or finding them in it as they look for pattern and coherence in what is being written. Recording what it itself is at any one juncture, the work effectively licenses and suggests any number of developments quite unanticipated by the author, while forbidding any number of the author's own contributions. However laboured and vestigial they may appear to many readers and critics, formal features regarded as 'constraints' (the three unities of neo-classical drama being a good example) can be generative in the same way as the most inviting 'opportunity', and at a surprisingly profound level.

That the centres of consciousness we find in poems, novels, or plays may have unconscious lives is an idea with which we are all familiar. The way in which a novel can, in the processes of writing and reading, serve as the bearer and provoker of tendencies, motives, and compulsions of a never wholly acknowledged kind is more difficult to describe. For example: we often find ourselves unable to decide whether some particular development has been 'forced' upon the author, or whether he or she has made room for it with conscious planning. In Jane Austen's *Emma*, a projected ball is anticipated in great detail, then suddenly cancelled, then equally suddenly revived eight chapters later. The gap appears to serve no purpose until we realize that it allows for the introduction of the presumptuous Mrs Elton, who intends to supplant the heroine as cock-of-the-walk (or hen-of-the-walk) in Highbury: an intention her conduct at the ball, when it finally does take place, makes nakedly apparent. Emma is forced to look to her defences under such a threat; her greatest defence being, of course, marriage with the novel's hero, Mr Knightley. Is this development is a conscious piece of foresight and planning on Jane Austen's part, or an opportunity (a 'gap') created by earlier events and developments in the novel (Frank Churchill's demanding aunt, say, or his own skittishness)? But in fact this way of framing the question itself falsifies the issue: foresight and planning on a novelist's, dramatist's, or poet's part *is* a response to opportunities of just this kind. As was suggested in Chapter 2, there really is no distinction to be made between constraints and opportunities in such cases. The planning and the opportunities for further plans or (every bit as important) for the revision of 'completed' work in the light of what has belatedly become apparent about the task as a whole: all these constantly arise and evanesce together.

If we have any doubts that this is so, Jane Austen's remarkably reflexive novel itself provides a description of the process, when the incorrigible Emma begins to plan a romance between Frank Churchill and her protégée, Harriet Smith. 'Could a linguist, could a grammarian, could even a mathematician have seen what she did,' Emma asks herself,

> without feeling that circumstances had been at work to make them [Harriet and Frank] peculiarly interesting to each other? – How much more must an imaginist, like herself, be on fire with speculation and foresight! – especially with such a ground-work of anticipation as her mind had already made.[22]

It is impossible to say, here, whether the novel is speaking through its heroine, or the heroine is speaking through the novel. It is equally impossible to say whether it is the novelist or the reader who becomes at this point more reflexively aware of himself or herself as an 'imaginist' of just Emma's type: a type with which, of course, the novel explicitly asks us to find fault. In fact these are not either/or questions at all. They are both/and questions, forced upon us by the 'ground-work of anticipation' common to novelist, reader, and character alike: a ground-work built up by *Emma* itself.

Novels are not minds. The dramatic significance they have is one we give them. We do not give works of literature the significance they possess under circumstances chosen strictly by ourselves, however, but under circumstances directly encountered, given and transmitted by those works themselves. A novel does not of itself privilege one set of circumstances it contains over another; but we do, and consequently we engage on any number of acts of forgetfulness, inadvertence, and even suppression. The more carefully we read, the more likely we are to come across elements in the work's structure we had previously ignored, and we are accordingly presented with classic instances of 'the return of the repressed'. For writers the case is a parallel one. The better they are, the less easy they will find it to ignore the unexpected dramatic demands their work makes of them. Novels may not have an unconscious; but from our point of view they behave as if they do.

For example: during a conventional rounding up of the characters' destinies at the end of Dickens' *Bleak House*, we are told that the heroine's friend Caddy and her husband have had a child. We also learn in passing and without comment that the baby is deaf and dumb. Many readers will explain this in terms of the writer's disinclination to have his novel end in utterly complacent satisfaction and good humour; this little child represents what Wordsworth called the 'still sad music of humanity', playing on beneath the novel's happy outcome. But others will be struck by the fact that Caddy's daughter is named Esther, after the heroine herself, and that her affliction takes us back to an episode near the beginning of the novel where the heroine, in leaving her guardian's house as a child, puts aside the doll on which she has lavished the love and attention she herself has never received: 'A day or two before, I had wrapped the dear old doll in her own shawl, and quietly laid her – I am half ashamed to tell it – in the garden-earth, under the tree that shaded my old window.'[23] Between them, the doll and Caddy's daughter are evidence of a latent, repressed concern, in novel and novelist alike, about the heroine's own emotional passivity, her strictly curtailed sexuality and her missing childhood. That so central a concern is admitted in so perfunctory a fashion will seem inexplicable until we realize that it does not emerge in isolation; that it reminds us not only of Esther Summerson's doll but also of the dead child Esther covers with her handkerchief at the brickmakers' cottage, and of Esther herself (put aside at birth and believed dead by her mother); and that the issue's emerging when it does, when no more can be said about it, is not so much an evasion of its implications as a more or less unpremeditated resurgence of them.

Another example is from *Jane Eyre*. On the night before Jane's attempted marriage to Rochester, she offloads in conversation with him (and for the reader's benefit) a number of portentous dreams and occurrences anticipating the next day's great disaster. She dreams of babies, for example, and she has a visitor at night whom she takes for a ghost, but whom Rochester knows to be his deranged wife: 'oh, sir, I never saw a face like it! It was a discoloured face – it was a savage face. I wish I could forget the roll of the red eyes and the fearful blackened inflation of the lineaments!' When Rochester points out that 'Ghosts are usually pale, Jane', she insists: 'This, sir, was purple: the lips were swelled and dark; the brow furrowed: the black eyebrows widely raised over the bloodshot eyes.'[24] To dream of babies is bad luck, as we know from an earlier incident in the novel, where Mrs Reed's fatal illness is presaged by Jane's dreaming of children every night for a week. On hearing that Mrs Reed has fallen ill, Jane hurries to her bedside where, it turns out, Mrs Reed has been having dreams too; also of children; but in this case of her adult son John, who lives the life of a spendthrift away from home. In getting money from his mother John threatens her, as she says, 'with his own death, or mine: and I dream sometimes that I see him laid out with a great wound in his throat, or with a swollen and blackened face'.[25] Mad Bertha Rochester, according to Jane's account, has a 'discoloured face' and swollen lips, whereas Rochester himself is wounded in the face and eyes by falling timbers during the fire at Thornfield. Like his mother, the little boy John Reed has dark skin; so has Rochester. Young Jane is injured in the head when John throws a book at her in the novel's first chapter. As I mentioned in Chapter 2, it so happens that Charlotte Brontë started work on her novel in a boarding house where she and her father were staying: her father was recuperating from an operation on his eyes, for cataracts. But even an explanation of this kind allows for the fact that a novel is more likely to spread, deepen, and re-transcribe a writer's fantasies and anxieties, than serve merely as a conduit for them.

It was mentioned above that the unconscious would be examined twice. What I have in mind is to press Freud on one aspect of his model of the unconscious that he felt to be quite uncontentious, but which bears on the very orientation of the science he originated. The 'written words of psychoanalytic literature', D.W. Winnicott once suggested,

> do not seem to tell us all that we want to know. What, for instance, are we doing when we are listening to a Beethoven symphony or making a pilgrimage to a picture gallery or reading *Troilus and Cressida* in bed, or playing tennis? What is a child doing when sitting on the floor playing with toys under the aegis of the mother?[26]

These questions may seem to have little to do with the specificities of the Freudian unconscious, but they are related to that idea, as I hope to show. Put bluntly, Freud was interested in those aspects of mental life which were congruent with his hydrostatic system, and only in them. What we are doing when we listen to Beethoven or play tennis concerned him hardly at all. But Freud's neglect of such activities of the mind was neither incidental nor unimportant. It had real implications for his understanding of literary and artistic creativity amongst other things, and it allows us some room to revise his thought on such issues: a revision which allows us to describe more fully the unconscious element in creativity.

In his early days, Freud habitually used two examples to disarm scepticism about the existence of the unconscious. Hypnosis was one – for where could hypnotic suggestions lie until acted upon but in the unconscious? The other was more everyday. In 'A Note on the Unconscious in Psychoanalysis' he wrote:

> A conception – or any other psychical element – which is now *present* to my consciousness may become *absent* the next moment, and may become *present again*, after an interval, unchanged, and, as we say, from memory, not as a result of a fresh perception by our senses. It is this fact which we are accustomed to account for by the supposition that during the interval the conception has been present in our mind, although *latent* in consciousness. In what shape it may have existed while present in the mind and latent in consciousness we have no means of guessing. (*PFL* xi. 50)

An unexceptionable notion. In pursuing a chain of thought, or cogitating some problem, we are distracted. Later the idea returns from a state of latency in exactly the same way as documents are returned to us on a word-processor: obediently, immediately, unchanged. Intent on exploring the potential of that grander vision of the unconscious discussed above, Freud passes over this unremarkable phenomenon, and so do his commentators. Freud, David Archard writes,

> appeals to the easily intuitable and unexceptionable fact that consciousness is 'discontinuous', that it is experienced as incomplete and containing gaps. Freud's simplest example is this. I am now thinking a particular idea. Momentarily distracted my concentration turns to the thought of something else and during this time I am not aware of the idea which previously occupied me. The source of distraction removed, I return to thinking of the original idea. The same idea is, while I am distracted by something else, 'missing' from consciousness but presumed intact between its first and second appearances. To answer such a case Freud proposes that the idea in question be regarded as 'unconscious' in the intervening period.[27]

The difference between ideas such as these and those suggested under hypnosis is that the latter are 'unconscious and *active*'. But this distinction between inert 'thoughts' and hypnotic 'suggestions' is not quite enough. Ideas simply placed in suspension by discontinuous consciousness, and 'presumed intact' meanwhile, do not belong to the Freudian unconscious properly understood; being 'merely latent' they must reside in the *pre*conscious. 'The term "unconscious" proper', Archard goes on, 'now designates those ideas which show evidence of having been *excluded from*, and thus remaining inadmissable and inaccessible to, consciousness.'[28]

We can see that a certain area of mental life is being moved around at the service of a view of the unconscious which is in turn being protected and given special status at that area's expense:

> Without being so named, it was the evidence of preconscious ideas that served the introductory argument for the use of the term 'unconscious'. Arguably then, the earlier examples [hypnosis and discontinuity] are relatively unimportant. What matters is not that an idea should be unconscious, but that it should be a certain kind of unconscious idea, namely one that has causal efficacy in relation to conscious ideas.[29]

All unconscious ideas are unconscious, but some are more unconscious than others. Some, that is, are unimportant, without causal efficacy, and come back unchanged, intact, and in their original state, whereas other unconscious ideas are charged with significance. Their significance or their efficacy, of course, is a function of their having been evicted or excluded from consciousness in the first place. Only by being judged worthy of suppression does a thought become active in the unconscious, and the unconscious is that place where suppressed thoughts are sent, to fester in the gloom.

The point is this. Thoughts which are suppressed are not the only important thoughts we have, though of course they have a special significance for the hydrostatic system. Streams of thought by no means deserving of or requiring suppression also disappear, either temporarily or for good. We are all familiar with thoughts and memories that we can summon up in all their banality or all their original intensity of shame and embarrassment more or less at will from wherever it is they come. We know equally well, however, that some ideas, once interrupted, never return; that the person from Porlock has become a figure of intellectual folklore for precisely this reason; and that there are few frustrations to match our inability to piece back together those thoughts or ideas Freud and Archard regard as being 'merely latent'.

But this is not the half of it. The negative aspects of discontinuity, distraction, or intermittence are a curse of which we are all sensible; the positive aspects of it are a blessing we have hardly bothered to think about. Certainly Freud left those positive aspects well alone. Perhaps the nearest we have come to such an enquiry is Michael Polanyi's discussion, in *Personal Knowledge*, of 'tacit coefficients' and of 'that curious persistence of heuristic tension through long periods of time, during which the problem is not consciously entertained'.[30] In intervals between periods of conscious thought we can and do lose the apparent benefits of concentration; but just as some problems defeat us by drifting outside our understanding in this way for good and all, so others meet their Waterloo in intellectual struggles and victories of which we are never aware until they are over. 'The fact that our intellectual strivings make effective progress during a period of Incubation without any effort on our part', Polanyi writes, 'is in line with the latent character of all knowledge.' And what Polanyi means by latency is quite different from what we have seen in Freud and David Archard. We should, he suggests,

acknowledge our capacity both to sense the accessibility of a hidden inference from given premises, and to invent transformations of the premises which increase the accessibility of the hidden inference. We should recognize that this foreknowledge biasses our guesses in the right direction, so that their probability of hitting the mark, which would otherwise be zero, becomes so high that we can definitely rely on it simply on the ground of a student's intelligence; or for higher performances, on the ground of the special gifts possessed by the professional mathematician.

In other words, 'the tension set up by the unfinished task continues to make progress towards its fulfilment'.[31] Suspended ideas do not come back unchanged and intact but altered, either radically or marginally. Nor does Polanyi's account have implications only for bright students and professional mathematicians. Whatever counts as thought depends in exactly the same way on multitudes of tacit premises built up with intellectual or professional expertise certainly, but in everyday life also as our interests and prepossessions dictate: premises which the mind is able to refer to and recast in advancing problems towards solution.[32] Writers and readers of literature invent, transform, and discard premisses of plausibility, and seek inferences reinforcing such premisses as a matter of course, by means of that host of unconscious and conscious perceptions and motivations mentioned earlier. That is what much of writing and reading amounts to.

It will be obvious, I think, why it is that there is so little room in Freud's version of the unconscious for mental life of this kind. It will be obvious, too, why Collingwood placed so much stress on the existence and function of that life. Freud's idea of rational reflective thought is marked by a strange lack of curiosity, generally speaking. 'Thought is after all', he wrote, 'nothing but a substitute for a hallucinatory wish' (*PFL* xiv. 721) – a remark which suggests how profoundly the notion of wish-fulfilment influenced his view of the mind. Without acknowledging the existence of such processes or something like them, Freud reduced the unconscious to a maelstrom of somatic instincts on the one hand, and what Richard Wollheim calls the infant's 'passionate but catastrophic relations with a loved parent' on the other.[33] Once those relations and instincts have settled into a pattern with the closure of the Oedipal phase, these archaic furies are battened down together, seeking escape where they can, while the maturational process continues precariously elsewhere. No wonder that Freud's interest in children was followed by Melanie Klein's in those younger still, and that psychoanalysis since her day (with some honourable exceptions of course) has continued to have an uneasy relationship with the very ideas of adulthood, adult thinking, and adult responsiveness, as the passage from Winnicott quoted above reminds us.

Freud's lack of interest in those potentialities of the unconscious not covered by the hydrostatic system amounts to a limitation of his account of the mind: especially when that account seeks to incorporate artistic creativity. In fact we might argue that it is around the axis of the unconscious and the conscious fields of the mind as envisaged by Polanyi, that creative thought in particular rotates (this perhaps is why 'flashes of inspiration' are so often regarded as part and parcel of the creative and scientific mystique). Again, the active but never wholly recognized participation of the literary work in the processes of its own construction is essential in directing the author's attention, conscious or unconscious, to certain developments and possibilities. What I call participation is only Polanyi's 'Incubation' in another form, and the 'heuristic tension' he describes is, for both writer and reader, the tension of their dialectical relationship to the work of literature upon which they are engaged. Writers and readers constantly 'sense the accessibility of a hidden inference from given premises' in a work of literature, and constantly 'invent transformations of the premises which increase the accessibility of the hidden inference'. They do so, by means of conscious and unconscious acts of understanding with practically every word they read or write.

With her attention more directly fixed than Polanyi's on imaginative problems, Marion Milner attempted to describe what she called the 'mood' instilled by the act of drawing:

> It was a mood which could be described as one of reciprocity; for although it was certainly a dreamy state of mind it was not a dreaminess that shuts itself off from the outside world or shuts out action. It was more a dreaminess that was the result of restraining conscious intention, or rather, a quick willingness to have it and then forgo it. Quite often there was some conscious intention of what to draw, at the beginning, but the point was that one had to be willing to give up this first idea as soon as the lines drawn suggested something else.[34]

The account remains a quintessentially psychoanalytical one in many respects. The form of intermittence Milner describes, for example (the 'quick willingness to have it and then forgo it') surely owes a great deal to the 'Fort/Da' game described by Freud in *Beyond the Pleasure Principle*. But it is at the same time a vivid account of that dialectical, reciprocal style of 'Incubation' I have extrapolated from Michael Polanyi. Milner's account also suggests the speed with which this style of incubation can work once it has been established between (in this case) the artist and her sketch. What Marion Milner says also reminds us of Virginia Woolf's detailed description (in *To the Lighthouse*) of a painter's thought processes. 'Where to begin?' Lily Briscoe asks herself, brush in hand:

> – that was the question; at what point to make the first mark? One line placed on the canvas committed her to innumerable risks, to frequent and irrevocable decisions. All that in idea seemed simple became in practice immediately complex; as the waves shape themselves symmetrically from the cliff top, but to the swimmer among them are divided by steep gulfs, and foaming crests. Still the risk must be run; the mark made.[35]

Which is by no means to say that conscious intention did not have a role also: 'will did come into it', Marion Milner's account continues, 'to the extent of the determination to go on drawing, to keep one's hand moving on the paper and one's eye watching with that peculiar kind of responsive alertness the shapes that it was producing.'[36]

If Milner's and Woolf's accounts thus far sound a little impressionistic, both writers were actually capable of going further, albeit in differing modes. Milner says of her drawings that 'they were certainly not like the usual waking dreams that one calls day-dreams, most of them were much more than wish-fulfilling fancies of what one might hope would happen; they seemed to be, some of them at least, very complicated reflections upon the central problems of being alive. The difference seemed to lie in the relation to action.'[37] Milner's bracketing of the wish-fulfilling element here allows her to escape the hydrostatic system altogether. Once she has left that behind, we notice, she is immediately able to acknowledge the moral element in creative thought which the hydrostatic system tends to ignore or subjugate. Her drawings 'seemed to be, some of them at least, very complicated reflections upon the central problems of being alive.' 'The main thing about this mood of reciprocity seemed to be', she wrote,

> that it was an interplay of differences that remained in contact; though it was often tempting to give up the contact, give up the effort of moving one's hand with the pencil and relapse into simple day-dreaming. The particular pair of differences that was in contact was ideas and action, thinking and making something happen by the movement of one's body, an inner image and the record of a movement represented by the line actually outside on the paper. And it was when these two interplayed, each taking the lead in turn in quick interchange or dialogue relation, that the drawings had appeared and had embodied in such concentrated form a whole set of ideas that I had never known I had.[38]

Lily Briscoe's first picture, too, is a reflection upon many of the problems of being alive, and above all their relation to action. Mrs Ramsay wants Lily to marry the elderly widower William Bankes; Lily resists Mrs Ramsay's interference on behalf of both herself and her putative husband. 'He has his work', she tells herself:

> She remembered, all of a sudden as if she had found a treasure, that she too had her work. In a flash she saw her picture, and thought, Yes, I shall put the tree further in the middle; then I shall avoid that awkward space. That's what I shall do. That's what has been puzzling me. She took up the salt cellar and put it down again on a

flower in the pattern of the table-cloth, so as to remind herself to move the tree.[39]

It is impossible to say which has come first here: a solution to the marriage problem or a solution to the artistic problem. That 'awkward space' in her picture is also the awkward space in her social life which concerned friends conspire to fill with a husband; she fills the one by moving the tree, the other by reminding herself, or perhaps discovering for the first time, that she has her work as Bankes has his. Ten years later she unfailingly remembers the importance and the coincidence of these two decisions: 'She had been looking at the tablecloth, and it had flashed upon her that she would move the tree to the middle, and need never marry anybody, and she had felt an enormous exultation.'[40]

But, the Freudian will say, this is simply a question of sublimation. What Virginia Woolf has described, unwittingly or not, is a sublimation of the kind art is particularly well-placed to provide. Lily does feel this 'awkward space' within herself, and she does wish to fill it, but for some determinable reason she chooses to fill it with a phallic symbol in a picture as opposed to a husband in actuality. Conversely, Lily's picture gives the literary critic a vivid example of the indivisibility of action-orientated moral thought from apparently 'aesthetic' formal issues in literature, such as Marion Milner tried to describe. That is to say, every formal reorganization of his or her work that the writer (or the artist) insists upon, or submits to, is also a moral reorganization of that work and of the writer's attitudes (conscious and unconscious) towards that work – a reorganization of the kind we see Lily Briscoe exhibit.

Are these two views irreconcilable or complementary? The latter, it seems to me. But they do return us to a position very like the one outlined by Collingwood, in which notions of the reflective mind, logic, morality, and ethics are regarded by Freud and his followers as merely a humanist superstructure: what Freud might tersely have summarized as 'resistance'. We appear to be left with a choice between Collingwood's view of the mind on the one hand, and Freud's on the other. That the choice need not be quite so stark has been suggested by the analogies already drawn between the dream and the work of art, as well as by the examination of some of those elements of the unconscious mind which failed to rouse Freud's interest or curiosity. It would be unfair both to psychoanalysis and to criticism, moreover, to consider the terms of their relationship frozen with Collingwood and Freud. As Winnicott's remarks quoted above suggest, one particular development in psychoanalysis – Object Relations – does require closer attention from literary critics, principally because it makes some allowance for those aspects of thought which Freud regarded with indifference, but which, as we have seen in this section, must be given room in an adequate account of literature.

3.2   Object relations

Melanie Klein's contribution to the humanistic evolution of psychoanalysis mentioned at the beginning of this chapter is hard to overestimate. Her work on infant sexuality is important enough in this respect, but even more so was her elaboration of two 'positions' in the mind, known as the paranoid–schizoid and the depressive. Paradoxically enough, what those positions actually are is almost less important than their existence as theoretical tools. That is to say: without becoming intellectually vacuous the theory of positions has proved more flexible in descriptive terms than Freud's theory of the complex. Not only is the position more open to and involved in the ongoing development of the individual than the complex; it is also more responsive to immediate experience. Where the complex tended to shape experience in a predetermined fashion, the position is always seen as part of a dialectical relationship to that experience. As a result it has the potential to incorporate and to comment usefully upon whole areas of mental life generally ignored by Freud: among them, the kind of intellectual processes described above by Michael Polanyi, Marion Milner, and Virginia Woolf. Melanie Klein did not go as far as D.W. Winnicott in this respect. She was no more interested in what we are doing when we play tennis or read *Troilus and Cressida* in bed than was Freud himself. But certain analysts who have learned from her – Winnicott himself but also, as I want to argue here, Hanna Segal – have been able to capitalize on the flexibility of the theory of positions to great effect.

In Klein's view, the newly-born infant has no sense of the mother as a distinct and separate individual. As far as the baby is concerned, the mother (and the breast in particular) is simply an extension of his own self. Whether he feels bliss or despair depends upon the presence or absence of this 'part-object', which is accordingly split in the mind into ideally good and horrifically persecutory forms (thus the 'paranoid–schizoid' position). The first of these the child wishes to engorge and possess utterly; the second he tries to keep at bay through various defences. He may, for example, try to split the bad breast into an infinity of smaller objects out of fear, or split the good breast out of envy. He may project his own well-being or hatred into either one, or he may introject (that is, incorporate) the good or bad breast in the same way. His omnipotent feeling that he is able to split, project, and introject fantasy objects in this way depends upon the very fact that he makes no distinction between himself and his mother.

The next stage takes place, Hanna Segal suggests, 'when the infant begins to relate to his mother and soon to other people in his environment as whole and separate persons, in contrast with an earlier stage, where no such clear perception exists':

> Confronted with the wholeness and separateness of the parents, the infant, and later the child, experiences the impact of his own ambivalence toward them. In his experience of separation, jealousy and envy, he hates them and, in his mind, attacks them. Since the infant at that early stage of development feels his wishes and phantasies to be omnipotent, he feels that the parents thus attacked become fragmented and destroyed, and he introjects them as such into his internal world.... But since he also loves his parents and needs them, this destruction brings about feelings of mourning, loss, guilt and a longing to undo the damage done and restore in his mind the parents to their original state. Reparative impulses come into play.[41]

This later 'depressive position' is in turn itself outgrown by the ongoing maturation and integration of the child's ego. The process is assisted by the child's stocking his mind with whole objects in this way and, in so doing, gradually recognizing and enforcing the distinction between internal and external reality. It is bound to remind us of that 'discipline of love' and 'apprehensive habitude' described by Wordsworth in a well-known passage from the second book of *The Prelude*. 'Blessed the infant Babe', Wordsworth wrote, whose mind,

> Even in the first trial of its powers,
> Is prompt and watchful, eager to combine
> In one appearance, all the elements
> And parts of the same object, else detached
> And loth to coalesce.

The reader may recognize the fluency and sophistication of this model of the mind when compared with, say, the Oedipus complex: though it could not have been achieved without that precedent idea. The two positions described are themselves relative to each other; the infant perceives parts first, and gradually wholes; his sense of omnipotence in deploying these perceptions is by turns greater and lesser; persecutory hatred and desirous love give way by degrees to ambivalence; the view of objects based on their presence or absence gives way to the testing of reality; and so on. Moreover, whereas both positions are superseded in turn, the depressive position can and often does reassert itself in adult life, and even the paranoid-schizoid position is reverted to at times of stress. The two positions 'are not only *stages* of development', Hanna Segal reminds us, but 'two *types* of ego integration and organization, and the ego has a constant struggle to maintain a state of integration' between them (*WHS* 16; my italics).

As Klein moved away from the Freudian structure of the unconscious and the complex, Freud's terminology was extended and a whole range of concepts for which he could find no use given life: fantasy and symbol in particular. The 'main thrust of Freud's thinking', according to Hanna Segal,

> is that phantasy is not a primary activity. It has the same roots as, and is comparable to dreams, symptoms, parapraxes, and art; it does not underlie dreams, symptoms, thought, and art. For Klein, on the contrary, unconscious phantasy is a core primary activity, an original expression of both impulses and defences, and it is continually interacting with perception, modifying it but also modified by it. With maturation and increasing experience, the phantasies become more complex, with more differentiated sensory components and motives, and elaborated in various ways.[42]

Where Freud decided that the role of fantasy in dreams was a secondary or parasitic one, Segal feels that dreams are, on the contrary, one of the forms of expression that fantasy takes. In moving from the paranoid–schizoid position to the depressive position,

> the nature of the phantasy changes from ideal and persecutory part-object relationships to whole objects such as the parental couple, siblings, and family, and the internal conflict worked out in phantasy is concerned more with reparation of damage done to these entities. It is also in the depressive position only that gradually repression replaces the more primitive defences of splitting, idealization, and projection. The infant becomes more separated and

differentiated from his object and capable of feeling guilty about his impulses and phantasies. He therefore represses them. And it is when repression functions that repressed impulses and phantasies can give rise to sublimation. (*DPA* 28–9)

Unconscious fantasy, as Hanna Segal describes it, is very close to that idea of the active, incubatory, unconscious put forward by Michael Polanyi in the previous section, except that she comes to it from the instinctual rather than the cognitive side of the coin, as it were:

> Higher mental activity, like thinking, is an interplay between phantasy and reality. We do not approach reality with a mind that is blank. We approach reality with expectations based on our preconscious or unconscious phantasies and experience reality … as a constant implementing and testing of our phantasies against reality. What is reality-testing? You can only test a hypothesis. Unconscious phantasies are like a series of hypotheses which can be tested by reality. (*DPA* 29)

Symbols, too, which Freud regarded with some mistrust, are seen in a new light. They have their place in mental life not in the traditional sense as a set of external, collective, and generalized signs, but as a flexible structure of interactions between fantasy and reality, necessarily unique to each individual. Symbol-formation originates in the infant's need to replace objects, the loss or damage of which brings him guilt: 'It is only when the infant can recognize the absence of the object that he can either symbolize or think' (*DPA* 57).

For the very reason that it is the basis of thought, symbol-formation is also the basis of communication between unconscious fantasy life and consciousness, the outside world, and other people:

> it could be asked what is meant when we speak of people being in touch with their unconscious. It is not that they have consciously primitive phantasies, like those which become evident in their analyses, but merely that they have some awareness of their own impulses and feelings. However, I think that we mean more than this; we mean that they have actual *communication* with their unconscious phantasies. And this, like any other form of communication can be done only with the help of symbols. So that in people who are 'in touch with themselves' there is a constant free symbol-formation,

whereby they can be consciously aware and in control of *symbolic expressions* of the underlying primitive phantasies. (*WHS* 57–8)

Dreams are communications of this kind. The 'capacity for nonconrete symbol formation', Segal suggests, 'is in itself an achievement of the ego – an achievement necessary for the formation of the kind of dreams covered by Freud's theory' (*WHS* 91). To this we are now in a position to add that works of literature also allow their authors a variety of 'communication with their unconscious phantasies' – except (and this is the important issue) such communication is one established in and mediated by the work itself, a fact which prevents the entire process becoming merely wish-fulfilling, self-serving, and internalized.

Which brings us to the last important point. The symbolic expressions associated with the depressive position (which Segal elsewhere calls 'representations'), are contrasted by her with the too-concrete 'symbolic equations' found in neuroses, psychoses, and paranoid–schizoid mental states. In symbolic equations, 'the symbol is so equated with the object symbolized that the two are felt to be identical' (*DPA* 35). On the other hand the 'symbol proper, available for sublimation and furthering the development of the ego, is felt to *represent* the object; its own characteristics are recognized, respected, and used' (*WHS* 57). In the former, reality-testing has broken down and introjections and projections have run wild; in the latter, that which has been lost or damaged has been replaced or repaired, and because it is seen to represent an external object it can be used in every aspect of mental life more or less indifferently, but in the creative aspect above all.

Enough has been said, perhaps, to suggest the strengths of the Kleinian view, especially with regard to those reservations about Freud expressed above. It has fought clear of that view of the unconscious and its products (dreams, parapraxes, et al.) which created so many critical problems and solved so few. The difficulties of the hydrostatic system, the constancy principle, and the distinction between primary and secondary mental processes have been overcome, to some extent at least. The unconscious no longer need be seen simply as a chthonic sump watched over by the censor, but as a creative agency in the production of symbols, and by means of them, a creative agency in subjectivity and conscious thought as well. The unconscious, for example, interacts with perception, 'modifying it but also modified by it'. Equally, the distinction between the latent and the manifest, has been replaced by a genuine dialectic between the two:

> Reality experience, in interaction with unconscious phantasy, gradually alters the character of phantasies, and memory traces of reality experiences are incorporated into phantasy life … the original phantasies are of a crude and primitive nature, directly concerned with the satisfaction of instincts. These phantasies are experienced in a somatic as well as a mental way, and, since our instincts are always active, a primitive layer of primary phantasies is active in all of us. From this core later phantasies evolve. They become altered by contact with reality, by conflict, by maturational growth. As instincts develop instinct derivatives, so the early primitive phantasies develop later derivatives. These can be displaced, symbolized and elaborated upon and even penetrate into consciousness as daydreams, imagination, etc.[43]

Once you start giving life to the unconscious beyond the drive for wish-fulfilment, it is hard to stop. Readers may be familiar with a climactic passage in the thirteenth book of *The Prelude*, in which Wordsworth recalls a walk he did in his youth to the summit of Mount Snowdon. After walking for many hours in fog-bound darkness, the poet suddenly climbs above the clouds, to see them laid out before him in the moonlight. The vision he receives is one of the mind – not 'the Mighty mind' as he says, but surely any mind. The fog spreads out ever further over the sea, just as consciousness – human knowledge and curiosity – spreads out over the world of nature. But there is also a tremendous *gap* in the clouds – 'a blue chasm':

> a fracture in the vapour,
> A deep and gloomy breathing-place, through which
> Mounted the roar of waters, torrents, streams
> Innumerable, roaring with one voice.

And it is in this 'deep dark thoroughfare', Wordsworth believes, that Nature 'had lodged/The Soul, the Imagination of the whole.' If it is appropriate to see Wordsworth's gulf as an analogue of the unconscious, is it clear how that analogue contains, alongside the sublimity and the fearfulness perennially associated with the unknown, an appreciation of it as the source of everything living and positive in mental life as well? The terms in which Hanna Segal discusses the mind may not owe much to that 'grandeur' and 'tragic courage' Trilling thought so highly of in Freud,[44] but (as I think the Wordsworthian analogy might show) they are infinitely more accessible to and descriptive of the kinds of moral interest literature represents. She is also able to supplement Polanyi's account of incubation in such a way as to make it clear that incubation includes artistic-creative concerns (which are fundamentally moral in character, as Marion Milner realized) as well as those scientific–creative ones which ultimately produce verifiable or refutable arguments. 'The richness, depth, and accuracy of a person's thinking', Segal writes, 'will depend on the quality and malleability of the unconscious phantasy life' he or she enjoys (*WHS* 46). (It is worth noting the richness, depth, and accuracy of Segal's own moral-evaluative language here, itself highly unusual in psychoanalytic discussion of the imagination.) Such fantasies determine 'the basic structure and character of the personality, as the matrix of our mental structure and life' (*DPA* 25), and our ability to learn from reality 'in turn is connected with the evolution and changes in [that] phantasy life' (*DPA* 26) which 'underlies and colours all our activities however realistic' (*DPA* 101). Her comments here suggest that you cannot speak about the '*character* of the personality' (as opposed to its structure, say) without reflecting upon what Milner called 'the central problems of being alive' and their relation to action.

Nor is this all. Freud believed that the writer aims 'to awaken in us the same emotional attitude, the same mental constellation as that which in him produced the impetus to create.' Where Hanna Segal is concerned, the emphasis is different. Certainly, she agrees with Freud that 'in order to move us deeply the artist must have embodied in his work some deep experience of his own' (*WHS* 202). Equally, she feels that the spectator of a tragedy 'identifies himself with the author, and the whole tragedy with the author's internal world' (*WHS* 199). She agrees with Freud on this point, with one extremely important difference: in her account the spectator of a tragedy does not simply identify himself with the author as a psychic whole, so to speak. On the contrary, the spectator 'identifies himself with the author *while the latter is facing and expressing his depression*' (*WHS* 199; my italics). What she calls 'aesthetic pleasure' always 'includes an unconscious reliving of the artist's *experience of creation*' (*WHS* 198; my italics). Literary critics may still have reservations about Segal's use of words like 'expression' and 'identification'. ('Identification', for example, is returned to in Chapter 5, below.) They may be sceptical about 'reliving' some aspect of the artist's experience, and as unhappy about an expression like 'aesthetic pleasure' coming from Hanna Segal as from Vladimir Nabokov and Richard Rorty (see Chapter 2). But her distinction between the artist 'as artist' and the artist 'as everyday individual' does allow her to discuss such things in terms of an actual work of art in which the expressions, identifications, relivings, and pleasures are assumed to take place. The 'experience of creation' is a distinct and separate *experience*, with ongoing mental consequences, and not a mere conduit for egoistic daydreams or otherwise inadmissible instincts, larded over with formal and aesthetic pleasures. The work of art, to put it bluntly, is an object to which we relate. In 'facing and expressing his depression' rather than merely succumbing to it more or less unwittingly the artist is able to take part in that debate or dialogue with his own work which I have tried to describe above.

I have placed so much emphasis on Hanna Segal's ideas of unconscious fantasy and the symbols by means of which that fantasy life is able to communicate itself because, just as Lionel Trilling felt about Freud, so I believe her importance for literary criticism lies less in her comments on individual authors than in that 'whole conception of the mind' she has to offer. Ever since her first important work on creativity, 'A Psycho-Analytic Approach to Aesthetics' (1952), Segal has felt that 'the artistic impulse is specifically related to the depressive position' (*DPA* 86), and that artists have, alongside a highly developed sense of reality which allows them to recognize psychic 'objects' as artistic material, a more powerful sense of loss with regard to those objects, and a more urgent wish to make reparation to them. The one sense implies the other. On the most abstract level, it may be this combination of factors that impels the writer to create, not those generalized types of human being that Samuel Johnson, for example, thought to be the essence of Shakespeare's achievement, but instance after instance of individuality and subjectivity. The writer does this not out of any crude sense of guilt towards his family, but out of an impulse to relive, rediscover, and confirm both the separate reality of those objects and his relationship to them.

And this is fine as far as it takes us. But practically speaking, Hanna Segal, as she is bound to by her vocation, moves in a direction I cannot follow here. If literary critics will always have to test theories such as hers against literature, she has another avenue: therapy. 'If the wish to create is rooted in the depressive position', she writes, 'and the capacity to create depends upon a successful working through it, it would follow that the inability to acknowledge and overcome depressive anxiety must lead to inhibitions in artistic expression' (*WHS* 190). She goes on to describe many cases in which writer's block and other creative strictures are eased by patients' eventual understanding of the sources of these problems. But is there an example that will suit us both? Is there a great writer (greater, that is to say, than William Golding, a novel of whose Segal does discuss at length)[45] who also strikes us as being the victim of the kind of 'depressive anxiety' she speaks of? No doubt there are many, but one in particular springs to mind: Joseph Conrad. If Segal's approach to literature can be seen to have descriptive value in a critical analysis of some of Conrad's work, then its status as an important development of Freud's thinking will have been demonstrated, in literary–critical terms at least.

3.3   'The Secret Sharer'

Like the rest of us, writers are subject to depression, whether originating in the depressive position or not. There is nothing in Hanna Segal's work to suggest that they are any more at risk than anybody else, though of course Dryden's notion that 'Great wits are sure to madness near allied' is as old as literary criticism itself.[46] Samuel Johnson suffered crippling bouts of melancholia, and T.S. Eliot, too, at various times in his life, found himself incapable of work in the face of acute depression. Conrad is an equally well-known instance. Indeed, no writer has testified so eloquently to the frustration and difficulty he went through in getting words on the page. In letter after letter to friends, fellow-novelists, publishers, and literary agents, he recounts his hypochondria, the feeble state of his nerves, the continual ill-health of his family, his financial worries – and his inability to write. In Conrad's case, too, we appear to have an open-and-shut case of a depressive position unresolved. An only child, Conrad lost his mother when aged seven and his father when aged twelve. He then lived with various family members until he broke away from his family and homeland to go to sea at the age of seventeen. Twenty years later, in 1894, he left the merchant service to become a writer. Four times he was resigned or he resigned himself to solitude: as orphan, exile, seaman (obtaining his master's ticket in 1884), and finally writer.

It would not be too outlandish a psychological guess to say that these four forms of solitude, utterly mingled and interdependent, came to have a powerful effect on Conrad's imagination, which was, in its nature, a centripetal and obsessive one. Loneliness in its stark and dominating form (what he called in *Lord Jim* 'a hard and absolute condition of existence')[47] was the subject of many of Conrad's books, reaching a climax with the hero of *Victory*. But the anxieties of loneliness combined with those of responsibility especially fascinated him, and his background being what it was, it was through the loneliness of *command* that he was able to dramatize this fascination.

Many stories will spring to mind in this connection: *Lord Jim* and 'Youth', for example. But *The Shadow-Line* and 'The Secret Sharer' have obvious similarities which Hanna Segal herself brings out in *Dream, Phantasy and Art*. Both are about a first command; both contain a double; both are 'dominated by the island of Koh-Ring' (*DPA* 88). Above all, and with the connection I have pointed to immediately above in mind, the anxious solitude of the first-time captains in both stories may be related to Conrad's own (quadruplicated) sense of isolation which he could resolve only in literature. 'It is while he was coping with his first command, and...in the throes of depression,' Segal suggests, 'that Conrad started writing.'[48]

And not only Conrad. The captain from *The Shadow-Line*, too, picks up his pen at the climax of his despair:

> It's the only period of my life in which I attempted to keep a diary. No, not the only one. Years later, in conditions of moral isolation, I did put down on paper the thoughts and events of a score of days. But this was the first time. I don't remember how it came about, or how the pocket-book and the pencil came into my hands. It's inconceivable that I should have looked for them on purpose. I suppose they saved me from the crazy trick of talking to myself.
>
> Strangely enough, in both cases I took to that sort of thing in circumstances in which I did not expect, in colloquial phrase, 'to come out of it.' Neither could I expect the record to outlast me. This shows that it was purely a personal need for intimate relief and not a call of egotism.[49]

We notice the captain's stress on involuntariness of his impulse, and on the distinction between 'intimate relief' on the one hand and 'egotism' on the other. In fact the captain's diary is, as we could only expect, an inextricable blend of the personal and the egotistic: 'My first command. Now I understand that strange sense of insecurity in my past. I always suspected that I might be no good. And here is proof positive. I am shirking it. I am no good.'[50]

Everything in human life is relative, in one sense at least. A child's first day at school or a naval captain taking his first command are commonplace occurrences, certainly – to everyone except the interested parties themselves. And the young captain of 'The Secret Sharer' is as alone as any schoolboy. Appointed to his command only two weeks before the opening of the story, the captain admits: 'my position was that of the only stranger on board. I mention this because it has some bearing on what is to follow. But what I felt most was my being a stranger to the ship; and if all the truth must be told, I was somewhat of a stranger to myself.'[51] 'I felt that it would take very little', he mentions later, 'to make me a suspect person in the eyes of the ship's company' ('SS' 102–3). The hope of 'quiet communion' with his first command, the captain feels, 'was gone for good' even on the night before the beginning of the voyage. He wonders 'how far I should turn out faithful to that ideal conception of one's own personality every man sets up for himself secretly' ('SS' 88–9). The captain's state of mind should not be exaggerated. The ideal conception of himself that he alludes to here, for example, is not evidence of schizophrenia; neither am I going to suggest that he reverts to the kind of infantile autism treated by Melanie Klein. But under 'the novel responsibility of command' ('SS' 91) the young man does suffer depressive anxiety, the evidence for which is the very defences he runs up against that anxiety: the paranoid–schizoid splitting and projection described by Klein and Segal.

Leggatt, the young man the captain takes from the sea and hides in his cabin, has committed murder on another ship, the *Sephora*, lying at anchor some miles away, on which ship Leggatt had served as chief mate before being put in irons pending trial on shore. One of the remarkable features of the story is the captain's immediate and unthinking acceptance of Leggatt's explanation of the crime's mitigating circumstances. Indeed, the captain comes to regard the stranger as his double with astonishing speed. Even while Leggatt is in the water, and before he has come on board, the captain feels that his 'self possession...had somehow induced a corresponding state in myself', and that a 'mysterious communication was established already between us two', the result of 'pure intuition' on his part ('SS' 93–4). 'I knew well enough' the captain records after only a few moments' conversation on deck, 'that my double there was no homicidal ruffian': 'I did not think of asking him for details, and he told me the story roughly in brusque, disconnected sentences. I needed no more. I saw it all going on as though I were myself inside that other sleeping-suit.'[52]

It is a remarkable occurrence, but not an inexplicable or a supernatural one. From the moment he hears Leggatt's voice in the water, the captain responds to something 'calm and resolute' in the stranger's manner. The more he hears and the more he learns, the deeper that response becomes. Leggatt had been a chief mate (and a level-headed and courageous one, it would appear) as the captain himself had been until a fortnight before; he is a younger man, but only by two years; he has even attended the same maritime school or college, Conway. Every fresh coincidence seems only the more natural, and serves to underwrite and extend the captain's instinctive identification with his guest. And if we ask ourselves why it should be that the captain identifies with him at all, and what the grounds are for this sympathy, we can only reply that Leggatt is for the captain what Frankenstein says Henry Clerval is for him in Mary Shelley's novel: 'the image of my former self'. Leggatt is *him*, in an earlier, younger incarnation. Calm and resolute Leggatt has projected onto him all the good aspects of chief mateship; all the authority and all the strictly demarcated responsibilities of that position which the captain himself, when junior in rank, used to fill. The very position, that is, he can no longer fall back on in actuality: for now his responsibilities are unlimited, his skill unproven, his ability to measure up to an ideal conception (not only of his own self but of captaincy) a matter of doubt for him and his crew. No wonder that he grasps at Leggatt so quickly, trusts him so implicitly – and hides him so anxiously.

The word Melanie Klein used for projective figures of the Leggatt kind is 'imago': a distorted version of a real object. In the earliest phase of infant development, she writes,

> the persecuting and the good objects … are kept wide apart in the child's mind. When, along with the introjection of the whole and real object, they come closer together, the ego has over and over again recourse to that mechanism – so important for the development of the relations to objects – namely, a splitting of its imagos into loved and hated, that is to say, into good and dangerous ones.[53]

It is the ship, the captaincy, the crew, the voyage, and the entire set of responsibilities they constitute that together have suddenly become a 'whole and real object' for the captain on taking up his command. In his anxiety he turns to his good imago, Leggatt: 'on the whole I felt less torn in two when I was with him' ('SS' 113). But where, or what, is the figure of persecution? What or who is it he hates? If his old position of mate is what he secretly hankers after, then, correspondingly, his anxieties are connected with that position he now holds without having proved his right to it: captaincy. Thus the captain from whom Leggatt has fled becomes the persecutory imago to whose badness Leggatt himself testifies by describing his cowardly behaviour during the storm in which the murder took place ('all his nerve went to pieces altogether in that hellish spell of bad weather we had'; 'SS' 100). And when this unfortunate soul comes on board in search of his escaped prisoner, we get a wonderfully vivid piece of projection:

> The skipper of the *Sephora* had a thin red whisker all round his face, and the sort of complexion that goes with hair of that colour; also the particular, rather smeary shade of blue in the eyes. He was not exactly a showy figure; his shoulders were high, his stature but middling – one leg slightly more bandy than the other. He shook hands, looking vaguely around. A spiritless tenacity was his main characteristic, I judged. I behaved with a politeness which seemed to disconcert him. Perhaps he was shy. He mumbled to me as if he were ashamed of what he was saying; gave his name (it was something like Archbold – but at this distance of years I hardly am sure), his ship's name, and a few other particulars of that sort, in the manner of a criminal making a reluctant and doleful confession. He had had terrible weather on the passage out – terrible – terrible – wife aboard, too. ('SS' 107)

These animadversions on his appearance are a ruse, of a kind. This is not distaste but fear, and what our captain really fears is the other's length and breadth of service: 'Seven-and-thirty virtuous years at sea', Archbold has to his credit, 'of which over twenty of immaculate command'. In the face of this the captain of a fortnight's standing jumps to the obvious conclusion: given the wealth of Archbold's experience, and the poverty of his own, Archbold (like his own crew) must be thinking him 'not the sort that would have done for the chief mate of a ship like the *Sephora*' ('SS' 110).

With his bad imago in the cuddy with him, it is the good imago the captain turns to: 'I looked politely at Captain Archbold but it was the other I saw' ('SS' 108). If Archbold had only known, he goes on, 'how afraid I was of his putting my feeling of identity with the other to the test'. All he had to do was to make a direct enquiry about Leggatt's whereabouts. The reason he did not, our captain feels, 'is that he was not a little disconcerted by the reverse side of that weird situation, by something in me that reminded him of the man he was seeking – suggested a mysterious similitude to the young fellow he had distrusted and disliked from the first' ('SS' 111). In this way the two projections are related to each other and to the captain himself. But once Archbold has been on board, and has been seen off, Conrad encounters a problem. Archbold has served the vital function of proving Leggatt's story, indeed his existence, not to the captain (who needs no proof) but to the reader. But when he pulls away from the ship's side the bad imago – the persecutory representative of captaincy and experienced seamanship – pulls away in his person. Archbold is no longer present as a psychological object to be disarmed, repaired, or introjected. How is the depressive drama to be sustained?

It is for this reason, I suggest, that we are given another hateful and hated projection in the story: not Archbold's equal in rank, certainly, but his equal in the kind of sniffy and paternalistic attitude Archbold adopts towards the narrator. In a manner that, were it not typical of narrative and dramatic organization generally, would remind us of Freud's notion of condensation, the two men share something else, too: whiskers. It is the mate of the narrator's own ship, with his 'round eyes and frightful whiskers' ('SS' 89), who takes on Archbold's role in his absence, commenting upon, exposing, and intruding upon the captain's insecurity, flitting around him 'in silent criticism' ('SS' 121) and surreptitiously alluding to the captain's sanity, sobriety, or both.[54] Through the agency of this 'absurdly whiskered mate', the bad as well as the good projection is preserved.

The wind stirs, the ship gets under way, and the story turns towards its climax. When the captain is informed of the breeze he feels 'the call of a new claim upon my thoughts and even upon my feelings': the claim, that is, of the ship herself, 'the whole and real object'. But while the stranger is on board, the captain feels 'not wholly alone with my command'. He feels safe, yes; but he is not in command. 'Part of me was absent'; 'all unconscious alertness had abandoned me. I had to make an effort of will to recall myself back (from the cabin) to the conditions of the moment. I felt that I was appearing an irresolute commander to those people who were watching me more or less critically' ('SS' 115–16). It is by means of passages like these that we come to see Leggatt as an ambivalent figure. Always 'perfectly self-controlled, more than calm – almost invulnerable' ('SS' 117), Leggatt eventually becomes 'something against nature, inhuman' ('SS' 123). He interferes with that natural, instinctive interdependence between the officer and his command for which the captain has yearned since the story's opening, and the lack of which he feels so strongly: 'all unconscious alertness had abandoned me'. However desirable and necessary a projection Leggatt may be, he remains a defence against reality and not a means of comprehending it.

The captain intends to bring his ship as close as possible to the volcanic island of Koh-ring, where his double will jump off and swim to shore. The only excuse he can offer for the danger in which he places the ship during this manoeuvre is the need to pick up a shore breeze. As the ship moves nearer and nearer to the hidden reefs, so his anxieties about his two chief-mates, above- and below-decks, are replaced by fear for *her*. His bad imago appears 'moaning' at his elbow: 'He was thunderstruck, and as it were deprived of the moral support of his whiskers. He clapped his hands and absolutely cried out, "Lost!"', to which the captain replies ('sternly') 'Be quiet'. Almost hysterical, the mate is unable to obey orders that we notice are now coming fluently:

> I hadn't let go the mate's arm and went on shaking it. 'Ready about, do you hear? You go forward' – shake – 'and stop there' – shake – 'and hold your noise' – shake – 'and see these head-sheets properly overhauled' – shake, shake – shake.[55]

Not knowing the ship, however, and having no landmark by which to gauge whether she is drifting or picking up the wind, the captain is at a loss to instruct the helmsman. Once again this anxiety outweighs any other: 'And now I forgot the secret stranger ready to depart, and remembered only that I was a total stranger to the ship. I did not know her. Would she do it? How was she to be handled?' ('SS' 128). He is given just such a mark by a hat in the water, left there by Leggatt in his swim to shore. By the hat's 'serving me for a mark to help out the ignorance of my strangeness' he is able to bring the ship around and establish for the first time that 'quiet communion' with her, unattainable so far, just as his projections recede – Leggatt to be 'hidden for ever from all friendly faces' in obscurity, the other, his bewhiskered chief mate, to proper subservience with the rest of the crew. 'And I was alone with her. Nothing! no one in the world should stand now between us, throwing a shadow on the way of silent knowledge and mute affection, the perfect communion of a seaman with his first command' ('SS' 129).

And that completes the analysis. The nameless captain of this nameless ship has resolved his depressive anxieties about his command, and so has Conrad about his infancy, his exile, his life at sea, and his work as a writer. The imaginary and the real man achieve their perfect communions, and the Kleinian pattern has found its literary apogee; or so it would appear.

The theory of the paranoid–schizoid and the depressive positions is particularly convincing when it comes to explaining two dramatically central elements in the Conrad's narrative. First, the hero's immediate empathy with Leggatt and the reasons for it; second, the hero's corollary sense of distrust emanating from both Captain Archbold and his own first mate, and the reasons for his paranoid attitude in that respect. Only when the ship and everything it represents (duty, exactitude, community, discipline both of self and others, the fabric of the vessel and the lives of its crew, the tradition of captaincy, the rule of law, and the force of custom) is integrated as a 'whole object', psychologically speaking, will these schizoid imagos disappear. Equally, only when the schizoid imagos disappear will the ship become so integrated.

Even in this flexible and sophisticated form, however, such an interpretation of 'The Secret Sharer' remains firmly based in the Freudian attitude towards literature in general. The assumption remains that Conrad was, for better or worse, the possessor of what Freud called a 'mental constellation': a more or less perennial group of unconscious forces which occasionally and irresistibly found vent in his writing. The only explanations Freud can offer for our taking an interest in the mental constellation of Joseph Conrad are, first, that it is one we all share (all of us being, to a certain extent, lonely 'exiles' of the Conradian type), and, second, that even if we do not share Conrad's idiosyncratic set of unconscious mental attitudes, such attitudes can be rendered palatable to us if we are offered a sufficient aesthetic reward to overcome our distaste. And Hanna Segal retains crucial elements of that account in providing her own. It is true that she speaks of an 'experience of creation': a distinct experience with which the reader identifies and in which the writer 'faces and expresses his depression'. But her choice of words is a revealing one. On the one hand, the writer merely 'faces' some sort of pre-existing, if not necessarily known, quantity: his or her depression. On the other, he or she merely 'expresses' that same fixed quantity, leaving it, so Hanna Segal's choice of word suggests, more or less unchanged in the process.

But 'The Secret Sharer', like any other work of literature, *transforms* the unconscious fantasies and depressive anxieties that lie behind its composition. If all that were involved were processes of 'facing' on the one hand and 'expressing' on the other, the writing of literature would be both easier and more common than it is. Again, though it may not be the first word we think of in relation to Conrad, 'pleasures' is by no means an inapposite term to describe these acts of transformation.

Comedy is not likely to be the first word we think of in relation to Conrad; yet even in tense dramas of depressive anxiety like *Lord Jim*, *The Shadow-Line*, *Heart of Darkness*, and 'The Secret Sharer', there are episodes of black humour which sit oddly with the psychological sources of those narratives. The most graphic example, perhaps, is in *Heart of Darkness*. Marlow, approaching Kurtz's camp, finds the steamboat under his command attacked by natives from the shore, and his helmsman knocked over by a cane entering the window of the pilot-house. He continues to concentrate on the river ahead, 'but my feet felt so very warm and wet that I had to look down':

> The man had rolled on his back and stared straight up at me; both hands clutched that cane. It was the shaft of a spear that, either thrown or lunged through the opening, had caught him in the side just below the ribs; the blade had gone in out of sight, after making a frightful gash; my shoes were full; a pool of blood lay very still, gleaming dark red under the wheel; his eyes shone with an amazing lustre.

The emergency passes and Marlow forces another passenger to steer: 'He looked very dubious; but I made a grab at his arm, and he understood at once I meant him to steer whether or no. To tell you the truth, I was morbidly anxious to change my shoes and socks.'[56] A more theatrical note is struck when the narrator of *The Shadow-Line*, his crew disabled by fever, discovers the ship's supply of quinine to be only worthless white powder: a scene that we cannot help visualizing in terms bordering on the melodramatically ridiculous. Aghast, he staggers over to the cabin of the chief mate, sick in bed:

> The wildness of his aspect checked my mental disorder. He was sitting up in his bunk, his body looking immensely long, his head

drooping a little sideways, with affected complacency. He flourished, in his trembling hand, on the end of a forearm no thicker than a stout walking-stick, a shining pair of scissors which he tried before my very eyes to jab at his throat.[57]

In fact the mate is simply trimming his beard. The crew of the *Patna* cut similarly ludicrous figures in their efforts to launch a lifeboat when abandoning their ship and their passengers. The 'turmoil of terror that had scattered their self-control like chaff before the wind', we are told, 'converted their desperate exertions into a bit of fooling, upon my word fit for knockabout clowns in a farce.'[58]

In 'The Secret Sharer' itself we are given a scene of equally farcical potential, in which the captain fears his steward is about to find the double hidden in his cabin, and gives increasingly irrational, helpless, and desperate orders to prevent the discovery:

> Suddenly I became aware ... that the fellow for some reason or other was opening the door of the bath-room. It was the end. The place was literally not big enough to swing a cat in. My voice died in my throat and I went stony all over. I expected to hear a yell of surprise and terror, and made a movement, but had not the strength to get on my legs. ('SS' 118)

The threatened explosion of Whitehall farce never takes place; if it did, the story would collapse. What is the function of such moments? How could Conrad have seized upon them in contexts like these? The pleasure and the relief in such situations, for both agent and witness, lay, Freud felt, in an *'economy in expenditure upon feeling'*.[59] There is in such moments as Conrad describes an element 'comparable to displacement, by means of which the release of affect that is already in preparation is disappointed and the cathexis diverted on to something else, often on to something of secondary importance' (*PFL* vi. 298): Marlow's socks, for example, or a pair of scissors. To put it more simply, 'humour is a means of obtaining pleasure in spite of the distressing affects that interfere with it; it acts as a substitute for the generation of these affects, it puts itself in their place' (*PFL* vi. 293).

In trying to define the phenomenon more closely Freud decided that humorous displacement was 'impossible under the glare of conscious attention', but was 'tied to the condition of remaining preconscious or automatic' (*PFL* vi. 298–9). By linking humour with both the automatic and with 'man's tenacious hold upon his customary self and his disregard of what might overthrow that self and drive it to despair' (*PFL* vi. 294), Freud can hardly help treading Conradian ground, however unawares. In each case – the shoes, the scissors, the 'turmoil of terror' on board the *Patna*, the mate in the bathroom – Conrad's heroes' attention is somehow stalled: pivoting, as it were, on the axis between consciousness and the 'preconscious or automatic' while being neither. (The pool of blood at Marlow's feet, we notice, lies 'very still'; Lord Jim's feet 'were glued to that remote spot' on the *Patna*; and the hero of 'The Secret Sharer' goes 'stony all over'.) It is not what the captain from *The Shadow-Line* calls 'mental disorder' which is checked in such moments of insensate panic, but the mind altogether. No one could call these men unconscious of what they see, but neither can we call their frozen attentions truly conscious ones. What we sense is a collision between the instinct to act on the one hand (to attend to the helmsman, to grab the scissors, to distract the steward), and the instinct to pause and to comprehend the situation on the other: instincts between which the mind finds itself unable to mediate. It is here that humour *is* able to provide mediation of a kind. On such occasions moral imperatives like the code of captaincy, or man's tenacious hold upon his customary self, actually forbid repression (what Freud calls elsewhere in this account 'the automatism of defence' or 'the flight reflex') and offer humour as a kind of substitution or compensation for this thwarted reflex.

Moreover, such jarring and kaleidoscopic impressions, being beyond Conrad's protagonists' control (just as developments up the Congo or at sea are beyond their control more generally speaking), reveal also an essential lability in the moral precepts, the codes, the inherited outlooks, and the frames of consciousness those protagonists inhabit. It was Henri Bergson who suggested that comedy depended on what he called 'un effet d'automatisme et de raideur [inelasticity]',[60] and that when we see an individual slip on a banana-skin he or she ceases to be human and becomes, however fleetingly, a mechanical object. Laughter, in Bergson's view, required 'une anesthésie momentanée du cœur'. 'Est comique', he wrote, 'tout incident qui appelle notre attention sur le physique d'une personne alors que le moral est en cause.'[61] On such occasions we see 'du mécanique plaqué sur du vivant'; where we expect 'la souplesse attentive et la vivante flexibilité d'une personne', we find instead 'une certaine *raideur de mécanique*'.[62] Transfixed and immobilized by the incongruity of instincts and impressions they have no choice but to admit, the protagonists of Conrad's tales witness the melt-down of their respective moral orders while remaining frozen themselves. In their admittedly humble way, such blackly humourous moments represent moral collisions of genuine intensity: the incompatibility, so to speak, of what Marion Milner called 'the central problems of being alive'. Conrad, Freud, and Bergson between them suggest that moral collisions of this kind are not restricted to the purely conscious sphere, and further that the humorous affect which such collisions generate in those situations is implicitly bound up with a resort to what is 'preconscious or automatic'.

This discussion brings me to a second important topic relating to Conrad in general and 'The Secret Sharer' in particular. I want to turn from the consideration of something which diverts and transforms unconscious obsessions to something that grows up alongside them and in dialogue with them, as it were, and which is manifestly a vital issue in Conrad's writing, but which psychoanalytic critics disregard all too often. What I have in mind here is the concept of tradition. Authors do not simply 'face' and 'express' depressive anxiety and unconscious fantasy; but then neither are they fortunate enough to encounter these things in neatly isolated and clearly labelled packages, which is what terms like 'face' and 'express' suggest. On the contrary, while the kind of quadruplicated depressive anxieties I have diagnosed in Conrad (orphan, exile, seaman, and writer) are themselves inter-related, each is also related to further entire webs of issues, abstract and intimately personal by turns: parents and parenthood, marriage, England and its language, Poland and its history, revolution and class, to name but a few. Tradition is one of those forces which straddles the unconscious and the moral spheres – modifying and being modified. Moreover it is precisely the kind of moral constraint which may, in certain circumstances, discourage or forbid repression.

We saw in Chapter 2 that Freud plays an important role in Richard Rorty's philosophy. According to Rorty, psychoanalysis allows us to 'catch hold of some crucial idiosyncratic contingencies in our past' and so 'make something worthwhile of ourselves'. Freudian psychoanalysis does indeed place a high emphasis on the 'idiosyncratic contingencies' underlying the individual's 'passionate but catastrophic relations with a loved parent' as Richard Wollheim describes them. For Freud as for

Rorty, tradition is by comparison with such contingencies not a subject of great importance except, perhaps, in providing one particular form of more or less institutionalized censorship and repression. But as the discussion of Conrad's twin consciousness of authorship and first command at the beginning of this section suggested, 'The Secret Sharer' and its analogues in Conrad's fiction are narratives to some extent *about* tradition: about captaincy, seamanship, command, and (explicitly in the case of *The Shadow-Line*) authorship. Traditions of these kinds, far from acting to repress anything in Conrad's fiction, restrained his imagination and his moral curiosity from attempting to do any such thing, as we have already seen. Conrad speaks in comparatively simple terms of carrying over an 'article of creed from the decks of ships to the more circumscribed space of my desk', and of the 'intimacy and the strain of a creative effort in which mind and will and conscience are engaged to the full, hour after hour, day after day, away from the world, and to the exclusion of all that makes life really lovable and gentle – something for which a material parallel can only be found in the everlasting sombre stress of the westward winter passage round Cape Horn.'[63] But such associations also involved those 'obscurer qualities and choices' mentioned earlier in this chapter. 'The fidelity to a special tradition may last through the events of an unrelated existence,' he wrote, 'following faithfully, too, the traced way of an inexplicable impulse'; and so it is that he finds himself 'compelled, unconsciously compelled, now to write volume after volume, as in past years I was compelled to go to sea, voyage after voyage.'[64] There is not much space for 'idiosyncratic contingencies' in Conrad's moral universe.

The stress on tradition in Conrad cannot be divorced from the elements of conservatism in his character and thought: his conviction, for example, that 'the temporal world, rests on a very few simple ideas; so simple they must be as old as the hills'; or his insistence that the writer, 'in his dealings with mankind', should 'be capable of giving a tender recognition to their obscure virtues'.[65] Another such belief, itself a conservative one if Freud is seen as a progressive, was that consciousness implied and necessitated *conscience*. 'J'ai vécu,' Conrad wrote (quoting Abbé Sieyès on the French Revolution),

> missing all along the varied forms of destruction by a hair's-breadth, saving my body, that's clear, and perhaps my soul also, but not without some damage here and there to the fine edge of my conscience, that heirloom of the ages, of the race, of the group, of the family,

colourable and plastic, fashioned by the words, the looks, the acts, and even by the silences and abstentions surrounding one's childhood; tinged in a complete scheme of delicate shades and crude colours by the inherited traditions, beliefs, or prejudices – unaccountable, despotic, persuasive, and often, in its texture, romantic.[66]

We would expect a conservative writer to see traditional influences as an 'heirloom' of the ages, the race, the group, and the family – as something to a degree externalized. What is surprising is the way such influences on the 'consciousness' which underlies 'conscience' are revealed to involve the *un*conscious, too; that the 'colourable and plastic' conscience is capable of being formed not only by conscious reference to collectivized heirlooms but 'even by the silences and abstentions' of childhood; and finally that such influences in fact form 'a complete scheme' in which 'delicate shades and crude colours' lie side by side indivisibly. Tradition can comprise an inert, externalized, and immutable set of laws, undoubtedly. It can form a 'code' the rigorous adherence to which may force individuals into moments of moral paralysis like those presented in Conrad's sea stories: moments in which Conrad's heroes experience what Bergson calls anaesthesia of the heart. But it is amenable, too, to influences across the entire spectrum of consciousness. If it were not amenable in this way it would not *be* a tradition. It can be 'fashioned by the words, the looks, the acts, and even by the silences and abstentions surrounding one's childhood' in an almost wholly unconscious way; but it can also be understood and evaluated, however partially, by the person who attempts to apprehend and integrate it. What Conrad calls its fine edge can be dulled in some places, but sharpened in others. It has its shaping role to play in consciousness as a whole (including conscience), and is itself shaped and adapted there in turn.

In particular, tradition is shaped and adapted when we see that is not enough. And credit must go to F.R. Leavis for demonstrating more or less once and for all that for Conrad tradition was *not* enough. On the basis of some passages from both *The Shadow-Line* and 'The Secret Sharer', for example, Leavis points out that for Conrad the tradition of the merchant marine and the master mariner is subject to a great deal of irony in both stories.[67] The hero of the former story has just lowered himself for the first time into the captain's seat in the ship's saloon, and is just indulging himself with a set of meditations on the dynastic series of captains who have enthroned themselves there before ('continuous not in blood, indeed, but in its experience, in its training, in its conception of duty, and in the blessed simplicity of its traditional point of view on life'),[68] when it is revealed that his predecessor died in the very same chair. ('I repressed a silly impulse to jump up'.) The hero of 'The Secret Sharer', having walked past his profoundly sleeping crew in the forecastle, is just congratulating himself on 'the elementary moral beauty' of life at sea ('presenting no disquieting problems'), and 'the singleness of its purpose', when his problematic double bobs up alongside.[69] Conrad may, in article written for the *Daily Mail* in 1918, have dwelt on 'the old tradition of the sea, which made by the work of men has in its turn created for them their simple ideal of conduct'.[70] But simple traditional ideals of exactly this kind are what his moral and dramatic attention is focused upon in stories like 'The Secret Sharer'. It is quite clear as a result that while such ideals may be admirable in themselves they do not amount to Conrad's final position on the conduct of life. Such ideals are where his stories begin, not where they end. Narratives like these suggest that there will always be occasions on which traditional modes of conduct reveal their inadequacy; occasions which in themselves require an appeal to a broader, more imaginative, and less prescriptive concept or understanding of the self, other individuals, or of humanity as a whole.

Of course, Leavis would have had little patience with the interpretation of 'The Secret Sharer' offered in the pages above. 'Some knowing psychological and esoteric subtlety has been written about the double', he wrote with characteristic waspishness: 'The significance, however, is not psychological but moral.'[71] I am trying to suggest that the significance is both psychological and moral, and that it cannot be anything else. Conrad's remarks about conscience and tradition in *A Personal Record*, for example, are surely an 'abstemious and silent' reference to the family tradition, which weighed so heavily on him during his childhood, of loyalty to the cause of Polish nationhood and independence: a tradition which he very strikingly abandoned.[72] Is the significance of that cause and his flight from it (a matter of reflex and automatism to some extent, no doubt) psychological or moral? So complex is that 'complete scheme of delicate shades and crude colours' Conrad describes that we find it impossible to separate the psychological from the moral elements it contains. But neither can we establish, as Freud often suggests we can, any ordered series of events in which the latter is a derivation or a concretion of the former.

These remarks in effect suggest that the distinction between the psychological and the moral is untenable. Since both Collingwood and I might appear to be committed to defend that distinction in order to defend the autonomies of moral philosophy and literature from psychoanalytical contamination, my finding it to collapse in this way appears serious indeed. But as I suggested in Chapter 1, such distinctions are the among very things which literature is determined to deconstruct. The 'obscurer qualities and choices' we have seen at work in the writings of Conrad, Virginia Woolf, Charlotte Brontë, Dickens, and Jane Austen are psychological and moral at the same time. But this does not mean that Freud was justified in making the sweeping institutional claims on moral philosophy and literature that he did ('the conflict in *Hamlet* is so effectively concealed that it was left to me to unearth it'). It is a major part of Hanna Segal's achievement that she is able to appreciate the significance, in their own terms, of those elements of experience with which fantasy inevitably concerns itself, amongst which are tradition, but also consciousness, reason, and will. By emphasizing the complexity of the relation between fantasy (the realm of the unconscious) and reality (the realm of 'conscience'), and the ultimate indivisibility of the two, Hanna Segal comes closer than any other psychoanalytic writer to an understanding of the unconscious element in literature. Precisely by virtue of achieving this level of understanding she is at the same time implicitly able to acknowledge the limits of psychoanalytical accounts of what Collingwood called 'mind in the proper traditional sense' even as she offers such an account herself:

What then is the freedom of thought? Nietzsche says 'The thought does not come when we want it, it comes when it wants.' We could add: It is not what we want, it is what it wants. This, of course, is personifying thought as though it were a being with a will of its own. There is such a category of thought – those attributed to and felt as emanating from an internal object – as an inspiration or a persecution. But more generally, thought and thinking are the outcome of a complex interaction of our impulses, wishes, phantasies and perceptions. And, as such, it is not necessarily what we would wish it to be. (*WHS* 227)

It is not necessarily what we would wish it to be. It is the particular responsibility (and pleasure) of artists to encounter not only the 'wishes, phantasies and perceptions' nurtured by themselves – the fulfilment of which Freud felt to to be the ultimate psychological motivation – but also those made plain to them by the work on which they have embarked, and which at first may have seemed a merely passive vehicle for their intents and purposes. Such wishes, inspirational and persecutory, enter into competition with the artist 'as though they had a will of their own', and until the work is brought to some kind of (frequently unexpected) conclusion, they restrain egoism, inhibit idle 'fantasy', and evade repression. Thus even thoughts taking a longed-for form, and recognized and welcomed for doing so, may evolve in unforeseen ways, not least in the hands of those who patiently and expectantly await their arrival.

4
'A Province of Truth':
Criticism and History

Chapters 2 and 3 have amounted to a series of brickbats and bouquets handed out to philosophers and psychoanalysts as a reward for their forays into literary criticism. I should now turn to some working historians, and bring their literary crimes and misdemeanours to the bar in similar fashion. But this I do not intend to do. Certainly there are historians who discuss literature: in Britain, Christopher Hill has written extensively on both Milton and Bunyan, and E.P. Thompson discusses literature in his influential study, *The Rise of the English Working Class*. There exist, also, social histories of Britain which include – perhaps out of a sense of duty rather than any more positive impulse – chapters on 'The Victorian Novel' or 'The Elizabethan Stage'. But histories of this kind have long since fallen out of fashion.

This chapter is concerned with working historians only indirectly: not as individuals making an explicit institutional claim on literature and criticism as philosophers like Martha Nussbaum and psychoanalysts like Hanna Segal have done, but as a group working in a particular intellectual tradition. Nor is this chapter concerned, directly at least, with the philosophical debate which bloomed and faded in the 1950s and 60s between the 'idealists' and the 'positivists' over history's status as a science. It is not the interface between history and science that is the object of study here, but the interface between history and literature, and I come at it from two directions: from the 'literary side' and the 'historical side' respectively. The former avenue of approach is represented by the New Historicist school of literary critics (including, in particular, Marilyn Butler, Jerome McGann, and Stephen Greenblatt); the latter by two theorists of history, historiography, and narrative (Hayden White and Paul Ricoeur). New Historicism and the historiographical-cum-narratological theories of White and Ricoeur do not form two sides of the same coin, I hasten to add. Still, readers are bound to be struck by a certain parallelism: just as the New Historicist seeks the historical component in literature (and so turns literature into history), so White and Ricoeur attempt to demonstrate an ineluctably 'literary' element in the writing of historical narratives (and so turn history into literature). The word history has two senses, of course: the past itself, and what is written about the past. New Historicists, as the summary given above suggests, are more interested in the past itself; historiographical narratologists are more interested in the writing of history: literature itself appears to stand in a state of suspension between the two. On the one hand it is in danger of being subsumed altogether within historical actuality; on the other it is flatteringly credited with providing the means by which that actuality is described and conveyed. The reader will hardly be surprised, by now, to learn that it is my intention with the arguments offered here to defend the autonomy of literature from both these fates.

Before doing this, however, I must trespass on the reader's patience by summarizing some ideas of R.G. Collingwood's for the second (and last) time. I must introduce him because his understanding of history is one which has implications for both the discussions I wish to carry out. In fact it is Collingwood who illustrates their connection.

4.1   R.G. Collingwood

Under the regime of common sense we assume that the imagination is a creative, inventive, fiction-producing faculty of the mind. When, in chapter two of his 'Epilegomena' to *The Idea of History*, R.G. Collingwood discusses the *historical* imagination, common sense demands, first, that he justify using the term at all, and second, that in justifying his use of the term he distinguish it from the imagination of the poet, the novelist, or the playwright. He meets both these demands, but in doing so he goes some way to undermining the view of history and literature from which they spring.

Collingwood does away completely, for example, with our common-sense notion that historians merely re-work and organize the versions of events given them by 'authorities' like documents or witnesses of historical events – authorities the historian must obey if he is not to fabricate the past. In fact, he writes, 'the historian is his own authority and his thought [is] autonomous, self-authorizing, possessed of a criterion by which his so-called authorities must conform and by reference to which they are criticized'.[1] Far from blindly copying out documents and eye-witness accounts, the historian 'is always selecting, simplifying, schematizing, leaving out what he thinks unimportant and putting in what he regards as essential' (*IH* 236), just as an imaginative writer does. Indeed, the historian can go further and, like a novelist, 'discover what, until he discovered it, no one ever knew to have happened at all' (*IH* 238).

How the historian does this is comprehensible enough. If we have evidence that Caesar was in Rome on one occasion and in Gaul on another, we can interpolate a historical event – his travelling from the one place to the other – even if we have no authoritative evidence to this effect. This 'act of interpolation', Collingwood reminds us, 'is in no way arbitrary or fanciful' (*IH* 240) so long as we do not embroider the account with inventions of our own for which we have no evidence. But though this act of interpolation is necessary (in the philosophical sense) it remains 'essentially something *imagined*' (*IH* 241; my italics). Collingwood calls an act of imagination constrained by evidence in this way an act of the '*a priori* imagination' (*IH* 241), and here, we might think, will come the anticipated distinction between the historical imagination ('*a priori*') and the imagination properly-so-called, belonging, say, to novelists.

But we would be wrong. For it transpires that the novelist works in exactly the same way and under the same rule of necessity as does the historian. 'A man writing a novel', Collingwood goes on,

> composes a story where parts are played by various characters. Characters and incidents are all alike imaginary; yet the whole aim of the novelist is to show the characters acting and the incidents developing in a manner determined by a necessity internal to themselves. The story, if it is a good story, cannot develop otherwise than as it does; the novelist in imagining it cannot imagine it developing except as it does develop. Here, and equally in all other kinds of art, the *a priori* imagination is at work.[2]

To imagine a counter-factual hypothesis concerning *The Pickwick Papers*, for example, Charles Dickens can no more arbitrarily transform the life of Samuel Pickwick by elevating him to the House of Lords, than a historian can arbitrarily have Caesar travel from Rome to Gaul by way of Vladivostok. Dickens' imagination is 'pure or free', as Collingwood puts it ('but by no means arbitrary'; *IH* 241), only in the sense that he can invent Pickwick to begin with. Having done so, Pickwick is to him as Caesar is to the historian of Rome. 'The imaginary, simply as such,' Collingwood maintains, 'is neither unreal nor real' (*IH* 241).

So far we are still on relatively familar ground. 'The historian's picture of his subject ... thus appears as a web of imaginative construction stretched between certain fixed points provided by the statements of his authorities' (*IH* 241). Caesar is in Rome, Caesar arrives in Gaul: *ergo* we can infer his travelling between the two places. But as we have seen it was a premiss of Collingwood's account that the historian has an autonomy which allows him to criticize his authorities. If the historian comes to depend on 'pegs' or 'fixed points' called 'data' (the emperor's presence in Rome and in Gaul, as documented), that autonomy is sacrificed. So it is that Collingwood takes a step apparently reducing still further the possibilities for an effective distinction between the historical and other kinds of imagination. 'I am now driven to confess', he writes, 'that there are for historical thought no fixed points thus given: in other words, that in history, just as there are properly speaking no authorities, so there are properly speaking no data' (*IH* 243). It is not a question of the historian imaginatively filling the gaps left between authoritative statements, or of imaginatively spinning a web between fixed points. There *are* no fixed points. For data do not come from 'outside' the writing of history: they are arrived at by critical historical thought itself. They are data only in the sense that they may be taken as read or believed to be settled for present purposes, but 'they remain settled only until he [an individual historian] or some one else decides to reopen them'. 'The web of imaginative construction', Collingwood goes on, 'is something far more solid and powerful than we have hitherto realized. So far from relying for its validity upon the support of given facts, it actually serves as the touchstone by which we decide whether alleged facts are genuine' (*IH* 244). Thus it is that the *a priori* imagination not only provides the historian with his narrative or his construction, but 'supplies the means of historical criticism as well' (*IH* 245).

By this stage in Collingwood's argument the chances of any real and operative distinction being made between the historian and the novelist seem slim indeed. On the contrary, the better history is recognized for what it is, the more it begins to resemble not our common-sense idea of it but art, fiction, novels. 'Freed from its dependence on fixed points supplied from without,' Collingwood concludes,

> the historian's picture of the past is thus in every detail an imaginary picture, and its necessity is at every point the necessity of the *a priori* imagination. Whatever goes into it goes into it not because his imagination passively accepts it, but because it actively demands it.

'The resemblance between the historian and the novelist,' he goes on, 'here reaches its culmination' (*IH* 245). So it does indeed: the resemblances, as Collingwood describes them, are so strong that we can see no difference between the imagination of the historian and the imagination of the novelist. Each provides imaginary pictures or narratives sharing an *a priori* nature; each is autonomous and free from 'authority'; and each decides exactly what must go into an account and what be rejected, not on the basis of some external influence, but as the imaginary and critical construction itself dictates.

How *do* they differ then, the novel and the history? The answer to the question is or appears to be a simple one: the latter is 'meant to be true' (*IH* 246). The novelist, Collingwood believes, has only to construct 'a coherent picture, one that makes sense'; the historian has to do this, too, but 'a picture of things as they really were, and of events as they really happened'.[3] The truth of history imposes three rules on the historian: 'his picture must be localized in space and time' whereas works of literature – or, more precisely, the 'pictures' found in works of literature – need not be; 'all history must be consistent with itself' in the sense that 'there is only one historical world' the various accounts of which must relate to each other (topographically or chronologically, for example), whereas individual works of literature 'cannot clash and need not agree'; and, most important, 'the historian's picture stands in a peculiar relation to something called evidence' (*IH* 246).

When Collingwood mentions evidence he does not, of course, mean those 'authorities' and 'sources' that he dispensed with earlier on. For these lie in the past itself, whereas the historian's evidence exists only in the present. At the very beginning of his discussion of the historical imagination Collingwood had made a distinction between historical *thought*, on the one hand, and those *perceptions* of the world, on the other, which the scientist seeks to circumscribe within natural laws. 'Historical thought', he wrote, 'is of something which can never be a this, because it is never a here and now. Its objects are events which have finished happening, and conditions no longer in existence. Only when they are no longer perceptible do they become objects for historical thought' (*IH* 233). If historical thought can only be thought about the past, the evidence for it can exist only in the present: 'something existing here and now, and perceived by the historian' (*IH* 244). Potentially, evidence can be literally any- and everything in the present world: 'this written page, this spoken utterance, this building, this finger-print' (*IH* 247). In actuality, evidence is restricted to those things in the world which assist the historian in answering questions: questions that are not only preconceived, but also ones to which he already suspects he knows the answer. The framing of some kind of critical question is essential, and is bound up with the historian's autonomy: 'anything is evidence which is used as evidence, and no one can know what is going to be useful as evidence until he has had occasion to use it' (*IH* 280). The historian alone decides what questions are worth asking for his purposes, and the problems he frames are not inherited passively from authorities in the past but take their origin in the present, where lies the only evidence he has for solving them. The present, in sum, is 'evidence for its own past': 'Every present has a past of its own, and any imaginative reconstruction of the past aims at reconstructing the past of this present, the present in which the act of [historical] imagination is going on, as here and now perceived' (*IH* 247). So it is that no problem in history 'is done once for all' (*IH* 248–9). For not only does each new present contain new evidence; it also demands new questions be framed for which that evidence may serve to support answers. In fact the very mode of questioning, influenced as it is by changes in other fields of knowledge and by changes of intellectual attitude both momentous and trivial, changes, too.

This is as far as I want to follow Collingwood's argument at the moment. It contains two ideas in particular which are of special importance to the arguments presented in the next two sections. The most obvious of these is Collingwood's conviction that history is meant to be *true*, whereas novels are not. It is this conviction and its implications that I want to consider in relation to the narratological and historiographical ideas of Hayden White and Paul Ricoeur, since clearly it may contribute to a distinction between a form of writing like history (or sociology or psychology or anthropology) and literature itself. The other idea of Collingwood's that must be considered is one that, at first sight, seems to have very little to do either with literature or with literary criticism: the *evidence* for historical thought and where it is found. It is to this that I will turn towards the end of the next section, on New Historicism.

4.2 New Historicism

At the very beginning of Chapter 2 I mentioned an essay of David Bromwich's called 'Literature and Theory': an essay that takes a disenchanted but combative view of the state of criticism at present. In it,

Bromwich provides a caricature of the articles currently filling the pages of 'Eng. Lit.' academic journals:

> If I set out tomorrow to connect the Victorian decline of satire with the rise of sentimental comedy, the repression of women's sexuality, and the dietary practices which, with many other practices, controlled the arbitrary differences of a social order, I would need perhaps the following bits of evidence: an essay of eighteenth-century criticism which identified the satirical genres with the 'acid' style; a textbook for young ladies, published between 1830 and 1880, asserting that acidulous foods were particularly improper for persons of the female gender; and a letter from a standard Victorian author (Thackeray, say), with a comment in passing that satires tended to exacerbate rather than comfort people's resentments about their condition, and besides his wife had never enjoyed reading them. Whether these wire-drawn and empirical-looking hints carried conviction or failed to, the article in which I published them would not be attacked on the ground that connections like these could not possibly add up to anything cogent. They are the stuff the practice of theory is made of.[4]

It is an exaggerated picture, but not unrecognizably so. If it is unfair at all, the unfairness lies in the last sentence: that this is the stuff the practice of theory is made of. Of some theory it may be, but by no means all. For what Bromwich describes could never be mistaken for a piece about *écriture féminine* by Hélène Cixous; or a piece of Marxist postmodernism in the Fredric Jameson mould; or an example of Derridean deconstruction; or a Bloomian meditation on the anxiety of influence; or a Lacanian one on the problem of the subject; or Bakhtinian dialogics; or reader-response; or speech act theory; or semiotics.

Of what is it representative then? Certain forms of Marxist criticism, possibly (liberal rather than radical); certain forms of feminist and post-colonialist criticism, certainly. But above all, Bromwich's caricature fits that particular kind of critical amalgam which Marxism, feminism, and post-colonialism all make use of freely, and which helps bind together the work they do: New Historicism. New Historicism does not only provide for itself; in an unacknowledged form – as I began to suggest in the Introduction – it also provides that neutral substance in which the active ingredients of other, more ostensibly radical critical approaches are bound.[5] It is for this reason that, from a practical point of view and as far as the writing of doctoral theses and articles in critical journals are concerned, New Historicism can with some justice regard itself as the dominant literary–critical mode at present, especially in the United States. For many it is nothing less than the acceptable face of literary theory: it studies books and writers generally familiar if by no means always classic; it is empirical almost by definition; it is (or at least purports to be) 'grounded', as it were, in historical reality; it has, as such, no axe to grind or political view to propound (apart from a general commitment to 'commitment'); and it displays little, if any, of that textual radicalism associated with post-structuralism generally and deconstruction in particular. It makes use of no complex jargon, requires no philosophical or linguistic expertise, and its gurus are on a distinctly human scale. It is home-grown, familiar, anodyne, plausible, and accessible: an oasis of traditionalism, some may feel, in a desert of critical speculation and sectarianism. Yet despite this aura of familiarity and empiricism, New Historicism is the one critical school with which this study must take issue bluntly and explicitly. I want to argue that there is in New Historicism an attitude to literature that is more inimical to it than is, say, the work of Derrida, Rorty, or Freud.

In practice, New Historicism is immensely influential. The theory that underlies that practice is surprisingly meagre – which second fact, of course, may go some way to explaining the first. His own work, Stephen Greenblatt writes, 'has always been done with a sense of just having to go about and do it, without establishing first exactly what my theoretical position is.' He professes himself 'quite giddy with amazement' at New Historicism's efflorescence; points out that New Historicists 'have on the whole been unwilling to enroll themselves in one or the other of the dominant theoretical camps'; and suggests that New Historicism best be described as 'a practice rather than a doctrine, since as far as I can tell ... it's no doctrine at all'.[6] Marilyn Butler puts a similar stress on practice as opposed to theory: 'The past, the historical point at which a particular book was produced,' she writes, 'is *different* from the present, in which it is being read. How fully should our theory (or, for my purposes, more urgent) our critical practice allow for that fact?'[7] Jerome McGann, who has done more theorizing than anyone else in this area, feels that a 'thoroughly elaborated methodology for a practical socio-historical hermeneutics is much needed'. He goes on to say, however, that 'How one decides which parts of the strategic programme need to be emphasized in particular case studies is always a difficult question. I am not even sure that one can theorize these sorts of problem at all.'[8] We hardly need invoke the shade of Terry Eagleton to suggest that those who say they have no theory occupy a theoretical position by the very fact of saying they do not. New Historicism is based on all sorts of theoretical presuppositions and predispositions – none of which are the weaker for being unarticulated – the most important of which for this study is that New Historicists are uniformly hostile to the idea of the autonomy of literature. For Marilyn Butler the New Historicist is above all sceptical 'of theories which exalt the autonomy of art and the magus-role of the artist'.[9] H. Aram Veeser regards 'the autonomous self and text' as 'mere holograms, effects that intersecting institutions produce'.[10] Stephen Greenblatt himself, in returning to the question of his practice and others' theories, feels that

> the most important effect of contemporary theory upon the practice of literary criticism, and certainly upon *my* practice, is to subvert the tendency to think of aesthetic representation as ultimately autonomous, separable from its cultural context and hence divorced from the social, ideological, and material matrix in which all art is produced and consumed.[11]

A negative attitude towards the autonomy of literature is one thing New Historicists share. Inseparable from it is the polar opposite of autonomy: context. 'For me', writes Greenblatt, 'the study of the literary is the study of contingent, particular, intended, and historically embedded works; if theory inevitably involves the desire to escape from contingency into a higher realm, a realm in which signs are purified of the slime of history, then this paper is written *against* theory' ('SE' 163). Critical acts of 'decontextualizing', Marilyn Butler argues, allow both critics and authors to escape 'into an unsocial, unspecific, timeless zone called art' – 'a tax haven,' indeed, 'where there is nothing to pay'.[12] With 'thin', pristine, and abstract language like 'timeless zone', 'higher realm', 'aesthetic', or 'autonomy', New Historicists almost inevitably contrast a 'thick', evocative, and apparently richly humanist vocabulary. 'Contingency' is one word in this vocabulary. 'Embedded' is another.[13] 'Context', however, remains the one found most thoroughly suggestive of an infinite panorama of embedded contingencies: the slime of history writ large.[14] Jerome McGann's analysis of Keats' 'La Belle Dame Sans Merci', for example, 'takes for its subject the idea of "context" and tries to explain the special relevance of this for poetry, as well as the necessity of an historical method for elucidating the specifically pertinent contexts which penetrate every poem we read' (*BI* 31). It is precisely the particularized historical method mentioned by McGann that Marilyn Butler has sought to supply. 'The writings of the past', she argues,

> ask for an educated reading, as far as possible from within their own discourse or code or cultural system. Texts have their specific and localized contexts, which include, but are not limited to, the literary context of an established genre and the linguistic context of a vocabulary at a certain stage of evolution. Intellectual issues and preoccupations also make up the language of a given group, as does the vaguer and broader concept, ideology. By looking at these systems, by which the material world and society are already selected and mediated, we can learn something, though not everything, of the language appropriate to a particular text. It follows that most of the best historical criticism is localized in respect of time and place, and directed to the understanding of specific works.[15]

At the very least this is not disingenuous: if it is not a theory of literature and literary criticism it is hard to know what would count as such. But it is representative for other reasons, too. First, there is the overdetermined emphasis on context: less richly humanist in this case than overtly scientist. The work of literature becomes a genre into which a vocabulary, 'at a certain stage of evolution', is poured, like milk into a jug.[16] Then there is the attitude which demands initially that we read 'from *within*' the 'discourse or code or cultural system' of any given text, only to abandon so impossible (and un-historical) an enterprise in favour of merely 'looking *at* these systems' like children through a sweetshop window. Equally obvious is the historicism in the critical equation: the preponderance of the historical impulse over the literary–critical one. 'The object of the intellectual historian ...', Butler writes elsewhere, 'is less concerned with evaluation than with making a record of the opinions held by people in actual historical situations' – as if making a record did not itself involve evaluation.[17] The historian's picture, Collingwood suggested, 'must be localized in space and time'; so, it would appear from Butler's 'specific and localized contexts', must the literary critic's. So, too, must be the imaginative writer's, if that picture is to reflect either the material world and society already selected and mediated for it, or the language of its given group.

Context literature must have, but what form does that context take? New Historicist critics tend to vacillate between flat assertions of the past's difference and of our duty to come to terms with it, on the one hand (read within), and rather less prescriptive suggestions, on the other (look at). Whether such critics operate by brute force or by inference makes little difference in the end, however. What we see in them is a set of narrowly restricted critical beliefs: a dogma. As is the case with most dogmas, there is little point in theorizing about it – which is not to say that New Historicists do not swallow their misgivings occasionally, and try. We have seen in Marilyn Butler's discussion of the 'discourse or code or cultural system' underlying every work of literature that New Historicism's dogmatic aspects cannot be separated from its quasi-scientific ones. Her use of the word 'code', for example, probably comes from Jerome McGann. For him, textual and bibliographical studies 'are the only disciplines which can elucidate that complex network of people, materials, and events which have produced and which continue to reproduce the literary works which history delivers into our hands' (*BI* 80). If Greenblatt offers us cultural poetics, McGann has textual, bibliographical, and 'documentary' poetics with which to supplement them. But his textualism and his historicism run close alongside each other – indeed, they are indivisible:

> When we read poems through their documentary codes, when we read out the meanings embodied in their bibliographical formulations, we confront poetical discourse as a particular deed of language – an institutionalized event in communication which takes place according to certain particular rules and possibilities, and which has particular ends in view. All these things change with time and circumstances, however, so the reading of the performative dimension of the poetic event has to seek the same kind of concreteness and specificity which grammatological readings have always insisted upon. The horizon of concreteness in the performative dimension is social and historical.[18]

I think most readers will need some help with this. For McGann, 'poetical systems [that is, poems] operate simultaneously in both grammatological and documentary modes' (*SV* 75). To invoke a massively brutal generalization, we can associate the former with traditional literary criticism's interest in the poem itself, as it were: with 'these words on this page'. The documentary modes, on the other hand, are McGann's domain. 'Although writing verse is itself a social act,' he tells us, 'only when the poem enters circulation – in manuscript copies, in private printings, or by publication – does it begin its poetic career' (*BI* 23). It is this documentary and bibliographic career with which he is most interested, and as the word 'career' itself suggests, the documentary mode is an inherently temporal one. Thus it is that 'we have to recover those traditional philological procedures for putting us in touch with worlds, people, and experiences from the past, and with the media in which those things embodied themselves' (*BI* 12).

The institutional 'rules and possibilities' McGann speaks of are the poem's 'Mastercode': preserved not only 'in the later surviving documents and editions' but also 'in the grammatology of the poems' so transmitted (*SV* 75). 'When we highlight the framing function of poetry's performative Mastercodes … ', McGann goes on,

> we establish the horizons within which textual heteroglossia will be operating in particular cases. These Mastercodes define the poem's communicative system: its parts, their relation to each other, and – ultimately – the object of the system as such (that is, in contradistinction to the objects of other communicative systems – say, predicative or propositional systems). These performative Mastercodes establish the poem's particular set of sociohistorical interests and engagements. (*SV* 77)

There is, I think, something circular about this argument. A decision on the critic's part to see a poem as a 'set of sociohistorical interests and engagements' ('an instutionalized event') has itself led him to evolve a category – the 'Mastercode' – which is the repository of 'those particular rules and possibilities' which generate those interests and engagements in the first place. The extent of the problem is revealed when McGann looks at a particular poem by Matthew Arnold. 'Sohrab and Rustum', he argues, took a definite 'ideological stance' on a certain problem exercising Victorian criticism (an aspect of the poem's 'productive Mastercode'). But the poem then 'proceeded along the representational lines which are specific to the poetic' (that is, the grammatological Mastercode) only to find that the 'representational structure of poetic discourse multiplies and complicates the communicative act' (*SV* 90–1). That poems do this is one of the arguments of this study. But granted that such a poem does 'multiply and complicate' matters in this way, what does that leave us to say about the relevance of Arnold's original communicative act or ideological stance? What are we to think of the productive Mastercode?

What conclusions does such multiplication and complication force us to reach about some of McGann's formulations – this one for example?

> Works descend to our hands in certain concrete and specific forms, and along a series of equally concrete and specific avenues. The textual history of literary works reflects the influence of these factors even as the specific texts give a visible (if unanalysed) form to the meaning and significance of that history. The critical analysis of texts discovers one of its chief intellectual justifications in that set of circumstances. Certain patterns of history are literalized in complete and finished forms in such texts; consequently, the critical analysis of such forms is an invaluable key to understanding those most elusive types of human phenomena, social and historical patterns. (*BI* 83)

Is this the promised land? That the textual history of published works may indeed shed light on the historical forces which led to those texts taking those printed forms is unexceptionable enough. But how much of human history can you hope to illuminate by such means? What does that history add up to, if 'poetic performativity overtakes and finally overcomes ideological performativity' (*SV* 91) in the very act of writing poetry? And why should we automatically regard 'social and historical patterns' as any more elusive than other human phenomena? McGann often accuses traditional literary critics of 'bracketing off' the documentary and bibliographical elements in criticism. But here he has clearly done some bracketing off of his own, and with equally serious implications. Where Matthew Arnold's poem is concerned, the grammatological mastercode has clearly had a quite radical effect on the poem's ideological, socio-historical, documentary-performative one. The patterns of history that may be 'literalized in complete and finished forms' in the text of a poem like 'Sohrab and Rustum' are transformed out of recognition by the poem itself.

It is precisely to avoid those elements in poetry which McGann calls 'incommensurable' (*SV* 91) that he adheres to the notion that a work of literature has a 'career'. To say that 'only when the poem enters circulation … does it begin its poetic career' may not sound like an attack on the autonomy of literature. It is one nevertheless. For McGann, 'the essential character of a work of art is not determined *sui generis* but is, rather, the result of a process involving the actions and interactions of a specific and socially integrated group of people' (*BI* 117). Those people are themselves divisible into two groups: one in complete and finished form in the past, the other at any point between that past and the present. A 'methodological scheme for a proper historical criticism' depends on such an organizational dichotomy, and 'should emerge out of a dialectic between the work of art's point of origin, on the one hand, and its point of reception on the other' (*BI* 22–3). Any other critical method is both uncritical and unhistorical:

> The historical particularity of a poem by Wordsworth or a novel by Austen have to be clearly specified in the act of criticism if that act is to proceed dialectically, that is, if that act is not simply to project upon 'the work' its own conceptual interests. (*SV* 124–5)

Which work of literature, we might ask, meekly allows us to 'project' our own conceptual interests on it in this way? And how could critics and readers avoid projecting their 'conceptual interests' in such a way? That is what reading is after all. Finally, to what extent does specifying its historical particularity in fact protect the work against expropriation of this kind? The reconstruction of any historical context proceeds, as Collingwood suggested, from present concerns; it cannot proceed from anything else. The more reconstruction we do the more idiosyncratic our reading of literature becomes, and our specifying the historical particularity of *Emma*, say, may be as profound an act of critical and historical appropriation as any other. For what does *Emma* itself have to say about its own historical particularity? ' "[C]ontext", *as something determinate* is,' F.R. Leavis suggested, 'nothing but his [the critic's] postulate; the wider he goes in his ambition to construct it from his reading in the period, the more it is *his* construction'.[19]

The careers of poems must have a beginning. It is from 'the pole of its origin', as McGann calls it (*BI* 24), that he stretches his system of critical differentials, and in which he can find one term of the critical dialectic he describes (the other being 'The Immediate Moment of Textual Criticism'). This pole is one he calls 'The Originary Textual Moment', and it has four parts:

1. Author
2. Other persons or groups involved in the initial process of production (e.g. collaborators; persons who may have commissioned the work; editors or ammanuenses; etc.)

3. Phases or stages in the initial productive process (e.g. distinct personal, textual, or social states along with their defining causes, functions, and characteristics)
4. Materials, means, and modes of the initial productive process (physical, psychological, ideological) (*BI* 82)

At first sight, this taxonomy must refer only to the production, documentary, or textual Mastercodes of the poem, and so, again, is unexceptionable enough. In the poem's bibliographical and publication history, items two, three, and four may indeed be larger issues than little item one. Only in terms of those performative Mastercodes does 'the initial historical moment of the poem's explicit and continuing social involvement' take place. Moreover, 'The special importance of this moment lies in its priority: whatever changes may occur in later readings of the poem, *all subsequent responses derive in some way from the initial event*' (*BI* 51; my italics). The 'initial moment of publication constitutes the first explicit appearance of the poem's meaning' – that is, in the communication between author and readers (*BI* 51).

We can see more clearly now, I think, why item one in McGann's list – the author – is such a nugatory presence. Poems, in his account of them, can have no meanings before they are distributed; they can be 'acts' only in the social world; and responses to the poem by readers derive only from that poem in 'documentary' form. Up to a point this is a truism. Everything that comes later derives from the beginning, and this is as true of the critical history of *King Lear* as it is of the history of the world itself. But it hardly follows that the *only* way to make sense of such things is painstakingly to reconstruct the originary textual moment – even if we could do such a thing, which we cannot. ('What do I care for first or last editions?', wrote D.H. Lawrence: 'To me, no book has a date, no book has a binding.')

But all this is also beside the point: a poem does not find its first reader in its first purchaser or recipient. Its first reader is the poet himself or herself, for whom the poem has most definitely a meaning, though by no means always the one he or she expected to find; which brings us to another fundamental point: there never can be an 'originary moment' in the life of a poem. Generally speaking, no writer can achieve maturity (for example) without having been immature to begin with. *Sense and Sensibility* and *Pride and Prejudice* (which arrived at more or less complete form around 1809) grew out of 'Elinor and Marianne' and 'First Impressions' (written in the mid-1790s), and *The Rainbow* and *Women in Love* are extrapolations of an original project called 'The Sisters'. Nor do we have to restrict ourselves to acknowledged instances such as these, where we have evidence of earlier drafts and 'dry runs': for just as *Don Juan* itself grew not only out of *Beppo* but also out of the entire Byronic myth of *weltschmerz* improvised upon in his earlier poems, so *Bleak House* and *Little Dorrit* are the direct outcomes of what Dickens learned in writing *The Pickwick Papers* and *Martin Chuzzlewit*, and the 'Ode on a Grecian Urn' is the result of what Keats learned in writing *Endymion*. Thus McGann's idea of an originary textual moment, and the performative and productive Mastercodes it embodies, though applicable to issues of publication and distribution, cannot be confused with or foisted upon that imaginative author-function at the top of his list. We cannot say, as McGann says of Keats' poem, 'To Fanny', that 'Poems like this one are, by virtue of certain pre-emptive definitions created out of their historical circumstances, formally and, as it were, "by nature", biographical works' (*BI* 47). ('Created out of their historical circumstances'? What does that mean? Created by who?) We are the ones who have decided what the historical circumstances of Keats' poem are; and we are the ones who have decided that 'To Fanny' is a biographical work. Conceivably, Keats might have agreed with us, and marshalled what he thought he knew of his life and times accordingly on sitting down to write; but no such pre-emptive decisions, definitions, or conditions can be said to have operated on 'To Fanny' itself, for in a poem such things are the first to go. This fact has less to do with the Romantic poets' peculiar (and historically determined) respect for spontaneity and sincerity in the writing process, than with the autonomy of the poem itself.

But perhaps we need some fuller examples. I began this section by pointing out how widespread and influential New Historicism is as a form of critical practice. Before closing it, I would like to examine briefly two examples of this practice: Jerome McGann's discussion of a poem of Emily Dickinson's, and Stephen Greenblatt's discussion of *King Lear*.

In considering Emily Dickinson's 'Because I could not Stop for Death', McGann suggests that the horses referred to in the poem are not, as critical tradition had assumed, pulling a carriage taken out to the country by the poet and a gentleman-friend. Such a carriage, McGann feels, would have been a one-horse affair. The horses are, he believes, pulling a hearse, the gentleman-friend is an undertaker, and the trip is to the cemetery, not the country:

> Because I could not stop for Death—
> He kindly stopped for me—
> The Carriage held but just Ourselves—
> And Immortality.
>
> We slowly drove—He knew no haste
> And I had put away
> My labor and my leisure too,
> For His Civility—
>
> We passed the School, where Children strove
> At Recess—in the Ring—
> We passed the Fields of Gazing Grain—
> We passed the Setting Sun—
>
> Or rather—He passed Us—
> The Dews drew quivering and chill—
> For only Gossamer, my Gown—
> My Tippet—only Tulle—
>
> We paused before a House that seemed
> A Swelling of the Ground—
> The Roof was scarcely visible—
> The Cornice—in the Ground—
>
> Since then—'tis Centuries—and yet
> Feels shorter than the Day
> I first surmised the Horses Heads
> Were toward Eternity—

The plurality of the horses, and the poem's entire mood (never mind its opening lines) are, we might think, all the evidence any critic could possibly want for such a conclusion. 'This small matter of fact' has, as McGann says, 'considerable importance for anyone wishing to develop an accurate critical account of the poem.' But he goes on:

It forces us to see, for example, that the journey being presented is not some unspecified drive in the country, but a funeral ride which is located quite specifically in relation to Emily Dickinson and her Amherst world. The hearse in the poem is on its way out from Pleasant Street, past Emily Dickinson's house, to the cemetery located at the northern edge of the town just beyond the Dickinson homestead. (*BI* 128)

In a note to this passage, McGann is even more specific. The hearse's journey would be, he says, 'from somewhere in the central part of Amherst out along Pleasant Street, past the schoolhouse on the left, and out to the beginning of the "Fields of Gazing Grain", at which point the undertaker would have turned to the right and driven past more fields to the gravesite' (*BI* 128). All that remains for the critic, we imagine, is further to specify that irritating and irreduceable 'somewhere in the central part of Amherst', which rather maims the effect of his researches. As McGann points out, 'these details are not verbalized into the Dickinson poem as explicit description. They are only present implicitly, as an originally evoked context which we ... can (*and must*) reconstitute if we wish to focus and explain the special emotional character of the work' (*BI* 128; my italics).

There are some important points that should be made here. First, McGann came to his new reading of Emily Dickinson's poem neither as the result of a visit to Amherst nor of poring over maps of the town. The poem itself suggested the reading and in turn provided all the evidence we need for it – which is an important aspect of the poem's autonomy. Second, we frequently reconstitute an author's works after seeing the surroundings in which they lived. That the route to the graveyard at Amherst led past Emily Dickinson's door is as interesting as the fact that Howarth parsonage looks out over a cemetery. But we are under no obligation to make any such reconstitutions, and we cannot possibly be sure either that Emily Dickinson did 'originally evoke' such a context, or that her having done so is of great importance in explaining 'the special emotional character' of her poem.

McGann's reconstruction of Amherst funerary arrangements is therefore factitious in two senses. It is supernumerary in that it comes after the real critical work has been done. In Collingwood's terms, for example, the question posed by the historical critic ('Are these horses pulling a hearse?') has already been solved by the poem itself. Maps of Amherst are not evidence at all, but mere data. It is self-contradictory to solve a critical problem about a poem by one means (textual; literary–critical) and then demand that other readers solve the same problem by other means (historical). McGann's reconstruction is also supererogatory in that it overdetermines the author's imaginative processes by insisting on the precise context the critic believes it was that Dickinson sought to evoke. It is not that the critic as historian has himself produced a 'picture' too 'localized in space and time'. The critic has forced such a picture upon the poet herself.

But McGann's 'context' has done more than this. It has forced our attention away from the dramatic and emotional detail which *is* in the poem; which is both constituted by the poem and constitutive of it. The life of social courtesies invoked in the first stanza only to be undone by all that follows (the world where neighbours 'kindly' give each other lifts, and show each other 'civility') is replaced by immortality, isolation, cold ('quivering chill'), and eternity. What goes on in such transitions is a process, a realizing by the protagonist as well as ourselves, of the truth – hence, a drama. The children at school (striving 'At Recess—in the Ring') are children anywhere: that is their point, so to speak. But it is also to the point that we should know just what they are doing ('playtime' or 'break'); they are innocent, uncaring, companionable (though somewhat trapped in that ring); so, in synecdochal fashion, they also figure for us the quotidian life the speaker is losing. And how we need that life! The very grave itself mimes the house that has been left behind, with its roof and cornice. All of this is illustrative of the way in which effective poetic localization *really* operates: making the local general, and vice versa.

If the critic begins to make that demand of the poet that Collingwood made of the critical historian – that his or her picture be localized in space and time – he or she goes some way to turning works of literature, not merely into historical documents (which is one of the things such works are) but into works of history. It is historians who, according to Collingwood's account, look to the present – to 'something existing here and now, and perceived by the historian'. What they are looking for is evidence about the historical past. For McGann, Emily Dickinson looked to the present – to the 'originally evoked context' of a funeral in Amherst in exactly the same way. But what Dickinson looked at was not a hypostatized 'present' at all: she looked at a poem – a poem free to range, as 'Because I could not Stop for Death' does, as close to and as far from immediate, temporal, and 'contextual' concerns as its imaginative preoccupations demanded.

Stephen Greenblatt's essay on *King Lear*, 'Shakespeare and the Exorcists', brings us to another aspect of the summary of Collingwood offered above. The essay has its origin in some lines given to Edgar while posing as Mad Tom (IV. i. 57–62):

> Five fiends have been in poor Tom at once; as Oberdicut, of lust; Hoberdidance, prince of dumbness; Mahu, of stealing; Modo, of murder; Flibbertigibbet, of mopping and mowing; who since possesses chamber-maids and waiting-women.

This demonic list – so literal-minded, but also so imaginative – suggests that it comes from a popular source or a real case of possession. And so it proves. The lines are an allusion to a hostile account of exorcisms carried out by Catholic priests in Buckinghamshire in 1585–86: Samuel Harsnett's *A Declaration of Egregious Popish Impostures*, published in 1603. It is a case Greenblatt seeks to re-open by asking the following questions:

> When Shakespeare borrows from Harsnett, who knows if Harsnett has not already, in a deep sense, borrowed from Shakespeare's theater what Shakespeare borrows back? Whose interests are served by the borrowing? And is there a larger cultural text produced by the exchange? ('SE' 165)

As it turns out, Harsnett did indeed borrow from Shakespeare's theatre: in a manner of speaking, anyway. The 'falsity, tawdriness, and rhetorical manipulation' Harsnett saw in the exorcism ceremonies he describes led him to compare them quite explicitly to a 'devil Theater' ('SE' 171). Greenblatt goes on to produce another example of cultural negotiation when he tells us that 'Catholic clerical garments ... were sold during the Reformation to the players' and that 'When an actor in a history play took the part of English bishop, he could', therefore, 'conceivably have worn the actual robes of the character he was representing' ('SE' 171).

What we have here are classic instances of what the anthropologiest Clifford Geertz would call thick description: 'an event or anecdote', as H. Aram Veeser calls it, which reveals 'through the analysis of tiny particulars the behavioural codes, logics, and motive forces controlling a whole society'.[20] The claims Greenblatt makes for his 'larger cultural text' are correspondingly grandiose. The 'transmigration of a single ecclesiastical cloak from the vestry to the wardrobe', he writes, 'may stand as an emblem of the more complex and elusive institutional exchanges that are my subject':

> a sacred sign, designed to be displayed before a crowd of men and women, is emptied, made negotiable, traded from one institution to

another. Such exchanges are rarely so tangible; they are not usually registered in inventories, not often sealed with a cash payment. Nonetheless they occur constantly, for it is precisely through the process of institutional negotiation and exchange that differentiated expressive systems, distinct cultural discourses, are fashioned. We may term such fashioning cultural poesis; the sale of clerical garments is an instance of the ideological labor that such poesis entails. ('SE' 171)

But is the idea of history Greenblatt has here a *critical* idea at all? He says that the possessed souls of Buckinghamshire in the mid-1580s 'gave voice to the rage, anxiety, and sexual frustration that built up particularly easily in the authoritarian, patriarchal, impoverished, and plague-ridden world of early modern England' ('SE' 168). The piling up of nouns and adjectives, the tendentious use of 'particularly', and the vague use of 'world', all tend to lull us into a state of credulity with regard to what is, after all, a piece of speculation. But it is not a simple one. On the contrary, it is based on countless predispositions we hold concerning the Tudor period: not merely that it was more superstitious and fideistic than our own, but that its fideism and superstition took a peculiarly 'outward', histrionic, imaginative, and radical form by comparison with our psychological *modus vivendi* – a response, that is to say, on the part of 'rage, anxiety, and sexual frustration' to the 'authoritarian, patriarchal, impoverished, and plague-ridden world' which created such rages, anxieties, and frustrations in the first place.

The same kind of *idée reçue* underlies Greenblatt's reconstruction of what he takes to be the response of Elizabethan theatre-goers to Catholic regalia on the stage.[21] Tudor theatre-goers seeing such things, for all we know, might have shrugged their shoulders in a gesture of historical and religious scepticism: a combination of 'how are the mighty fallen' and *'plus ça change, plus c'est la meme chose'*. In his fourth Satire John Donne talks about borrowed clothes in just this way, after all:

> 'For a King
> These hose are,' cry the flatterers; and bring
> Them next week to the theatre to sell;
> Wants reach all states; me seems they do as well
> At stage, as Court; all are players; who'ever looks
> (For themselves dare not go) o'er Cheapside books,
> Shall find their wardrobe's inventory.

We might equally well imagine the Tudor audience pointing in mischevious glee at the ignominous fate of such trappings of religious authority. All are players: everybody's inventory, king's or bishop's, Romanov's or Stalin's, can end up on Cheapside. But there is no room for attitudes of that kind in Greenblatt's account; on the contrary, the theatre audience understood themselves to be witnessing much more: a momentous and portentous instance of cultural poesis, no less, in which 'a consecrated object is reclassified, assigned a cash value, transferred from a sacred to a profane setting, deemed suitable to be staged' ('SE' 171), and so on and so forth.

That such signs could be taken for wonders – or the clothes be taken for the man – is by no means inconceivable; but the arguments often seem more ingenious than just. In his discussion of possession, for example, Greenblatt draws in material from all over the place: 'a northern Italian folk cult', for instance, 'who believed that their spirits went forth seasonally to battle with fennel stalks against their enemies, the witches'; some shamans from Siberia; and 'an illuminating study of possession among the Ethiopians of Gondar' by Michel Leiris ('SE' 167–8, 170). But if every instance of cultural poesis is so culturally *embedded*, we might ask, how can a case about early seventeenth-century England be supported with facts as far-fetched as these? Moreover, we cannot help feeling that Greenblatt's notion of historical evidence comes perilously close, if not to David Bromwich's 'wire-drawn and empirical-looking hints', then to that quasi-inferential system described by Collingwood: 'a web of imaginative construction stretched between certain fixed points provided by the statements of his authorities'. Edgar's speech, Harsnett's *Declaration*, and the sale of ecclesiastical vestments are 'data' of one kind; but so, in fact, are Greenblatt's visions of hyper-reflective theatre-goers and hyper-sensitive victims of possession. It comes as a shock to realize that nothing in *King Lear* or outside it stimulates Greenblatt to reflect critically on the nature of the fideism, superstition, suggestivity, and impressionability he ascribes to Elizabethan England, even though Shakespeare himself reflects critically upon such issues many times – in the first scene of *Hamlet*, for example, where superstitious soldiers are contrasted with sceptical courtier-intellectuals like Horatio, or in *Macbeth* as a whole.[22]

If 'Shakespeare and the Exorcists' is, or may be, something less than good history it also presents a highly partial literary–critical perspective. (Not as partial as Jerome McGann on Emily Dickinson, certainly, but partial nonetheless.) Greenblatt's Harsnett-and-vestments material is fascinating, to be sure. His idea of literary theory and *its* history is a highly schematic one by contrast. There is 'mainstream Anglo-American criticism in the mid-twentieth century', for example, safely in the remote past, a 'root assumption' of which was 'the *absolute disjunction* of the literary and the nonliterary'.[23] In Greenblatt's own day there is 'theory' (which is deconstruction) and there is the real McCoy. The former 'lead[s] too readily and predictably to the void':

> in actual literary practice the perplexities into which one is led are not moments of pure, untrammeled aporia but localized strategies in particular historical encounters. ('SE' 164)

The absolute primacy of historical reasoning is self-evident: 'the institutional strategies in which both *King Lear* and Harsnett's *Declaration* are embedded...are part of an intense and sustained struggle in late sixteenth- and early seventeenth-century England to redefine the central values of society' ('SE' 165) – and the devil take anyone who sees Shakespeare's play in other terms.

> Those in the audience who had read Harsnett's book or heard of the notorious Buckinghamshire exorcisms would recognize in Edgar's lines an odd, joking allusion to the chambermaids, Sara and Friswood Williams, and the waiting woman, Ann Smith, principal actors in Father Edmund's 'Devil Theater.' ('SE' 175)

Mine is not just a case of wondering how many (or how few) of Shakespeare's audience would have got the joke at all – given the intensity of the drama they were in fact witnessing on stage – but of wondering exactly how they would have taken it if they did. For just as there was a context in 'Because I could not Stop for Death' effectively suppressed by McGann, so there is an immediate context in *King Lear* looming infinitely larger, from the audience's point of view, than the goings-on at a Buckinghamshire manor house in 1585. And that is that King Lear is mad in earnest, Edgar only in show.

Now Greenblatt knows this. Harsnett's book, he writes, 'supplies Shakespeare not only with an uncanny anachronism but with the model for Edgar's histrionic disguise. For it is not the *authenticity* of the demonology that the playwright finds in Harsnett...but rather the inauthenticity of a theatrical role' ('SE' 175). Neither am I suggesting that he must drop the task in hand and take fuller account of this issue. But somebody must, because even if we went so far as to say that the *most* significant bit of 'poesis' going on in Lear's mad scene is a cultural one, we would have to acknowledge that some dramatic poesis takes place, too; that there are some localized strategies in particular dramatic encounters as well as particular historical ones. Edgar's act is one of self-preservation ('Whiles I may scape', he says before choosing the Mad Tom disguise, 'I will preserve myself'); Lear's predicament is one of self-destruction. One finds shelter in being nothing; the other finds exposure. The whole contrast between them in the scenes on the heath serves to bring out Edgar's moral passivity and complacency (which is consistent with being suddenly 'possessed' by an arbitrary external force like 'the foul fiend') in contrast to the imaginative activity and strength abiding in Lear still, despite his insanity. 'Poor naked wretches, wheresoe'er you are,' says Lear,

> That bide the pelting of this pitiless storm,
> How shall your houseless heads and unfed sides,
> Your loop'd and window'd raggedness, defend you
> From seasons such as these? O, I have ta'en
> Too little care of this! Take physic, pomp,
> Expose thyself to feel what wretches feel,
> That thou mayst shake the superflux to them,
> And show the heavens more just.
>
> (III. iv. 27–36)

Truly adrift, Lear ascribes not only his own madness but Tom's also to natural causes ('Has his daughters brought him to this pass?'). As Mad Tom, Edgar ascribes his insanity to supernatural possession, and our awareness that all this is a charade is underwritten by the hocus-pocus lifted from Harsnett. So there is a dramatic as well as a historical process taking place.

But Greenblatt's essay suggests that what New Historicist critics actually mean, as often as not, by 'context' is something purely institutional. For New Historicism, institutions (government, the church, the theatre, the press, or what Marilyn Butler calls 'the intellectual ambience which is the actual seedbed of intellectual discussion') simply *are* what Greenblatt calls 'the social, ideological, and material matrix in which all art is produced and consumed'. Anything else tends to get sidelined; neither can what Jerome McGann calls these 'specifically pertinent contexts' be changed or rethought by writers and readers themselves. The boot is on the other foot, permanently. The context is always a social one: never anything else. This notion of context, though, far from being rich, deep, and mulchy, as its inventors believe, demonstrably needs to be supplemented by something else, or the critic ends up talking about (and to) the tiny handful of people in Shakespeare's audience who took – or take – Edgar's allusion to Harsnett's *Declaration* as the critic himself did.

All this happens, more to the point, in the very face of works of literature which harbour the possibility of broader understanding than a merely institutional one. Just as Catholic regalia is 'emptied' of significance by moving from the vestry to the wardrobe, Greenblatt argues, so *'King Lear* is haunted by a sense of rituals and beliefs that are no longer efficacious, that have been *emptied out'* ('SE' 177). He is certainly right to say of this play that in it the characters' oft-repeated appeals to the gods remain unanswered, as they do in every other play of Shakespeare's. ('I can call spirits from the vasty deep', Glendower tells Hotspur in *1 Henry IV*. 'Why so can I, or so can any man', is Hotspur's reply; 'But will they come when you do call for them?') But is it really true to say that belief in justice, or in filial piety, or in family and civic loyalty, or in accountability – never mind in love – has been emptied out either *in King Lear* or *of* it as a result of the gods' indifference? And if these are not beliefs, what are they? If people like him would expose themselves to feel what wretches feel, after all, they would show the heavens more just – or so Lear believes. You may see the kind of urgent demand for justice made by some of the leading characters in *King Lear* as homage to a religious institution and nothing more – a concept thoroughly in need of emptying out. You may see the play as a 'massive display of mimed suffering and fraudulent exorcism', similar to the now discredited ceremonies described by Harsnett; a play which we revisit nonetheless only because it 'recuperates and intensifies our need for those ceremonies, even though we do not believe in them, and performs them, carefully marked out for us as frauds, for our continued consumption' ('SE' 183). If you choose to see it in such terms, the chances are you will write about it much as Greenblatt has done, and in doing so contribute further to what he calls 'a salutary return of the literary text to the condition of all other texts' ('SE' 164).

In Chapter 1 I suggested that New Historicism seeks 'to revive a mode of criticism that is not merely old, but antiquated', and I must try and make good that observation in the space remaining. I was not referring, for example, to the philological tradition from which Jerome McGann draws so much of his expertise, as well as his prose-style. The antiquated mode of criticism I have in mind is in fact barely a critical mode at all, but a network of beliefs about literature that are probably buried deep in many readers, and which resurface perennially in literary criticism.[24] These beliefs have their origin in the feeling that reading literature critically is not easy, and that criticism could be improved if it became more scientific or more disciplined or more objective. Add to this feeling a tendency towards common-sense empiricism with which the Anglo-Saxon mind has constantly to struggle, and those occasional resurfacings of impatience with traditional literary criticism are easily understood.

I have already alluded to one such instance: F.R. Leavis' row with F.W. Bateson over the 'discipline of contextual reading'[25] which Bateson (as editor of the magazine) sought to associate with *Essays in Criticism* back in 1953. There is no need to revisit the debate in detail: only to see, in Bateson's own particularized historical method, some features with which we are now thoroughly familiar. Having discussed the intellectual contexts of Alexander Pope and Andrew Marvell, Bateson went on to say:

> But this intellectual context, important though it certainly is for understanding Marvell and Pope, does not seem to provide the ultimate framework of reference within which their poems need to be read. Behind the intellectual context lies a complex of religious, political and economic factors that can be called the social context.[26]

The 'culminating desideratum, the final criterion of correctness' in criticism, Bateson believed, 'is the awareness of the appropriate social context'. To discover the meaning of poems 'we have to ask what they meant to their author and his original readers'. 'There is no alternative – *except to invent the meanings ourselves.*'[27]

The similarities between historicism's old and new varieties are as we would expect: both find evaluative criticism difficult to accomodate, even where they try to accomodate it at all; both, despite intense moralistic urgings of their own, are profoundly indifferent to the moral element in literature; both cover dogmatic beliefs with a veneer of disciplinary rigour. Bateson, it is true, still thought he could squeeze an autonomous work of literature into his scheme. His discipline of contextual reading, he wrote, 'should result in the reconstruction of a human situation that is demonstrably implicit in the particular literary work under discussion'.[28] Jerome McGann, by contrast, found a human situation more implicit in a map of Amherst than a poem of Emily Dickinson's. The other main difference between Bateson and his successors is that the latter are more sceptical about the entire notion of 'reconstruction'. They *want* reconstruction, certainly but they realize the difficulties involved in such processes. New Historicists also realize that mere reconstruction looks like mere history. 'The aim is not to reconstruct the past, which could not be done innocently, even if it were worth doing at all', writes Marilyn Butler: 'It is to understand how writing functions in its world, in order to understand writing, the world, and ourselves.'[29]

The concept of context to which Leavis responded in his essay was, therefore, a more forthright and possibly more naïve one than that on offer today. And he was forthright in turn. Whereas 'the study of literature should', he believed, 'be associated with extra-literary studies':

> To suggest that their *purpose* should be to reconstruct a postulated 'social context' that once enclosed the poem and gave it its meaning is to set the student after something that no study of history, social, economic, political, intellectual, religious, can yield. The poem, as I've said, is a determinate thing; it is *there*; but there is nothing to correspond – nothing answering Mr Bateson's 'social context' that can be set over against the poem, or induced to re-establish itself round it as a kind of framework or completion, and there never *was* anything.[30]

What we have here is clearly anathema – and not just to historicists, but to one of our most deeply held and rarely analysed preconceptions about literature and its relation to society. We are all aware that the historical contexts of literary works may be difficult to reconstruct, and that their reconstruction involves a necessary and inevitable degree of idiosyncrasy. But we simply cannot believe that such contexts never existed, when every element in our intellectual frame is orientated towards the opposite assumption.

Still, I think there is something genuinely salutary in what Leavis had to say, if only by virtue of its setting us on our heels. There are two arguments I want to introduce here: one of my own, following on what has been said in Chapter 1 in particular, and one that returns us to Collingwood and *The Idea of History*. Together they may allow us to make sense of Leavis' unexpected argument.

First. I suggested in Chapter 1 that while works of literature are inevitably in dialogue with the historical developments surrounding them, the psychological occurrences preceding them, and the institutional structures moulding them, the dialogue that provides literature with its autonomy is that dialogue that the poem, play, or novel originates with its author and readers about itself and those external forces operating upon it. This is only the long way of saying something we could put in the form of a question. Is the context in which Marvell started to write the 'Horatian Ode' the same context as that in which he completed it? Leavis has the reader, not the writer, in mind when he writes that 'if the poem is an important challenge, it engages, in the response that "reconstructs" it, and as an inseparable part of the response, the profoundest and completest sense of relative value that one brings from one's experience.'[31] I suggested earlier, in discussing Jerome McGann's 'primary textual moment', that the writer is a reader, too. But in fact so reciprocal are the processes of reading and writing that we can say of Marvell himself, as Leavis said of the reader in general, that the 'Horatian Ode' involved 'the profoundest and completest sense of relative value' that Marvell brought from his *own* experience. Where that sense of relative value would take him, Marvell could not have told us in advance, since he himself only encountered its operation in the poem, and could have discovered them nowhere else. Even a poem like this, therefore, is contingent upon itself. In corollary fashion, we may be sure that Marvell's own personal historical context, as he understood and experienced it, was utterly 'reconstructed' – to use the word in another sense – by the 'Horatian Ode'. (And deconstructed, too.) No one, I think, would dispute that the 'ultimate framework of reference' of Alexander Solzhenitsyn's work, from *A Day in the Life of Ivan Denisovich* to *The Gulag Archipelago* in particular, is Soviet totalitarianism. Removed from that context, either in the West itself or indeed in post-Soviet Russia, Solzhenitsyn has found his moral and intellectual compass much harder to set with accuracy. But Solzhenitsyn's embeddedness in that framework – as successively Marxist apostate, prisoner, and dissident – was precisely that which enabled him to transform the framework, aesthetically and politically. It was precisely that which *impelled* him to transform the framework in the directions he did: from socialist realism to the steepest historical irony, and from the Gulag seen as an aberration associated with 'the cult of personality' to the Gulag as an abiding and inextinguishable element in the Soviet state. The more closely authors are bound up with the historical frameworks in which they find themselves, the more urgent their need to transform such frameworks, in fiction and therefore (within the limits of their calling) in reality. From both our point of view and that of writers like Marvell and Solzhenitsyn, it is the poem that determines the context quite as much as the other way around. What the poem provides, to adapt a phrase of Nietzsche's, is a recontextualization of all contexts.

Second. Readers familiar with *The Idea of History* will realize that one particular element of Collingwood's theory of historical explanation is missing from the summary offered above: re-enactment. The historian, Collingwood felt, 'must re-enact the past in his *own mind*' (*IH* 282; my italics). What makes the human world historical and the natural world un-historical is the fact that the former is a world of purpose and of thought. Past thought, and not simply past events, are the historian's aim: 'To discover what this thought was, the historian must think it again for himself' (*IH* 283). As we might have guessed, the re-enact-ment of past thought and experience brings Collingwood to the notion of context, and here he has some useful points to make:

> An act of thought is certainly a part of the thinker's experience. It occurs at a certain time, and in a certain context of other acts of thought, emotions, sensations, and so forth. Its presence in this con-text I call its immediacy; for although thought is not mere immedi-acy it is not devoid of immediacy. The peculiarity of thought is that, in addition to occurring here and now in this context, it can sustain itself through a change of context and revive in a different one. This power to sustain and revive itself is what makes an act of thought more than a mere 'event' or 'situation'... (*IH* 297)

'The immediate, as such,' Collingwood goes on, 'cannot be re-enacted. Consequently, those elements in experience whose being is just their immediacy (sensations, feelings, &c. as such) cannot be re-enacted; not only that, but thought itself can never be re-enacted in its immediacy' (*IH* 297). Put crudely, Collingwood is defending the autonomy of thought: what he calls 'the self-identity of the act of thinking' (*IH* 298). 'It has been said', he goes on, 'that anything torn from its context is thereby mutilated and falsified; and that in consequence, to know any one thing, we must know its context, which implies knowing the whole universe' (*IH* 298). Not even the most ambitious or blindly self-infatuated New Historicist claims to know that much, but the tendency in thought Collingwood is considering is recognizably of a historicist cast, whether new or perennial.

That is one trap into which we might fall in re-enacting past thought – the Milman Parry trap, perhaps: to commit ourselves to the dogmatic pursuit of a hopeless degree of specificity, ultimately and in theory entailing a knowledge of the whole universe (or the whole of Amherst, to start with). The other is its opposite, which, were it not for the qualification he enters ('as something determinate') we might almost call the Leavis view: under which it is both 'easy and legitimate' to detach thoughts from their context, 'for there is no context' (*IH* 299). Both errors have their origin, Collingwood believed, in a false dilemma.

> That dilemma rests on the disjunction that thought is either pure immediacy, in which case it is inextricably involved in the flow of consciousness, or pure mediation, in which case it is utterly detached from that flow. Actually it is both immediacy and mediation. (*IH* 300)

Acts of thought take place in an immediate context which is irrecoverable: the flow of consciousness. However, they are also capable of sustaining themselves outside that context: that is what makes them thought, as opposed to consciousness as it might be studied by a psychologist. But if such acts of thought are to be revived they must be revived in a context (the mind of a reader, for example) willing and able to support them, and this indeed requires some knowledge:

> Thus, the mere fact that someone has expressed his thoughts in writing, and that we possess his works, does not enable us to understand his thoughts. In order that we may be able to do so, we must come to the reading of them *prepared with an experience sufficiently like his own to make those thoughts organic to it*. (*IH* 300; my italics)

But is this required knowledge of context itself or of other thought; of immediacy or mediation?

> If I now re-think a thought of Plato's, is my act of thought identical with Plato's or different from it? Unless it is identical, my alleged knowledge of Plato's philosophy is sheer error. But unless it is different, my knowledge of Plato's philosophy implies oblivion of my own. (*IH* 300-1)

What makes my re-thinking a thought of Plato's 'different' is not a question of the inadequacies and distortions created by historical reconstruction, for as we have seen thought 'is capable of sustaining itself and being revived or repeated without loss of its identity' (*IH* 300). It is not a passive or irremediable element of contingency (entropic or generative) at work which makes such a difference, but an active principle of the mind: a principle that creates for the mind *its own context*, in which Plato's thought is not merely reconstituted but evaluated by each and every human individual according to their experience and interests. In Plato's mind, according to Collingwood, Plato's arguments 'existed in a certain context of discussion and theory'; indeed without such a context those arguments could never have arisen (*IH* 301). In the reader's mind, conversely, Plato's arguments exist in quite another context: that of the reader's own intellectual training (the context of his or her 'discussion and theory').

This 'double character of thought' (*IH* 300) in which we all live and have our being, intellectually speaking, allows us both to acknowledge the primacy of context as a matrix of thought, and to preserve the integrity of thought outside such a matrix (leaving thought's capacity to transform such matrices aside for the moment). Like philosophical arguments, works of literature exist in at least two contexts: the immediate one of their coming to be written, and the mediate context of their coming to be read. In denying that any such distinction can be made between immediate and mediate contexts, and insisting that criticism must, in McGann's words, 'establish the ground for a whole system of critical differentials that stretch across the continuing social life of a literary work from its point of origin to its current operations' (*SV* 125), New Historicism really does begin to commit itself to a totalizing fallacy of the 'everything is historical' kind. That works of literature begin their lives in historical circumstances peculiar to them is self-evident. Research into such circumstances will always have an explanatory function in criticism, nor should critics ever come to regard the historical environment as a form of slime poetry should rinse off as soon as possible. The death penalty for murder was abolished in Russia during the reign of Catherine the Great. Clearly, a fact of this kind is of great importance to the way we interpret a novel like *Crime and Punishment*; it rules out, for instance, the possibility that Raskolnikov turns himself in to satisfy the death wish. But to convert criticism to a 'particularized historical method' as McGann, Marilyn Butler, and Stephen Greenblatt suggest we should, asks us to re-live the past rather than understand it. Such a programme would remove literature's own interpretative function and award it to the 'informed' student of cultural poetics. Such a programme would, in effect, turn literature and criticism into varieties of history, and deny to literature its capacity to transcend its own immediacy (see *IH* 303) and thus to transform the contexts in which it finds itself, whether those contexts belong to the writer or the reader.

4.3   Hayden White and Paul Ricoeur

So much for that perennial critical impulse to regard works of literature as historical artifacts and little more. I want now to turn to a critical tactic less time-honoured and apparently wholly different in intention, but which is an attack on the autonomy of literature that takes a parallel or corollary form. This critical mode is not to do with history as a set of events in the past, but with history as a written discourse, and its ultimate aim is to blur the distinction between history and literature by identifying both with a larger, all-encompassing function: narrative.

The work of the two critics to be discussed here is highly sophisticated by comparison with New Historicism, which has achieved its influence more or less by appealing to the lowest common denominator. It remains to be seen, however, whether Hayden White or Paul Ricoeur have done anything likely to unseat the feeling that we know the difference between a work of history and one of literature. Samuel Richardson's novel is called *Clarissa: or, the History of a Young Lady*. But when Richardson came to write his postscript dealing with various critical objections levelled at the story, he called himself 'The author of the history' only to add immediately afterwards, in brackets, 'or rather *dramatic narrative*'. How do we know we are reading a 'dramatic narrative' as opposed to a 'history'? What is the difference between them? And is that difference one of degree or of kind? Clearly the answers to such questions will bear heavily on the autonomy of imaginative, 'dramatic' literature. If there is no hard and fast distinction to be made between literature and the narratives we find in history then there may be none between it and the 'non-fictional' narratives we find throughout the human sciences.

There are two answers to this set of questions that will not be considered here. The first is a simple one. It says, in effect, that a work of art is what one finds in a gallery. That is to say, we know the difference between a novel and a history because each comes appropriately 'labelled' by some kind of external authority: authors themselves, the engines of publication and distribution, or cultural authorities more generally conceived. Ultimately this is what Richard Wollheim would call the institutional theory of art;[32] and it comes as no surprise that institutional critics like Jacques Derrida place much critical emphasis on matters of rules and conventions, of law, and of judgement: an emphasis that itself slips from considerations of a broad nature ('What then decides that *Before the Law* [a story by Kafka] belongs to what we think we understand under the name of literature?') to more accusatory, *ad hominem* kinds of finger-pointing ('And who decides? Who judges?').[33] All I would say about such a theory is what has been said by countless others: that obviously it is true; but equally obviously it is inadequate. It does not, for example, explain on what basis items *become* labelled in the ways they do.

The second answer left to one side is of an entirely different character. It says that works of literature are distinct from discursive writing by virtue of the fact that they do not, or need not, refer to anything outside themselves – whereas history, psychology, anthropology, and so forth evidently do. This, too, is an old idea about imaginative literature, but it has been advanced in a most sophisticated form recently by Michael Riffaterre, among others. '[N]arrative truth', Riffaterre writes, 'is born of tautology. As a consequence of the fact that this overdetermination [of literary as opposed to discursive language] is entirely contained in the text and therefore self-sufficient, and that it is an exclusively linguistic phenomenon, readers need not be familiar with the reality that the text is about in order to believe it true.' Whereas 'verisimilitude presupposes things, concepts, or sign systems against which the text may be tested for accuracy and evaluated in the light of their authority, fictional truth spurns referentiality that raises the specter of whether or not the reader acknowledges its accuracy. Instead, fictional truth relies entirely on the text itself as if the latter were self-sufficient.'[34] Literary texts do possess what Riffaterre calls 'a frame of referentiality': but that frame is the so-called 'subtext', held *within* the work of literature, and which is unique to the imaginative narrative mode.[35]

Readers might expect that the defence of the autonomy of literature offered in this study as a whole will fall in with this argument of Riffaterre's: particularly as Collingwood's dictum that history is meant to be true has already been quoted in order to differentiate history from literature. From this might be derived, for example, a relatively neat distinction between an externally orientated 'frame of referentiality' proper to history, and a 'self-sufficient', 'autonomous', internally orientated one ('an exclusively linguistic phenomenon') proper to literature. Such a distinction accords with both common sense and some highly distinguished critical theory. It may be made to fit Collingwood's account. It also seems to provide a basis for further whittling away at the institutionalist position – along the lines of 'what we need to know about about Jane Austen's society to understand her novels is contained within the novels themselves; we need not refer to contemporary codes, intellectual seedbeds, etc.' But it seems to me that, familiar and reassuring as it undoubtedly is, the concept of internal and external frames of referentiality advanced by Riffaterre (and others) is just as inadequate as the institutional theory advanced by Derrida (and others) – for reasons that I hope will become clear.

Brief mention was made, in the previous section, of empiricism and its fatal attraction for the Anglo-Saxon mind. But just as dangerous is structuralism – which, it is worth making clear immediately, is a phenomenon by no means confined to the post-war intellectual movement bearing that name. (It is obviously present to a large degree in Freud's work, for example.) And the work of Hayden White is a latter-day monument to structuralism. We only to have to read that

> every history is first and foremost a verbal artifact, a product of a special kind of language-use. And this suggests that, if historical discourse is to be comprehended as productive of a distinctive kind of knowledge, it must first be analyzed as a structure of language,[36]

to be made aware of the fact. 'Recent theories of discourse', White writes,

> dissolve the distinction between realistic and fictional discourses based on the presumption of an ontological difference between their respective referents, real and imaginary, in favor of stressing their common aspect as semiological apparatuses that produce meanings by the systematic substitution of signifieds (conceptual contents) for the extra-discursive entities that serve as their referents. In these semiological theories of discourse, narrative is revealed to be a particularly effective system of discursive meaning production by which individuals can be taught to live a distinctively 'imaginary relation to their real conditions of existence,' that is to say, an unreal but meaningful relation to the social formations in which they are indentured to live out their lives and realize their destinies as social subjects.[37]

'The beginning of all understanding is classification'.[38] The progenitors of this intellectual attitude are not hard to find: Roman Jakobson, Jean Piaget, Kenneth Burke, Karl Mannheim, Northrop Frye, and Stephen Pepper are all acknowledged by White. These he regards as being on the 'positive' or 'integrative' wing of structuralism, as opposed to the 'eschatological' or 'dispersive' bunch: Lévi-Strauss, Barthes,

Foucault, Lacan. 'The positive wing has been concerned', he feels, 'with the scientific determination of the structures of consciousness by which men form a conception of the world they inhabit and on the basis of which they contrive modes of praxis for coming to terms with that world' (*TD* 258) – and it is clear where White's intellectual loyalties lie.

It is White's belief that 'even in the simplest prose discourse, and even in one in which the object of representation is intended to be nothing but fact, the use of language itself projects a level of secondary meaning below or behind the phenomenon being "described." ' So it is that 'The facts and their formal explanation or interpretation appear as the manifest or literal "surface" of the discourse, while the figurative language used to characterize the facts points to a deep-structural meaning' (*TD* 110). It is not only imaginative, literary narratives, as Riffaterre might have it, that are 'overdetermined', but all narratives, ostensibly true or not.

In their line of work historians confront an 'unprocessed "historical field" ', that may or may not be chronicled in an 'unprocessed historical record' (say, a mere list of dates and events).[39] Confronted in this way, White postulates 'a deep level of consciousness on which a historical thinker chooses conceptual strategies by which to explain or represent his data. On this level the historian performs an essentially *poetic* act, in which he *pre*figures the historical field and constitutes it as a domain upon which to bring to bear the specific theories he will use to explain "what was *really* happening" in it' (*Mh* x): 'a linguistic act which is tropological in nature' (*Mh* 430). What happens is that the events become 'motifically encoded' (*Mh* 6) in such a way as to grant them meaning. (This process, indeed, is what distinguishes an 'event' from a mere 'fact'.) In order for the historian to 'bring to bear upon the data of the historical field the conceptual apparatus he will use to represent and explain it, he must first … constitute it as an object of mental perception'; 'before a given domain can be interpreted, it must first be construed as a ground inhabited by discernible figures.' 'In other words',

the historian confronts the historical field in much the same way that the grammarian might confront a new language. His first problem is to distinguish among the lexical, grammatical, and syntactical elements of the field. Only then can he undertake to interpret what any given configuration of elements or transformations of their relationships mean. In short, the historian's problem is to construct a linguistic protocol, complete with lexical, grammatical, syntactical, and semantic dimensions, by which to characterize the field and its elements in *his own terms* (rather than in the terms in which they come labeled in the documents themselves), and thus to prepare them for the explanation and representation he will subsequently offer of them in his narrative. This preconceptual linguistic protocol will in turn be – by virtue of its essentially *prefigurative* nature – characterizable in terms of the dominant tropological mode in which it is cast. (*Mh* 30)

This, clearly, is 'integrative' structuralism with a vengeance. It is also full of problems, most of which involve reconciling the idea of 'poetic' preconceptual prefiguration with so hyper-conceptualist a discussion of quasi-grammatical classification, linguistic protocols, and the rest. Can any intellectual act be said to be *pre*figurative, especially when it involves construal and discernment (not to mention construction and constitution)? When could either the historical field or the historian be said to be a *tabula rasa*, awaiting the experience of prefiguration? Surely to discern figures and construe a ground is already, unavoidably, to begin the act of interpretation. You cannot constitute something as a domain without already entertaining strong suspicions about what is going in within it – and vice versa. Similarly, White speaks elsewhere of 'the generic story-form chosen by the historian to guide the articulation of the story' being by definition 'a *distortion* of the whole factual field of which the discourse purports to be a *representation*' (*TD* 111; my italics). There is the logical inconsistency of the historian choosing a story-form to guide (as opposed to initiate, say) a story which (since it needs guiding) must therefore already be in existence; there is also the logical problem of how an un-prefigured 'factual field' can be distorted if it has yet to be given a form in the first place. But White is quite clear on these related issues: history has 'its origins in the literary imagination' (*TD* 99) and, just as 'we find the categories for analyzing the different modes of thought, representation, and explanation met with in such nonscientific fields as historiography in the modalities of poetic language itself' (*Mh* 31), so 'historians must employ the same strategies of linguistic figuration used by imaginative writers'.[40]

Novelists might be dealing only with imaginary events whereas historians are dealing with real ones, but the process of fusing events, as the *object* of a representation, is a poetic process. Here the historian must utilize precisely the same tropological strategies, the same modalities of representing relationships in words, that the poet or novelist uses. (*TD* 125)

At first sight, this sounds like Collingwood on the *a priori* imagination. But that is not how the theory develops. The 'facts', for example, are only 'congeries of contiguously related fragments' which 'are put together in the same ways that novelists use to put together figments of their imaginations' (*TD* 125) – a remark that speaks volumes about the structuralist intellectual attitude, towards novelists' working habits at least. 'Although historians and writers of fiction may be interested in different kinds of events, both the forms of their respective discourses and their aims in writing are often the same' (*TD* 121). 'Viewed simply as verbal artifacts histories and novels are indistinguishable from one another.' Only if we approach them 'with specific preconceptions about the kinds of truth that each is supposed to deal in' can we make such a distinction. 'Both', for example, 'wish to provide a verbal image of "reality"', though the novelist works by 'indirect' or 'figurative' means as opposed to the historian's 'point-by-point' correspondence. In both cases 'the discourse taken in its totality as an image of some reality bears a relationship of correspondence to that *of which* it is an image': 'history is no less a form of fiction than the novel is a form of historical representation' (*TD* 122). 'In point of fact':

> history – the real world as it evolves in time – is made sense of in the same way that the poet or novelist tries to make sense of it, i.e., by endowing what originally appears to be problematical and mysterious with the aspect of a recognizable, because it is familiar, form. It does not matter whether the world is conceived to be real or only imagined; the manner of making sense of it is the same. (*TD* 98)

Thus 'the differences between a history and a fictional account of reality are matters of degree rather than of kind' (*TD* 78).

The change in direction from Collingwood is clear enough, I hope. His fundamental distinction (that history is meant to be true) has disappeared. The aims of historians and the aims of novelists are essentially the same – to provide a verbal image of reality.

Two things are needed above all others if White's account is to hold water. First there must be an iron-clad distinction between 'the facts' out there in the unprocessed field (which are facts, of course, because they are true: they really happened), the nature of which White does not dispute, and the idea that historical accounts based on such facts are meant to be true. Because clearly the traditional conception of history is built on the understanding that no such distinction can be made: that the truth of the facts (the 'point-by-point correspondence') spills over into and validates, but also impels and demands, the truth of the narrative. The second thing needed for White's account to make sense is an explanation of how 'what originally appears to be problematical and mysterious' in both history and literature is endowed with a recognizable, familiar form.

It is precisely by means of his distinction between the 'unprocessed historical field' and the motific encodations applied to it that White achieves a prophylactic *cordon sanitaire* between individual facts and narrative truth. Motific encodation allows him to turn towards that which is poetic and metaphorical, and by these means substitute significance for truth. What happens when the virgin historical field is 'prefiguratively grasped and prepared for conscious apprehension' (*Mh* 34) is an ultimately 'poetic' or 'linguistic' act of choice on the part of the historian between four types of prefiguration: Metaphor, Metonymy, Synecdoche, and Irony. These are ways of relating events to each other in such a way as to make them comprehensible, and to turn a list of events like a chronicle into a recognizable story along Aristotelian lines:

> The arrangement of selected events of the chronicle into a story raises the kinds of questions the historian must anticipate and answer in the course of constructing his narrative. These questions are of the sort: 'What happened next?' 'How did that happen?' 'Why did things happen this way rather than that?' 'How did it all come out in the end?' These questions determine the narrative tactics the historian must use in the construction of his story. (*Mh* 7)

Thus the historian moves 'from an original metaphorical characterization of a domain of experience, through metonymic deconstructions of of its elements, to synecdochic representations of the relations between its superficial attributes and its presumed essence' before finishing up with 'a representation of whatever contrasts or oppositions can legitimately be identified' by ironic means (*TD* 5). How all these phases, given their nature, their orientation, and their sequence, can be said to be 'preconceptual' (*Mh* 30) is not clear. Nor is the distinction between such 'prefigurative acts' and 'narrative tactics' (and the two kinds of choice they imply: unconscious and conscious). But again, such a distinction is central to White's platform:

> such questions about the connections between events which make of them elements in a *followable* story should be distinguished from

questions of another sort: 'What does it all add up to?' 'What is the point of it all?' These questions have to do with the structure of the *entire set of events* considered as a *completed* story and call for a synoptic judgment of the relationship between a given story and other stories that might be 'found,' 'identified,' or 'uncovered' in the chronicle. (*Mh* 7)

Several important questions arise about this *cordon sanitaire*. Can the two sets of questions White outlines ever, in fact, be separated? Is it possible to ask what happens 'next' without also and at the same time asking what it 'all' adds up to? For any individual event in a followable story can only take its place and be 'followable' if it coheres with something we believe (on current evidence) to be the whole; and each event added to the narrative will change the final destination: such an indefeasible relationship is the condition of plausibility. But we can see now how White's distinction serves in fact to underwrite a particular view of truth: that it is in fact a matter of 'meaning' or 'significance'. If there are other stories that can be found, identified, or uncovered in the chronicle by means of other motific encodations, why should we believe this one in particular? Why indeed should the *historian* believe it? The answer is, in the end, not much more than 'because he believes it', or 'because that's the way he sees the world', or 'because that's the way we see the world', or 'because it fits'. To borrow Richard Rorty's invaluable phrase, 'there is nothing beyond vocabularies which serves as a criterion of choice between them': the choice is a choice of vocabulary (or motif), and nothing more. In fact, even belief may not be the right word; it, too, is subject to the hermeneutics of suspicion. What propels the motific encodation may be a matter of ideological or intellectual predisposition, inheritance, or prejudice – and nothing the historian writes, it seems, is going to change those. 'When it is a matter of choosing among these alternative visions of history,' White declares, 'the only grounds for preferring one over another are *moral* or *aesthetic* ones' (*Mh* 433). The truth or otherwise of such visions is simply beside the point.

At the beginning of this chapter I said that I would not discuss working historians, but I want to give a brief example of where thinking of this kind can lead. Edward Said's *Orientalism* is explicitly a study of historical bias, among other things: of the fact that the Orient of the Western academic, politician, poet, or artist, 'is not the Orient as it is, but the Orient as it has been Orientalized.'[41] As a direct result, Said is as keen as Hayden White to deconstruct the notion that historical accounts (of the kind provided by Western Orientalists) can be true. 'I believe it needs to be made clear about cultural discourse and exchange within a culture', he writes,

> that what is commonly circulated by it is not 'truth' but representations. It hardly needs to be demonstrated again that language itself is a highly organized and encoded system, which employs many devices to express, indicate, exchange messages and information, represent, and so forth. In any instance of at least written language, there is no such thing as delivered presence, but a *re-presence*, or a representation. The value, efficacy, strength, apparent veracity of a written statement about the Orient therefore relies very little, and cannot instrumentally depend, on the Orient as such.

'And these representations', needless to say, 'rely upon institutions, traditions, conventions, agreed-upon codes of understanding for their effects, not upon a distant and amorphous Orient.' All this is utterly conventional institutionalism: that because language is a device-employing human institution it can have only an arbitrary relationship to an untouched, pre-existing historical reality – and that as a result everything stated in that language 'relies very little, and cannot instrumentally depend' upon reality at all. Such a view betrays itself out of its own mouth; just as we might expect, there are some facts which Said *does* want us to take at face value, not simply where his argument is concerned, but regarding the Orient itself:

> When around the turn of the eighteenth century the Orient definitely revealed the age of its languages – thus outdating Hebrew's divine pedigree – it was a group of Europeans who made the discovery, passed it on to other scholars, and preserved the discovery in the new science of Indo-European philology.[42]

It is important for Said that we accept the fact of the antiquity of oriental languages: our doing so underwrites his sneer at Hebrew's 'divine pedigree', and also represents 'the Orient as it is'. When it is a matter of choosing among alternative versions of history it transpires that some *are* true: not on moral or aesthetic grounds, but true, period, despite being expressed in a device-employing means of communication. The Orient definitely revealed the age of its languages. So it turns out that 'a written statement about the Orient' can rely and depend on the Orient as such, provided it is written by Edward Said. But it is also a fact that this definite revelation did not simply reveal itself: by Said's own account, it was discovered by Orientalist scholars who apparently should have been wholly committed at the ideological level to its suppression; and not only discovered, but passed on and preserved as the basis of an entire new science. Said goes on to say that we must 'ask how one can study other cultures and peoples from a libertarian, or a nonrepressive and nonmanipulative, perspective'.[43] Given the fact that 'there is no such thing as delivered presence', no such thing as an 'Orient as it is' (despite the fact that Said's entire project depends upon his consistently comparing such a thing with the distortions of Western writers), I think a non-manipulative human science (like an un-prefigured historical field) is a pipe-dream. Anything we say about anything – orientalism included – is going to be in language and therefore subject to language's expressive tendency. A degree of non-manipulativeness is all you can ask of a historian. But the absence of delivered presence in history, and the recognition that language is ineluctably a persuasive medium, has never constituted an excuse for playing around with the status of facts at your convenience.

The set of reflective choices that, in White's view, answers the question 'what does it all add up to?' (as opposed to 'what comes next?') is itself a threefold one, coming in logical and temporal sequence after poetic prefiguration by Metaphor, Metonymy, and the rest. Moreover, it is this set of choices that lends recognizable and familiar form to problematical and mysterious events. There is explanation by emplotment, explanation by argument, and explanation by 'ideological implication' (*Mh* 7), and each of these, like its prefigurative ancestor, has four strings to its bow.[44] The motific encoding of the historical field by means of emplotment is imaginative but by no means arbitrary: not because the act of imagination is of a special kind in the case of history (being constrained, that is, by respect for the truth), but for the much simpler reason that there are comparatively few motifs available. 'The types of stories that can be told about the French Revolution', for example, 'are limited to the number of modes of emplotment which the myths of the Western literary tradition sanction as appropriate ways of endowing human processes with meanings' (*TD* 60–1). In fact the 'fund of culturally provided *mythoi*' (*TD* 60) is disappointingly (or reassuringly) small: there are only four, so that

> [a] given historian is forced to emplot the whole set of stories making up his narrative in comprehensive or *archetypal* story-form. For example, Michelet cast all of his histories in the Romantic mode, Ranke cast his in the Comic mode, Tocqueville used the Tragic mode, and Burckhardt used Satire. (*Mh* 8)

All of this ties in, of course, with White's view that there are 'only events under different descriptions'; that 'a discourse is regarded as an apparatus for the production of meaning rather than as only a vehicle for the transmission of information about an extrinsic referent' (*CF* 42); and that all we have is a choice between the various pre-determined tropological distortions of the virgin historical field allowed us by the mega-institution, 'the Western literary tradition'. To put it at its simplest, 'What one historian may emplot as a tragedy, another may emplot as a comedy or romance' (*TD* 58). The potential for new histories of the Holocaust or the Black Death expands accordingly.

After all of which it will come as a disappointment to find that in general White is scathing about historians' 'artistic abilities'. Historians are, in his view, 'naive storytellers' (*Mh* 8) compared with imaginative writers, and rightly accused of being 'unwilling to probe the more arcane strata of human consciousness' or 'utilize contemporary modes of literary representation' (*TD* 27). As with Richard Rorty and Alasdair MacIntyre, the literary critic may feel a faint blush of pride coming on. At last: here is a theorist of history who values the special capacities of literature, and so on. 'There have been no significant attempts at surrealistic, expressionistic, or existentialist historiography', White reminds us; on the contrary,

> when historians claim that history is a combination of science and art, they generally mean that it is a combination of *late-nineteenth-century* social science and *mid-nineteenth-century* art. That is to say, they seem to be aspiring to little more than a synthesis of modes of analysis and expression that have their antiquity alone to commend them. If this is the case, then artists and scientists alike are justified in criticizing historians, *not because they study the past*, but because they are studying it with *bad* science and *bad* art. (*TD* 43)

On late nineteenth-century social science I cannot comment; but if by 'mid-nineteenth-century art' White means the realist novel developed by writers like Jane Austen, Stendhal, Dickens, Balzac, Flaubert, Tolstoy, George Eliot, and Henry James, that has often been judged to be good art, in its way, and certainly not a mode of expression valued only for its antiquity: but like Rorty, White is an enthusiastic Modernist.

Two points in particular arise here. First, as we have seen, White places emphasis on the need for both novelists and historians to endow what originally appears to be problematical and mysterious with recognizable and familiar form; but he does not reconcile this requirement with the literary experimentalism he feels historians should emulate.

> The original strangeness, mystery, or exoticism of the events is dispelled, and they take on a familiar aspect ... as elements of a familar kind of configuration. They are rendered comprehensible by being subsumed under the categories of the plot structure in which they are encoded as a story of a particular kind. They are familiarized, not only because the reader now has more *information* about the events, but also because he has been shown how the data conform to an *icon* of a comprehensible finished process, a plot structure with which he is familiar as a part of his cultural endowment. (*TD* 86)

In what way, though, would our 'cultural endowment' prepare us for surrealist, expressionist, or existentialist historiography, and how are such innovations consistent with the need for historians to invoke 'recognizable archetypal story-forms' (*TD* 106)? One of the main aims of surrrealism, after all, was precisely to undermine our cultural endowment by every means at the artist's disposal. Dali would have been genuinely scandalized if you told him one of his pictures constituted an icon of a comprehensible finished process – and his is only an extreme case: there would be a long queue of artists and writers, differing from Dali in every possible respect *except* their disbelief in such 'icons', who would want to take White up on the issue.

The second and graver issue concerns White's own understanding of literary experimentalism, an understanding which is sufficiently shaky to make us wonder what he thinks he intends in advancing such a requirement of history in the first place. Modernists like James, Woolf, Joyce, and Proust, he argues, represent 'realism's imminent unmasking and the writer's surrender to the free play of language itself as the true function of literature' (*CF* 206). Moreover, 'One can narrativize without dramatizing, as the whole of modernist literature demonstrates, and dramatize without theatricalizing, as the modern theater since Pirandello and Brecht makes eminently clear' (*CF* 33). But it is not 'eminently clear' in the least that Joyce or Proust 'surrender to the free play of language' (if any such thing can be said to exist in the first place, or if any such thing could be said to be the true function of literature), or that Modernism has found the means to divorce drama from narrative (of Samuel Beckett least of all is this true), or that a writer like Pirandello 'dramatizes without theatricalizing'. (Indeed there are few great playwrights more self-consciously 'theatrical' than Pirandello.) Where literature and criticism in general are concerned, White is similarly flat-footed. He speaks, for example, of historical discourse being endowed 'with a quality of "thinginess" similar to poetic utterance'. In the same essay he decides that 'from the standpoint of traditional literary theory, the notion that the form of a discourse might be one of its contents would have to be treated as either a paradox or a mystery'. Not only is he unaware that critics like Coleridge, Henry James, and D.H. Lawrence all, repeatedly and emphatically, argued for the indivisibility of form and content; he himself, in the very same piece of writing, enforces such a distinction, speaking as he does of tropology being 'concerned more with codes than with whatever contingent messages can be transmitted by specific uses of them'.[45]

Nor is this simply a question of hazy memories of Coleridge, Joyce, or *Six Characters in Search of an Author*. As in the case of Richard Rorty, the problem lies deeper than this. White's understanding of narrative is rhetorical; essentially it concerns an instrumental, mechanistic mode of communication. It is 'rhetorical analysis', in his view, that 'will disclose the poetical understructure' (*TD* 105) of history, and it is the illusorily scientific promise held out by rhetorical analysis that allows him to identify 'the techniques of poetry in general' with the 'rhetorical devices, tropes, figures, and schemata of words and thoughts ... described by the Classical and Renaissance rhetoricians' (*TD* 123), as if 'the techniques of poetry in general' (whatever they might be) have been frozen in time for good and all and can be translated into the historical sphere with similar ease. To put it simply, he is drawing history alongside not literature itself, but alongside an unrecognizable, 'rhetorical' simulacrum: 'insofar as a historian's discourse is literary it seems to *be* rhetorical' (*CF* 227). To the extent that White does this, he does not clarify the profound relation between the two spheres of interest at all: he obscures it. The higher, the more all-encompassing, and the more scientifically ambitious the structuralist pyramid he raises, the deeper he buries the relation he is seeking to discover. The more he pulls history towards what he takes literature to be, the more he pulls history away from what literature actually is.

As I intimated at the beginning of this discussion, the outcome of it may be an unexpected one. I believe that Hayden White, far from bringing history and literature together under the umbrella of 'the poetic' or 'the linguistic' or 'the rhetorical' has actually driven them apart by such means. But this has not meant that this study commits itself as a result a common-sense distinction between the two. When history and literature are looked at as they are, without the 'tropological' and 'scientific' distortions introduced by Hayden White, their similarity is at least as striking as their difference. Like atomic particles, they carry the same charge. Therefore they refuse to coalesce; they repel each other; but only after they have been brought very close indeed – closer in fact than either Collingwood or White envisage.

The reader will be relieved to learn that an exhaustive analysis of Paul Ricoeur's narratological theories – particularly as represented in his three-volume *chef d'oeuvre*, *Time and Narrative* – will not be presented here. Such an analysis has been rendered unnecessary because what has been said about Hayden White itself acts as a focus for what is to be said here about Ricoeur's work. That is to say, a great part of his theory simply does not concern me. Like the seven-eighths of an iceberg, I will let it float past undisturbed.

Still, I must indicate, however sketchily, what *Time and Narrative* is about. I want to remind the reader that the foundation of the argument presented here is Collingwood's remark that the difference between history and literature is that history is meant to be true. We have seen that Hayden White retained this distinction, but only for decency's sake: 'facts' may be true but 'events' are already marked by tropological distortion and by the search for meaning, and since 'meaning' and 'significance' can be found more or less indifferently in history and literature, why bother to lay much stress on their differences? Ricoeur retains Collingwood's distinction, too: more emphatically as it happens. 'Only history', he writes, 'can claim a reference inscribed in empirical reality, inasmuch as historical intentionality aims at events that have actually occurred.'[46] He speaks, at one point, of 'historical narrative's ambition to constitute a *true* narrative' (*TN* ii. 3; my italics).

But while Ricoeur accepts what Collingwood has to say more or less at face value he also draws the entire issue into a new sphere, anticipated neither by Collingwood, nor White, nor perhaps any other theorist of narrative and historiography. Historical intentionality may aim at events that have actually occurred; but, as Ricoeur goes on to say,

> Is not every narrative told as though it had taken place, as is evident from the ordinary usage of verbal past tenses to narrate the unreal? In this sense, fiction would borrow as much from history as history borrows from fiction. It is this reciprocal borrowing that authorizes my posing the problem of the *interweaving* reference between history and narrative fiction. This problem can be avoided only by a positivist conception of history that would not recognize the aspect of fiction in its reference through traces, and by an antireferential conception of literature that would not recognize the importance of the metaphorical reference in all poetry. (*TN* ii. 82)

Thus the imaginative construction of historical narratives from traces (documentary or otherwise) suggests a borrowing from literature, whereas literature's metaphorical references to the world remain references nonetheless, on a par with the historian's own orientation.

This is the area I want to explore. But Ricoeur's reference to the use of verbal past tenses in narrative itself indicates, in however tiny a fashion, where the preponderance of his interest lies. For him, both the question of truth and the question of the interweaving reference between history and literature are bound up with time, or what he would call the aporias of temporality. For whereas it is clear that he agrees with Collingwood (and with White) that history is made up in an imaginative, 'fictional' sort of a way out of 'evidence' and 'facts', he sees an all-embracing issue behind that state of affairs. The 'epistemological break between fiction and history, or between myth and history,' in his view, 'turned attention to the question of *evidence*, at the expense of the more fundamental question of what accounts for the *interest* of a work of history. It is this interest', he goes on, 'that assures the continuity between history based on historiography and ordinary narration' (*TN* i. 151; my italics).

For Ricoeur the interest which unites history and literature is *time*, and the argument of his study takes a form conveniently outlined in an earlier essay of his:

> The argument divides into three steps. (1) It is necessary to establish that there is more *fiction in history* than the positivist conception of history admits. (2) Then it must be shown that fiction in general, and narrative fiction in particular, are more *mimetic* than the same positivism allows. (3) These two prior points being granted, I shall

suggest that the references of empirical [i.e. historical] narrative and fictional narrative *cross upon* what I provisionally called historicity or the historical condition of man. The concept of *crossed reference* provides, in my view, the key to the fundamental relation between narrativity and historicity.[47]

Thus, as Hayden White puts it, the crossed referent or 'the ultimate referent' of narrative, in Ricoeur's view, 'is the human experience of time or "the structures of temporality"' (*CF* 175). Where in White's view we continue to read Gibbon long after his use-by date because of his prose style, in Ricoeur's view we do so because of the insight Gibbon gives us into 'the deep structure of historical consciousness' – at least that is how White himself summarizes the difference between his analysis and Ricoeur's own (*CF* 180). This ultimate referent is what history and literature share, and which makes them subjects of overriding human interest, since our being in time is a first-order condition of humanity. What distinguishes history from literature, and therefore preserves either from mere redundancy, is 'the difference between the solutions contributed by each of them to the aporias of time' (*TN* iii. 138): aporias between phenomenological and cosmic time, for example.

Like White, Ricoeur wants to bring history and literature together: to find the point at which they interweave or share a referent. But for him it is not enough to say that history is meant to be true whereas literature is not. *Both are true*; not in their relation to evidence or 'facts' or 'what really happened', but in their shared reference to time, which constitutes their interest for us. 'The relation between fiction and history', he writes,

> is assuredly more complex than we will ever be able to put into words. And, of course, we have to combat the prejudice that the historian's language can be made entirely transparent, to the point of allowing the things themselves to speak; as if it sufficed to eliminate the ornaments of prose to be done with the figures of poetry. But we cannot combat this initial prejudice without also struggling against a second one, which holds that the literature of imagination, because it always makes use of fiction, can have no hold on reality. (*TN* iii. 154–5)

The whole overt emphasis of Ricoeur's enterprise in *Time and Narrative* serves the idea that both history and literature 'aspire to present a verbal image of reality' (*TN* iii. 312; White's phrase exactly). An image, that is to say, the vital truth-claim of which is directed less towards the factual and 'the real' than towards the temporal. 'Verisimilitude', Ricoeur insists, almost in direct contradiction to Collingwood (and reducing still further, if you like, the diaphragm that separates history from literature), 'is still a province of truth' (*TN* ii. 13). For Ricoeur history and literature are both true – with respect to *time*.

The overt and avowed emphasis of *Time and Narrative*, however, is not the whole story. In fact, Ricoeur's acknowledgment that history concerns the real whereas literature concerns the imaginary is something he does not convert into an essential parity between the two in the metaphysical, temporal sphere. While striving to do the latter Ricoeur's very vocabulary and mode of argument betray him – more and more so, it must be said, as his long study gradually forsakes the summary of others' ideas (Augustine's, Frank Kermode's, etc.) for the articulation of his own.

What I have in mind is a residual element in Ricoeur which privileges historical reality over fictional reality. We have already seen this feature at work, albeit in a most fugitive way, in his discussion of the two prejudices his study aims to combat. Is it pedantic to point out that there is a predisposition in Ricoeur's very ranking of the prejudices concerned? For a hierarchy there undoubtedly is, between the '*initial*' misunderstanding of history ('that the historian's language can be made entirely transparent') and the '*second*' one relating to fiction ('that the literature of imagination … can have no hold on reality'). Why initial? Why second? Then there is the fact that his crossover-point, his interweaving reference, where 'empirical' narratives and fictional narratives meet, is itself called 'historicity or the historical condition of man'. Again, history is the senior partner. Something of the way Ricoeur is still committed to keeping literature and history in a hierarchical relation is also suggested by the idea of literature ('verisimilitude') being a mere 'province' of the truth. Not only is verisimilitude a province of truth: the word itself is a 'province' of the whole family of words having *verus* as its root (verity, verify, veritable). When push comes to shove, the fact that history deals with empirically real events for him means that history is the truer mode.

On the everyday question of truth first. Ricoeur feels that history is in a state of indebtedness to what has really happened. He speaks of 'the feeling of a debt' experienced by historians with respect to their specific relation to the past, which he calls 'standing-for' (*TN* iii. 177). He invokes a term of Karl Heussi's, the *Gegenüber* (meaning, loosely, 'opposite number' or even 'opponent'), which 'imposes a directive and a corrective on historical research, removing it from the arbitrariness that seems to affect the work of selection and organization that the historian performs' (*TN* iii. 305). This work of selection and organization we have already seen described by Collingwood: the historian in his view 'is always selecting, simplifying, schematizing, leaving out what he thinks unimportant and putting in what he regards as essential', and such autonomous and self-authorizing activities were ones Collingwood compared directly with the writing of fiction. The *Gegenüber* of history functions as both background and constraint, chaos and structure, in this respect. It is utterly gone, other, and past; yet it leaves traces, and a need for such traces to be rendered coherent by means of 'standing-for' and the historian's sense of indebtedness. Heussi's is a concept Ricoeur places in the foreground of his analysis, using it to emphasize one aspect of Collingwood's dictum (in contrast to literature, history is meant to be true), while at the same time illustrating his own manner of 'posing the problem'. 'Only historians' he writes,

> can, absolutely speaking, be said to refer to something 'real,' in the sense that that about which they speak was observable to witnesses in the past. In comparison, the characters of the novelist are themselves quite simply 'unreal'; 'unreal,' too, is the experience described by fiction. Between the 'reality of the past' and the 'unreality of fiction,' the dissymmetry is total. (*TN* iii. 157)

In effect, Ricoeur has substituted the historical *Gegenüber* for Collingwood's 'picture of things as they really were, and of events as they really happened'. Our access to history is not access to things *wie es eigentlich gewesen* but to a reconstruction elicited and interpellated by the past both as chaos and as order. History not only abhors a vacuum; it also supplies the means with which to fill it. While the *Gegenüber* may include other, new epistemological and metaphysical responsibilities which are real enough, it also includes 'the dead': it also includes, that is, those events 'observable to witnesses in the past' which constitute historical reality.

However, this manner of 'posing the problem' itself raises other questions. Is 'reality' made up of simply of observable events? Is 'reality' only that to which witnesses can testify? That is a very important slice of it, certainly, for historians in particular no doubt; but it is not all of it, not by a long chalk. Are abstract nouns real? Or unconscious changes in attitude which no one 'witnesses' as such – the 'hundred visions and revisions' J. Alfred Prufrock famously speaks of, which can be experienced before toast and tea? And if these things are real yet they are not included in the *Gegenüber* of history, where do they find a home?

Ricoeur does have a parallel version of the *Gegenüber* up his sleeve where literature is concerned, but a disappointment awaits anyone assuming that that is where, for example, Prufrock's excruciating dilemmas are experienced by him and found by us. Literature's *Gegenüber*, it turns out – the thing to which it is indebted by way of background and constraint; the reality it stands-for; the thing to which it must 'correspond in an appropriate manner' (*TN* iii. 143) – is the opposite to its historical one. That was to be found in the past, among the dead, as a kind of moral pressure that the past be recorded and made sense of; this is found in the future, with the living *readers* of a work of literature, as a corollary kind of moral pressure to illuminate those readers' lives. '[I]t is only through the mediation of reading', Ricoeur writes, 'that the literary work attains complete significance, which would be to fiction what standing-for is to history' (*TN* iii. 158). Come back Jerome McGann, all is forgiven.

Ricoeur wishes to lead the reader a step further than Collingwood was prepared to go. For him, history and literature are equally true, albeit only with regard to mankind's experience of time. I wish to go a step further than Ricoeur. Here is what he says of literature's effect on its *Gegenüber*, the readership:

> This critique of the naive concept of 'reality' applied to the pastness of the past calls for a systematic critique of the no less naive concept of 'unreality' applied to the projections of fiction. The function of standing-for or of taking-the-place-of is paralleled in fiction by the function it possesses, with respect to everyday practice, of being undividedly revealing and transforming. Revealing, in the sense that it brings features to light that were concealed and yet already sketched out at the heart of our experience, our praxis. Transforming, in the sense that a life examined in this way is a changed life, another life.

'You must', my reader will surely feel, 'be happy with this.' Literature's capacity to bring features to life that were concealed; transformation; what more could this particular defence of the autonomy of literature ask for, given what has been said in previous chapters?

But Ricoeur goes on. 'Here we reach the point', he says:

> where discovering and inventing are indistinguishable, the point, therefore, where the notion of reference no longer works, no more

than does that of redescription. The point where ... the problematic of [literary] refiguration must free itself, once and for all, from the vocabulary of reference. (*TN* iii. 158)

It is here, therefore, where Ricoeur's discussion of revelation and transformation seems to be most thoroughly in tune with the account offered by this study, that the illusion of like-mindedness is shattered, and the way is opened for us to take the extra step of which I have spoken. As Ricoeur, in seeking to define the *Gegenüber* of literature, adds concepts like revelation and transformation to the Socratic-cum-Arnoldian critical attitude to literature ('the unexamined life is not worth living'), he reveals his own position to be in itself, in my view, a piece of humanist, 'Victorian' piety and naïvete. Literature may constitute a clarifying examination and illumination of life, *à la* Matthew Arnold, it is true; but it is also just as capable of constituting a fantasy, an evasion, a distortion, and a misconstrual. For neither the writer nor the reader does literature function merely as a moral one way street, examining life from a position of elevation and intellectual privilege, criticizing it, or laying on moral utilities for hard-pressed modern mankind. Yet this role is what Ricoeur sees literature fulfilling. And history, too, in its fashion. He quotes Socrates again at the conclusion of his study, when discussing the relation of self-knowledge to the cultural role of narrative, as follows:

> The self of self-knowledge is the fruit of an examined life, to recall Socrates' phrase in the *Apology*. And an examined life is, in large part, one purged, one clarified by the cathartic effects of the narratives, be they historical or fictional, conveyed by our culture. So self-constancy refers to a self instructed by the works of a culture that it has applied to itself. (*TN* iii. 247)

The whole remedial and unproblematically beneficent process is strongly reminiscent, not only of Matthew Arnold ('the best that has been thought and said in the world'; 'Sweetness and Light'), but also of Hayden White and the literary codes and *mythoi* he believes are stored in culture, and of Alasdair MacIntyre and the 'stock of stories' we encountered in Chapter 2, which he believes constitute the 'initial dramatic resources' of society.

Ricoeur's moral naïvete on this point arises directly from his belief that the point of revelation, transformation, examination, and change at which literature arrives is also the point 'where the notion of reference no longer works' and where literature 'must free itself, once and for all, from the vocabulary of reference'. His, Rorty's, MacIntyre's, and

White's views of literature and its relation to its readers all depend on this idea of literary 'freedom' – and so does Matthew Arnold's to some extent, though his familiarity with literature was more intimate and profound than any of these later commentators. In Ricoeur's view what works of literature refer to, so to speak, is (much to the horror of New Historicists everywhere) a *future*: 'It is only in reading that the dynamism of configuration completes its course. And it is beyond reading, in effective action, instructed by the works handed down, that the configuration to the text is transformed into refiguration' (*TN* iii. 159). Once again: I have spoken (not in such sanguine terms, it is true) about literature transcending its own immediacy; but the state of affairs Ricoeur describes is very far from what I have in mind. His comments on reading, for example, are revealingly Rorty-esque. 'The ideal type of reading', he believes, is 'figured by the fusion but not confusion of the horizons of expectation of the text and those of the reader' (*TN* iii. 179), a state which is itself 'a provocation to be and to act differently' (*TN* iii. 249). What is unsatisfactory about accounts like these is precisely their idealism. For that which prevents a kind of weightless fusion between texts and readers is the fact that neither is completely orientated towards the other; that both in fact are intent on contexts of their own: present contexts; contexts which are transformed, certainly, but which are not rendered any the less real for either party by being so.

I can complete the argument by turning to what Ricoeur has to say about the temporal plane, the aporias literature and history encounter there, and their different solutions to them. The first thing that strikes us is his emphasis on what he calls the 'emancipation' of literary narrative. '[F]rom the epic to the novel, by way of tragedy and the ancient and modern forms of comedy,' he says, 'the time of fictional narrative has been freed from the constraints requiring it to be referred back to the time of the universe. ... Each fictive temporal experience unfolds its world, and each of these worlds is singular, incomparable, unique' (*TN* iii. 128). This is perfectly true if by it we mean that works of literature need not be related to each other in time any more than in space. But it does not follow from this that the temporal emancipation of literature is anything like as complete as Ricoeur believes. Individual works of literature may unfold worlds that are different from other individual works of literature. But the worlds they each unfold refer to our own just the same. The fact that novels do not have to be consistent with each other in this respect does not mean they are not consistent with a 'realistic' notion of time – even when that notion is one they deliberately flout. If it were not there, not referred to, how could they flout it?

Works of literature are no more emancipated from 'reality' (time, space, probability, etc. *ad infinitum*) than are works of history. The 'images of reality' literature and history provide both seek to be true in *every* respect (not merely the temporal one) – only in different ways. Literature involves events that are invented, history involves events that really took place. The former is, whatever its ostensible subject-matter, orientated towards the present, the latter towards the past. But these considerations are, where my argument is concerned, neither here nor there. The fact that history refers directly to empirically real events does not, as Ricoeur cannot help implying, make it any 'more' real; only real in a different way. The fact that the *Gegenüber* of history is in the past whereas that of literature is (*pace* Ricoeur) in the present and its concerns, is equally by the by. It is not the case that in a work of fiction 'All the specific connectors set in place by history can…be neutralized and simply mentioned' (*TN* iii. 129). It is not the case that 'novelists have no material proof' (*TN* iii. 162), nor that because objects in works of literature 'are not to be denoted but are to be transformed' that they are 'depragmatized' as a result (*TN* iii. 168). Nor is it the case that 'The horizon of expectation peculiar to literature does not coincide with that of everyday life'; nor that 'a new work is able to create an aesthetic distance…because a prior distance exists between the whole of literary life and everyday practice' (*TN* iii. 173); nor that because '[the work] is "refractory" to anything other than itself', it asserts its ability to transfigure the everyday and to transgress accepted standards' (*TN* iii. 176). All this returns us to that Riffaterrean notion of the difference between history and literature: that a work of literature 'tends to assume the status of a self-sufficient system of symbols'.[48] It even leads us further back still, to Aristotle's idea that literature is more philosophical than history: as Ricoeur puts it, that 'history opens us to the possible, whereas fiction, by opening us to the unreal, leads us to what is *essential* in reality'.[49]

Let me say it once again: the reader might have expected me to approve Ricoeur's conclusions. Do they not, after all, suggest a kind of autonomy for literature – emancipated from historical and social reality and from practical language? Do they not speak of self-sufficiency? Above all, does Ricoeur not suggest that literature's capacity 'to transfigure the everyday and to transgress accepted standards' depends upon its being '*refractory to anything other than itself*'? Well; if the autonomy of literature could be won by such means, that would be a pyrrhic victory indeed. The operation would be a success, but the patient would die. Literature is indeed a refractory thing, stubbornly resistant to institutional contamination even as it welcomes it. It does, as readers have often testified, transfigure the everyday and transgress accepted standards. That is why it is of value to us. But it does not achieve any of these things by adopting 'aesthetic distance' or by circumscribing 'aesthetic experience', by laying claim to self-sufficiency or contrasting itself to everyday experience. By no means does literature emancipate itself from historical and social reality, or from 'practical language'. That literature deals with metaphors does not for one moment imply that it relates to the world, in Hayden White's phrase, 'in the most indirect and allegorical manner' (*CF* 170). The truth is exactly the reverse. Literature transforms reality; but its capacity to do so reality depends upon its utter involvement with it.

The best example I can give of this is Jane Austen's *Northanger Abbey*, where reality is shown to conform to a Gothic novel. Catherine Morland's Gothic fantasies about the villainous General Tilney are not entirely absurd; he may not have killed his wife, but he is cruel to his children, and he does indeed wake Catherine at dawn to send her packing in a lonely coach, and so on and so forth. Yet none of this in any way invalidates what Austen has to say elsewhere about her novel in particular, about novels in general, and about their proper relation to everyday reality. 'Gothic' insecurity, 'Gothic' hysteria, 'Gothic' over-suggestivity, 'Gothic' cruelty, and 'Gothic' mystery exist side-by-side with the England Henry Tilney describes, where 'Murder was not tolerated, servants were not slaves, and neither poison nor sleeping potions to be procured, like rhubarb, from every druggist.'[50] *Northanger Abbey* is a transfiguration of the everyday and a transgression of accepted standards which cuts in two directions: it asks that the novel in general apply itself to 'the common feelings of common life', certainly (and Jane Austen's affinity with Wordsworth and the preface to *Lyrical Ballads* is by no means insignificant in her choice of such an expression),[51] but (like *Lyrical Ballads* again) it also recognizes that feelings of Gothic extremity and mystery *are* common feelings of common life. So Jane Austen is doubly refractory, to use Ricoeur's expression; she transgresses two sets of expectations. First, she writes the 'realist' novel of everyday English life instead of the Radcliffean fantasy the title of her novel might lead us to expect, were we to browse in the catalogue of the circulating library; second, at the very moment we overcome our disappointment and learn to cultivate a blasé and dismissive attitude to the illicit pleasures we had anticipated, she reveals the Radcliffean fantasy to be a part of the very reality she has campaigned for and induced us to prefer. For that fantasy is an indubitably real element in Catherine Morland's experience as an anxious teenager on the brink of social and sexual experience ('parentless' in Bath). At no stage is the novel's absolute engagement with telling the truth about common feelings of common life compromised. On the contrary, the two 'transgressions' I have described are, taken as an indivisible whole, the truth (the 'psychological' truth, if you like) the book has to communicate.

No matter how many warnings to the contrary he issues, Ricoeur still clings, ultimately, to an antireferential conception of literature. For him 'metaphorical reference' can never be a genuine reference, one 'observable to witnesses'. It is always a neutralized, de-pragmatized, fictionalized poor relation: 'only imagined' as Hayden White says. Like many another similar account of literature Ricoeur's comes to depend on 'aesthetic distance' and 'aesthetic experience'; but once that particular finger is pulled out of the dyke, the entire argument begins to crumble. When, as George Eliot says, she tells the truth about loobies, we are indeed free (novels being novels) to think about lords.[52] But neither loobies nor lords become 'neutralized' as a result; they do not become part of our 'aesthetic' experience as opposed to the rest of it. That which is true of a so-called 'realist' writer like George Eliot is true in exactly the same way of Andrei Sinyavsky's bewildering fictions, which are 'set' nowhere at all but which are so clearly concerned with totalitarianism in general and Soviet life in particular; of Kafka's stories; of Gogol's; of *The Faerie Queen*; or of a science-fiction fantasy like Marge Piercy's *Woman on the Edge of Time*, the heroine of which is a thirty-seven year-old Mexican American in the grip of poverty, whose lover has been killed, whose daughter has been taken away from her by the authorities on the grounds of her mother's mental instability, and who finds herself incarcerated in an asylum where she is subjected to electronic implants in her brain. The entire fantasy, the entire 'pack of lies' to be found in each of these works could interest us only if it were rooted in and woven into reality. The experience of writing and reading stories not only helps us understand what reality is; it helps make reality for us, not only in the sense of fundamental perceptions (of temporal relatedness in particular of course) but also and at the same time in the evaluative sense Henry James had in mind when, in a letter to H.G. Wells of July 1915, he argued that art '*makes* life, makes interest, makes importance, for our consideration and application of these things', seeing as he did 'no substitute whatever for the force and beauty of its process.'

So it is that literature is always open to both the criticism that it is untrue ('books', in Philip Larkin's memorable phrase, 'are a load of crap'), and the response of many readers that it is more interesting than history. 'I can read poetry and plays, and things of that sort,' says Catherine Morland, 'and do not dislike travels. But history, real solemn history, I cannot be interested in.'

I read it a little as a duty, but it tells me nothing that does not either vex or weary me. The quarrels of popes and kings, with wars or pestilences, in every page; the men all so good for nothing, and hardly any women at all – it is very tiresome: and yet I often think it odd that it should be so dull, for a great deal of it must be invention. The speeches that are put into the heroes' mouths, their thoughts and designs – the chief of all this must be invention, and invention is what delights me in other books.

'Historians, you think,' Eleanor Tilney replies, 'are not happy in their flights of fancy. They display imagination without raising interest.'[53] A great deal of history is indeed invention, as Hayden White would be the first to point out, though it remains invention designed and intended to show what really happened. But the inventions we find in literature, while they, too, are designed and intended to show what really happens, do so not by displacing or de-pragmatizing reality but – to borrow two phrases of Pierre Macherey's I have already used in Chapter 1 – by wresting it in a new direction according to an internal principle of elaboration.

5
Four Objections

Books of this kind always achieve less than their authors hope. There will be readers whose thoughts already run along similar lines to the arguments presented here. For them a defence of the autonomy of literature may be faulty in many respects and still remain welcome. There will be a second group of readers who will find it temperamentally and intellectually alien to their interests, and for whom the errors they may find in it will be sufficient proof of its dispensability.

Still, I should like to anticipate some reservations that might be held about this study, not so much with the aim of disarming critics in prophylactic fashion by such means, but to complete the argument which has been introduced in the preceding chapters, and to introduce some issues that could not naturally be accommodated in them. In examining these objections, I repeat, my primary aim is less to pre-empt them (though obviously I will seek to defend what has been written here) than to describe the autonomy of literature in greater breadth.

5.1 'Approaching' literature

The first objection might take this form, in which the reader is imagined to think that this study has not gone far enough. Such readers will have agreed that the theories of literature offered (implicitly or explicitly) by the institutionalist critics discussed above are inadequate in differing but central aspects. They will agree that the dialogue which takes place between the work and its writer and readers as it develops is as important as that which takes place between the work and its origins in philosophical, psychological, and historical causation. They will agree, in short, that works of literature are capable of resisting and transforming institutional contamination as well as succumbing to it.

But such readers may also have been frustrated by this critical formulation. 'Why is it', they may ask, 'that you are unwilling to press the theoretical implications of this view home? Why is it that, faced with the institutional claims of a Rorty, or a Freud, or a Greenblatt, you are only able to go so far as to say that literature transforms, or diverts, or redirects such claims? Why are you unwilling to give a theoretical account of *how* such transformations take place, given that they indeed do? You suggested in Chapter 1 that something in contemporary criticism remains *au dessus de la mêlée* – where the *mêlée* was seen, in terms borrowed from Dan Jacobson, as "the ebb and flow of the events in the story or poem itself" – but you, too, have proved yourself incapable of providing a theoretical account of the process. You have repeatedly said that literature does not arise in the mere passive reflection of some forms of "external" causation, but you have given no general description of the springs of "internal" causation; you have not told us what their sources are and how they operate (apart, possibly, from some ideas to be gathered in your discussion of Marion Milner and Michael Polanyi in the Psychoanalysis chapter). Instead you have only offered some examples of what might be called now transformations-from-within: *Lolita*, 'The Secret Sharer', *King Lear*, and so on.'

Such questions go some way towards answering themselves. Claims for autonomy are in part untheorizable. As Hayden White puts it:

> claims for the autonomy of a way of thinking or a discipline are not really theoretically arbitratable, since in order for such claims to be assessed, one must assume a point of view outside the way of thinking of the discipline being so defended, which already begs the question of autonomy itself. In this respect, claims for the autonomy of a discipline are like claims for the autonomy of a community, folk, or state, establishable finally only in the practical realization thereof.[1]

It is true, as was suggested in Chapter 1, that this study's theoretical side provides an essentially negative definition of the autonomy of literature. Starting with the kinds of institutional claims made by Jacques Derrida, the ideas of literature offered by some philosophers, psychoanalysts, and theorists of history have been criticized, whereas nothing has been offered in the place of such ideas but an inherent propensity to evasion without which literature would hardly exist: what might otherwise be called intractability, lability, 'mobility', or inexhaustiveness. No sustained attempt has been made to reduce this principle to theoretical cohesion, or even to begin such a task by providing a taxonomic survey of the varying ways and degrees in which any particular work of literature, or literature considered as a whole, evades institutional contamination. What is such a taxonomy to do? Distinguish between art-for-art's-sake attitudes on the one hand, and Socialist realism on the other? or between a psychologically motivated poem like 'The Love Song of J. Alfred Prufrock', a historically motivated one like Marvell's 'Horatian Ode', and a philosophically motivated one like *The Man With the Blue Guitar*?

Even as such a taxonomic project is outlined it is clear how impossible it would be of success. Nor would it be countenanced by the theoretical critics with whom I have taken issue. But its more sophisticated variant – expressed in the wish to reduce that general principle of evasion to theoretical cohesion and expression – is equally unattainable. One of the things the principle of evasion is bound to evade, after all, is cohesion. This study is by no means the first concerned with the autonomy of literature to meet this difficulty: if I suggest that the series of objections offered above on the part of some of them might be summarized as 'I could wish that you had made your assumptions more explicitly and defended them systematically', then it will be clear that I see such objections in the same light as F.R. Leavis saw those raised to *Revaluation* by René Wellek – objections which Leavis attempted to counter in his essay 'Literary Criticism and Philosophy'.

With this difference: where Leavis felt 'the critic must *guard against* abstracting improperly from what is in front of him and against any premature or irrelevant generalizing'[2] – in effect thus making it a matter of choice for the critic – I find myself unable to offer such generalizations even should I want to. I cannot offer any theoretical description of how it is literature evades or transforms institutional contamination. There is no such a description to be offered. We cannot say how literature 'generally', or 'theoretically', or 'normally', or even 'typically' makes the transformations it does to the claims made upon it by other areas of human knowledge or activity, because literature can only make such transformations uniquely, occasionally, and individually. Literature has a large part of its existence in confronting what Derrida calls institutional contaminations, but it does not confront claims upon its autonomy on abstract, theoretical grounds, nor can such grounds be discovered *ex post facto*.

Of course this amounts to a theory of the transformative effect of literature. But it is not the kind of theory that René Wellek had in mind where *Revaluation* was concerned – and this brings us to the question of the relationship between theory and practice in literary criticism, and how much theory can really be said to achieve, vital as it is. The first point to make is that Leavis' own statements in relation to this question should not be taken altogether at face-value: 'the story put about that Leavis is not interested in "theory"', S.L. Goldberg has suggested, 'strikes me as a myth that Leavis put about himself, and a most unfortunate one.'[3] And he went on:

> If like Leavis we're talking about the tradition of English literary criticism – about what I should insist is an historically deep-rooted cultural practice, a 'form of life' in the sort of Wittgensteinian sense – then you can't do what most contemporary 'theorists' want to: transform it into a rationalistically, deductively-derived, set of methods or approaches. We don't 'approach' literature – like geologists, or even 'study' it like anthropologists; we read it. The notion of 'approaches' suggests that in some sense you stand in a postion to literature and to reading, rather like a surgeon in front of his instruments deciding which of them you're going to use on the patient. And too many courses in 'theory' ... suggest – in fact, positively insist – that we do, or we should, adopt that external, if not instrumental, conception of literature and of reading. Most of the stress on 'interpretation', for instance, seems to me based on that highly dubious presupposition.[4]

We are obviously free to transform the 'form of life' which is to be found in 'the tradition of English literary criticism' 'into a rationalistically, deductively-derived, set of methods or approaches' if we wish. We can graft an 'external, if not instrumental, conception of literature and of reading' onto that 'historically deep-rooted cultural practice'. But is it possible for us to choose our instruments where literature is concerned, or is literature invasive in a more radical sense than we have understood it to be?

Let me come at this another way. In his study of Tolstoy's view of history, Isaiah Berlin concludes that the novelist, despite his scepticism regarding the limitations of human knowledge, did manage to secure, however tenuously, 'a moment of revelation which in some sense explains and reconciles, a theodicy, a justification of what exists and happens, as well as its elucidation'.[5] Moreover, Tolstoy's intellectual position, far from having its basis in 'a yearning for mystical illumination', was in Berlin's view 'scrupulously empirical, rational, tough-minded and realistic'.[6] Tolstoy's theoretical view of intellectual progress in general and history in particular had its origin in what we can only call practice – the practice of a novelist in particular:

> We – sentient creatures – are in part living in a world the con-
> stituents of which we can discover, classify and act upon by ratio-
> nal, scientific, deliberately planned methods; but in part … we are
> immersed and submerged in a medium that, precisely to the degree
> to which we inevitably take it for granted as part of ourselves, we do
> not and cannot observe as if from the outside; cannot identify, mea-
> sure and seek to manipulate; cannot even be wholly aware of, inas-
> much as it enters too intimately into all our experience, is itself too
> closely interwoven with all that we are and do to be lifted out of the
> flow (it *is* the flow) and observed with scientific detachment, as an
> object. It – the medium in which we are – determines our most per-
> manent categories, our standards of truth and falsehood, of reality
> and appearance, of the good and the bad, of the central and the
> peripheral, of the subjective and the objective, of the beautiful and
> the ugly, of movement and rest, of past, present and future, of one
> and many; hence neither these, nor any other explicitly conceived
> categories or concepts can be applied to it – for it is itself but a
> vague name for the totality that includes these categories, these con-
> cepts, the ultimate framework, the basic presuppositions wherewith
> we function.[7]

The reader will recognize the extent to which this passage reformulates
principles considered elsewhere in this study. The flow of intimate
experience Berlin describes in mental life is directly comparable with
'the ebb and flow of the events in the story or poem itself' described by
Dan Jacobson, and 'the medium in which we are' that moulds those
categories we live by is similarly comparable with those 'tacit coefficients' described by Michael Polanyi in Chapter 3. On the negative
side, we might want to register reservations with regard to Berlin's 'ultimate framework' of the same kind registered with regard to the New
Historicists' 'ultimate context' of socio-historical determinism. And it is
not true (to extend the analogy a little further) that we are utterly
'immersed and submerged' in literature, or by literature; that we cannot observe it 'as if from the outside'; 'cannot identify, measure and
seek to manipulate' literature, because it is 'too closely interwoven with
all that we are and do to be lifted out of the flow … and observed with
scientific detachment, as an object'. To adopt such a position *vis-à-vis*
literature (which Berlin does not, of course) would be to annihilate its

autonomy at a stroke: literature's function depends upon its being, in an essential respect, 'an object', for writers as well as readers. Not every object, however, depends for its existence on 'scientific detachment' – which brings us to back to the question of theory and its limitations. It might be worthwhile at this stage to introduce a writer at the furthest possible remove from one like Isaiah Berlin, and one for whom 'scientific detachment' was explicitly a desideratum. For Louis Althusser a work of literature, like any other cultural manifestation, is what he called an Ideological State Apparatus.[8] And in regarding works of literature in this way, Althusser is right. Novels, poems, and plays are certainly the agents of ideology, bourgeois or otherwise. What else could they be? Autonomy, as has been pointed out before, is not independence. Undoubtedly, works of literature are able not only to reflect, illustrate, or synthesize the dominant ideology of their times, but by these means actually to intensify, symbolize, and otherwise reinforce the political unconscious, right across the board. Indeed, literature is able to carry ideological conviction into areas it could have penetrated in no other way: to persuade, mollify, and anaesthetize its audience in ways beyond the politician's or the theorist's (or the author's) wildest dream. Who would have guessed, for example, that novels like *Brideshead Revisited* and *A Room With a View*, albeit in their cinematic new clothes, could in recent years have proved so astonishingly successful among audiences with apparently little or no emotional investment in the British ruling classes of the early twentieth century?

It is unlikely that members of the British ruling classes would themselves have anticipated such a phenomenon. As Althusser points out, ideology is an unreliable political ally at the best of times; its action, he points out, 'can never be purely *instrumental*'. In fact, 'the men who would use an ideology purely as a means of action, as a tool, find that they have been caught by it, implicated by it, just when they are using it and believe themselves to be absolute masters of it.'[9] But still – and here a peculiarly divided note of frustration and evasion enters Althusser's account – ideology remains 'not an aberration or a contingent excrescence of History: it is a structure essential to the historical life of societies. Further, only the existence and recognition of its necessity enable us to act on ideology and transform ideology into *an instrument of deliberate action on history*' ('MH' 232; my italics). It is not the historical over-determination in such a passage that I want to comment upon here, though views like Althusser's have clearly had an influence on New Historicist literary criticism. Nor is it the implication that structures invisible to some are, or can be made, transparent to others.

Least of all do I want to labour the obvious: that to see literature as an Ideological State Apparatus is to curtail its autonomy drastically, not because literature does not serve this function but because it serves so many other functions besides.[10] What is relevant here is Althusser's elision between practice and theory. Like a piece of string, ideology may be pulled (by Marxists) but not pushed (by bourgeois humanists). What is mistakenly regarded as a tool in the hands of some may be made 'an instrument of deliberate action' in those of others. Ideology, Althusser suggests, 'is distinguised from science in that in it the practico-social function is more important than the theoretical function' ('MH' 231).

That we have come a long way from Isaiah Berlin is obvious; but, putting the political differences between the two writers aside, it is clear that their positions have something important in common. Ideology, according to Althusser's account, 'is profoundly *unconscious*, even when it presents itself in a reflected form':

> Ideology is indeed a system of representations, but in the majority of cases these representations have nothing to do with 'consciousness': they are usually images and occasionally concepts, but it is above all as *structures* that they impose on the vast majority of men, not via their 'consciousness'. They are perceived – accepted – suffered cultural objects and they act functionally on men via a process that escapes them. ('MH' 233)

It might seem an act of gross critical irresponsibility to bring Althusser and Tolstoy together in a context such as this. But in fact the Marxist theorist and the novelist-thinker as defined by Isaiah Berlin share some basic intellectual predispositions, though from them they head in entirely different directions. Both believe mankind to be acted upon unconsciously by forces beyond its knowledge or control: what Tolstoy might have called God or History, and Althusser Ideology. Such forces 'act functionally on men via a process that escapes them', as Althusser puts it. When, on Tolstoy's behalf, Isaiah Berlin writes about 'the medium in which we are' which 'determines our most permanent categories, our standards of truth and falsehood, of reality and appearance, of the good and the bad, of the central and the peripheral' and the rest of it, all the while acknowledging that such 'permanent categories' are pretty contingent entities after all, we are clearly close to Althusser's notion of 'the very element and atmosphere' human societies find 'indispensable to their historical respiration and life' ('MH' 232).

It is at this point, where it is strongest, that the comparison breaks down. For the medium Berlin describes as representing Tolstoy's most vital interest (*pace* Tolstoy's own view of his work, needless to say) is quintessentially a matter internal to the individual subject, whereas for Althusser, the individual subject is above all that which is called forth – literally 'hailed and interpellated'[11] – by 'the element and atmosphere' of society, history, and class. But Althusser creates a problem for himself here: for how could an individual subject calling himself a Marxist be called forth by bourgeois ideology? How can theorists lift themselves out of the element and atmosphere in which they have their historical existence? And if they do – as they obviously can – to what extent is that ideological medium really omnipresent, after all? How is it, if ideology operates at the subliminal level, that its 'structure' can even be detected, let alone criticized and transformed 'into an instrument of deliberate action on history'? How is it that whereas no individual can stand with scientific detachment outside the 'flow' or 'the medium which we are' described by Isaiah Berlin, the theorist can, in Archimedean fashion, reflect upon 'the very element and atmosphere' of the society of which he is an anomalous product?

It is the co-existence of contradictions like these that underlies Althusser's trite conclusion where the theory and practice of ideology are concerned. 'Marx's philosophical anti-humanism', he writes,

> does provide an understanding of the necessity of existing ideologies, including humanism. But at the same time, because it is a critical and revolutionary theory, it also provides an understanding of the tactics to be adopted towards them; whether they should be supported, transformed or combated. And Marxists know that there can be no tactics that do not depend on a strategy – and no strategy that does not depend on theory. ('MH' 241)

The problem here is not one relating to Marxism *per se*, but rather to Althusser's understanding of the relation of theory to practice. The tactics–strategy–theory hierarchy is indicative enough. Effectively he asks us to believe that such hierarchical problems disappear in the case of Marxism for no better reason than the fact that the latter is 'a critical and revolutionary theory', as opposed to some non-critical and reactionary alternative. Marxists are able to achieve a scientifically detached, reflective, and theoretical understanding of ideology, in a way others cannot, because (or so the theory goes) they possess a scientifically detached, reflective, and theoretical understanding of everything else: of the meta-structure, so to speak, of which the ideological structure is a sub-set. The problem is that every theory can make the same claim. In essence, the predominance of Althusser's theory depends on a theory: that his is better than anyone else's. In fact the relationships between his various theories and theoretical elements is thoroughly incestuous, and empty references to the dependence of tactics on strategy hardly serve to disguise the fact. (Tactics are determined by strategy, certainly: at least to some extent. But tactical considerations are strategic ones in action and actuality. Neither is given the upper hand.)

Unsurprisingly, there is a similar problem to be found in the work of Althusser's follower, Pierre Macherey. Like Althusser, Macherey makes a basic distinction between traditional bourgeois criticism and its 'harder' Marxist cognate. In Macherey's case this distinction depends on the familiar ambiguity latent in the word 'criticism' itself: 'on the one hand, a gesture of refusal, a denunciation, a hostile judgment; and on the other hand … (*in its more fundamental sense*) the positive knowledge of limits, the study of the conditions and possibilities of an activity.' The former sense of the word, he argues, produces 'the negative judgment of criticism-as-condemnation', or 'criticism as appreciation (the education of taste)'; the latter produces 'the positive knowledge of … criticism-as-explanation', or 'criticism as knowledge ("the science of literary production")'.[12] Needless to say, the two senses of the word find their historical and political avatars without much ceremony. The bourgeois critic is associated with negative, bloody-minded judgementalism, but also with rather more effete qualities like 'appreciation' and 'taste'. Equally inevitably, the Marxist critic is associated with positive, scientific knowledge. The Marxist gets the chicken; the bourgeois gets the feathers.

What is surprising is that Macherey, despite burdening himself with shop-soiled pieces of 'dialectic' like these (positive versus negative, judgement versus knowledge, taste versus science, and the rest), shows himself able to retain an awareness of what is involved in traditional literary criticism. 'There can be no adequate empirical description of the enterprise of criticism', he writes, and goes on to say why not:

> There ought rather to be a rational justification, a demonstration that it can take a specific deductive form, applying an appropriate method to the object under consideration. Obviously, though, neither method

nor object is given *a priori*. They are mutually determining. The method is necessary to construe the object, but the authority of the method is itself derived from the existence of the object. (*TLP* 8)

This is a good summary of the dilemma in which traditional criticism often finds itself when it seeks a theoretical explanation of the kind demanded by writers like Althusser and Macherey (and René Wellek). The problem is related to our ability to see literature as an object, and whether that ability necessarily demands 'scientific detachment'. Althusser and Macherey say yes; Leavis and Goldberg say no. For Macherey, traditional, bourgeois criticism's unwillingness or refusal to take up a posture of scientific detachment boils down to its treating works of literature as objects of consumption rather than production: 'its tendency [that is] to fall into the natural fallacy of empiricism, [and] to treat the work ... as factually given, spontaneously isolated for inspection' (*TLP* 13).

It will be obvious why institutionalist critics are attracted to such a theory: the notion of anything whatsoever being 'spontaneously isolated' is anathema to institutionalism. (No work of literature can ever wriggle free of the slime of history.) But whereas traditional criticism may occasionally have regarded works of literature as spontaneously isolated factual givens, or objects of consumption rather than production, that has never been the essential tenor of its practice, and this study in particular has striven to do exactly what Macherey says traditional criticism cannot do because of its theoretical inadequacy, naïvete, and bad faith. This study has attempted to provide an account of literary production ('the actual conditions of its possibility') without falling either into Marxist scientism about 'laws', or bourgeois empiricist fallacies about factual givens. Traditional criticism does not depend on there being factual givens in the world, labelled *Jane Eyre* or *Paradise Lost*, waiting like so much cattle, 'only to be received, described, and assimilated through the procedures of criticism' (*TLP* 13). But neither does its existence depend on its providing theoretical laws governing the emergence-cum-production of the material it studies. In other words, traditional criticism has been interested in the question of how a work of literature is produced ever since Aristotle; but it has never been able to formulate laws governing such activity without incorporating itself within a prior theory: Marxism, for example, or Aristotelianism. This study has been expressly devoted to the question of 'literary production', as opposed to consumption. But the attempt to answer the question has not allowed me to prescribe theoretical and generally operative laws governing such activity, of the kind Macherey regards as essential; and this in turn suggests that the *kinds* of distinctions by means of which his theory operates, from the simplistic (judgement versus knowledge) to the complex (production versus consumption) are either merely irrelevant to literature, or themselves self-generating and self-sustaining, or both. For this study has been intent on arguing, on a case-by-case basis, that the production and consumption of literature cannot be opposed in this heavy-handed way.

Certainly, works of literature are objects. In some respects, no doubt, they are objects about which we can be scientifically detached in the way Althusser and Macherey suggest the Marxist critic can with respect to ideology and its productions. But it is also true that we cannot 'approach' works of literature without them 'approaching' us, and that we cannot always choose our instruments in the comparatively leisurely way the surgeon or the theorist might.

5.2   What institutionalists say and what they mean

The second objection is at least as radical as the first – more so, if anything. This study has tried to describe and illustrate, in theoretical and practical terms, one principle in particular: the capacity of works of literature to hatch and to generate unexpected patterns of meaning which the author comes to recognize and respond to. Authors may be suffering from delusions when they themselves draw attention to this principle, but certainly there is a large amount of evidence to the effect that they see it at work in what they do. (In Chapter 1 I quoted comments by Henry James, Thomas Mann, Isaac Babel, Nadezhda Mandelstam, and Keats; but here are two more: one from Keats again, 'That which is creative must create itself'; and one from Dickens, 'I don't invent it – really do not – *but see it* and write it down'.) It is this capacity to hatch and generate unexpected patterns of meaning, I have suggested, that allows works of literature to transform institutional or 'contaminatory' pressure and influence.

But what if this principle – putting to one side the value and centrality granted to it by imaginative writers themselves – is insufficient adequately to underwrite a genuine autonomy for literature? Or, to put the point another way, what if critics like Freud and Greenblatt, Hayden White and Richard Rorty, Jerome McGann and Hanna Segal, were quite prepared to accept such a principle, without accepting either that it committed them to the autonomy of literature argued for here or that it necessarily contradicted the critical positions they themselves have adopted? None of them, surely, believes that literature is wholly conta-minated – by history, by psychology, by philosophy; and if there is some freedom for literature of the kind this study argues for, why should that be inconsistent with the work other critics have carried out and the issues to which they have drawn attention?

All of which is well and good: but let me return to two issues out-lined earlier on in this study. A genuine acceptance and understanding of the autonomy of literature, in my view (and in Derrida's view if I have understood him correctly), is much less to do with finding and defending some 'purely literary' trace-element than it is to do with accepting and understanding literature's own activity: its ability actively to hatch and generate and so on. If there is no such activity taking place, then what we have is really not a piece of literature in the full sense of the word. Its literary value will not be its *most* important aspect for either its author or its readers. Its most important aspect will be its relation to 'the actual seedbed of intellectual discus-sion' in Marilyn Butler's priceless phrase, or to Harsnett's *Declaration of Egregious Popish Impostures* (or something similar), or to the depressive position, or to mankind as a storytelling animal. For surely what makes literature worth reading in the first place is that its relation to things of these kinds is *not* what is most important about it: that such rela-tions are subject to certain inner principles of development, unique to each work.

But never mind what Freud or Greenblatt might be prepared to con-cede to literature along these lines: that 'of course' it has the potential to hatch and generate unexpected lines of development, lying along-side its institutional debts and obligations. The fact is that as a general matter of fact such writers concede no such thing, and that the overall effect of their work is substantially to downgrade this capacity in litera-ture. No matter how many times poems demonstrate that the gramma-tological mastercode overrides, overwrites, and otherwise destabilizes the documentary one, Jerome McGann still insists that we positi-vely must reconstitute the 'originally evoked context' if we wish to make any sense of the work whatever. ('There is no alternative', wrote F.W. Bateson, 'except to invent the meanings ourselves' – as if the only condition preventing the random invention of meaning is historical context, never mind what a poem itself may allow or disallow.) Despite finding novelists better servants of human liberty than philosophers, Richard Rorty still argues that we should 'work ourselves out of our jobs by conscientiously blurring the literature–philosophy distinction and promoting the idea of a seamless, undifferentiated "general text" '. Despite spending so much time on Shakespeare, Stephen Greenblatt still anticipates 'a salutary return of the literary text to the condition of all other texts'. (Historians, as Hayden White puts it, 'must employ the same strategies of linguistic figuration used by imaginative writers'.) 'We are perfectly aware that very many imaginative writings are far removed from the model of the naive day-dream', Freud wrote; '*and yet* [my italics] I cannot suppress the suspicion that even the most extreme deviations from that model could be linked with it through an uninterrupted series of transitional cases.' (A 'piece of creative writing', it follows, 'like a day-dream, is a continuation of, and a substitute for, what was once the play of childhood'.) What Freud says about 'suppressing suspicions', needless to say, is a polite fiction: a diplomatic nod to the autonomy of literature. He has no intention of suppressing his suspicions in this regard: he would not dream of suppressing them; he is bent on our acknowledging their validity. For Hanna Segal, too, writers merely face and express their depression: the act of writing does not make any more decisive a contribution than that.

For critics holding these kinds of views to turn around and say that 'of course' literature also possesses more active, more transformative, more transgressive capacities than their accounts taken in isolation would suggest, seems to me to be disingenuous. It is certainly true that some of the critics I have discussed are more sophisticated than others, more able to intimate and to realize alternative ways of seeing the issue. Stephen Greenblatt is to Jerome McGann much as Hanna Segal is to Freud, Charles Taylor to Richard Rorty, or Paul Ricoeur to Hayden White. But they all in fact on occasion and repeatedly make sweeping or manifestly reductive claims on the basis of evidently limited premises and preconceptions: from Hayden White's absolute determination to prove that there is no worthwhile distinction to be made between the writing of history and the writing of literature, to Martha Nussbaum's conversion of fiction to a socially sanctioned mode of Aristotelian analysis. No one – not even in this day and age – goes to see *King Lear* because of its historical embeddedness, or reads Byron's *Don Juan* because it is 'fundamentally an autobiographical poem which comments upon and interprets the course of European history between 1787 and 1824':[13] yet to read Greenblatt and McGann is strongly to get the impression that these are the primary critical issues presented by such works: in short that 'cultural poetics' – as Hillis Miller suggested in the MLA address quoted in the Introduction – have replaced 'dramatic poetics' as the driving force and focus of interest in literature.

So if such writers were explicitly to acknowledge the capacity of literature to 'create itself', in Keats' phrase, we would have to wonder if they had considered all the implications for the positions they hold. If the grammatological mastercode overrides the documentary one, that has implications for the latter's centrality. There may *not* be an uninterrupted series of transitional cases between imaginative writing and naïve day dreams. *Don Juan* may *not* be fundamentally a biographical poem interpretive of European history. The strategies of linguistic figuration used by imaginative writers may be quite different from those used by historians or philosophers, and there may be no 'general text' of the kind anticipated by Rorty and Greenblatt.

The notion of autonomy I am arguing for here is not the least bit massive or monolithic: quite the reverse, as I hope my examples have shown. But then neither is it a matter of indifference. To displace contamination by a hair's breadth is enough to transform it out of recognition: as readers of Swift or Pirandello or Chaucer or Andrei Sinyavsky will recognize. But once it is displaced the effect is decisive. In the end the critics I have discussed in this book tend, whether they know it or not, to see literature as a passive thing. (And this is just as true, I am sorry to say, of a person as well-intentioned and well-read as Martha Nussbaum as it is true of Hayden White.) Seeing it as such, no acknowledgement on their part of literature's own activity, however well-meant and sincere, can be altogether meaningful, because if literature is active in anything like the way I have tried to outline then the *most* important reasons for our continuing to take an interest in it lie in quite other areas than the ones indicated by the critics I have discussed.

There is a fallacy of misplaced – or myopic – interest, then, to which institutionalist readers are remarkably prone. But it is also true that an individual work of literature is itself a source of interest: itself a seedbed. *Jane Eyre* may have existed in near relation to the actual seedbed of intellectual discussion in mid nineteenth-century England; it may be a form of 'moral commentary', comparable to Diderot or Kierkegaard; it may even be a continuation of and substitute for the play of childhood, though that would more obviously be true of Brontë's rather stunted juvenilia than it is of *Jane Eyre*. It may be true that the dangerous supplement means that nothing said in the novel can be in identical relation to anything outside it and that as a direct result it can never achieve moral, ontological, or epistemological closure, that it uses strategies of linguistic figuration which other story-telling animals (like historians) also habitually employ, that in it Brontë faced and expressed her depression, that it is an Aristotelian enquiry into the richness and diversity of the positive commitments of a good person living in a world of uncontrolled happening, and so on. But the *most* important thing about the book – for Charlotte Brontë even more than for us her readers – is that it constitutes an experience in itself: shattering, confusing, exasperating, enthralling, humiliating, building up and laying waste to the innumerable influences converging on it, undoing and enforcing the categories and hierarchies of everyday understanding that underpin it only when and if it does become an experience in itself, and only by doing so becoming one. It is an experience that subordinates all the factors listed above to the ebb and flow of the events in the story itself. When a critic, or a school, or a mode or mood of criticism goes further than merely presenting and pursuing a special interest, but in doing so denies such processes – whether wittingly or otherwise, implicitly or explicitly, by intention or in effect – they have arrested the interest of literature at its source. That having been done the critic discovers a kind of *terra nullius*. Anything can be done there, and any line of enquiry can swell to dominate the horizon, but the context which gives such things real meaning and substance is absent. Anything can be said about the body in front of you, but nothing you can say will bring it back to life.

5.3 Who, we? Effects on readers

Objection number three is best summarized by the Derridean question: 'who, we?'[14] That is to say, the objection involves the common use by traditional literary critics of the first person plural in formulating literary arguments. An instance was provided in Chapter 2, where *Lolita* came under discussion. I quoted a passage from the novel in which Humbert Humbert momentarily considers allowing Lolita to fall out of his clutches and offering her, instead of 1001 nights in cheap motels, 'a sound education, a healthy and happy childhood, a clean home', and the rest. I went on:

> We can recognize easily enough how disappointed we should be as readers if Humbert obeyed this momentary instinct, abandoned his plot on Lolita's innocence, and transformed himself into a model father. We should surely accuse the novelist of arousing expectations he has no intention of satisfying. And in feeling this – in feeling that to let Lolita go now would be a complete anti-climax – we have … joined the circle of paedophilic child-abusers for whom this

novel offers pornographic stimulation of the most reprehensible and disgusting kind. For we can be fairly sure ...

For readers to ask 'who, we?' of such a passage, or 'on whose behalf do you imagine you are talking here?', suggests one thing straight away. The ubiquitous use of 'we', the argument might run, is based on the critic's assumption that all readers would respond in the same way to *Lolita* were they to encounter it, and that all Nabokov's readers (including Nabokov himself) are or would become 'complicit in Humbert's pursuit of his nymphet – wholly, intently, excitedly': the suggestion being that the novel appeals to some quality latent in each and every human being, irrespective of race, age, gender, sexual orientation, etc., etc. A large part of traditional literary criticism (so the argument might continue) depends upon the implicit belief in, or sometimes insistence upon, inherent qualities of this kind – which is what makes it both so collusive and so surreptitiously imperialistic, ideologically speaking.

Such an assumption, it is argued, reveals its falsity and partiality the moment it is reflected upon. Not many children of Lolita's age are likely to read *Lolita*, let alone a bit of criticism devoted to it. But if they did, they would surely demur as emphatically as they could from those acts of readerly complicity described in Chapter 2. Similarly, those readers who have been victims of child abuse might strongly deny any such implicit alliance or sense of fraternity on their part with the repulsive Humbert. Women, well aware of patriarchal predation on females of whatever age, and more sensitive to questions of sexual coercion than men can ever be, perhaps, might also argue that far from being complicit with Humbert in the way I have described they observe the unfolding of the narrative with an entirely different set of emotions and allegiancies.

Two points about the first-person plural in criticism arise immediately and can themselves be illustrated by two quotations. First, that traditional literary critics have often felt that their use of 'we' is a moral imperative where their work is concerned. In closing his biography of Thomas Gray, for example, Samuel Johnson has this to say:

> In the character of his *Elegy* I rejoice to concur with the common reader; for by the common sense of readers uncorrupted with literary prejudices, after all the refinements of subtilty and the dogmatism of learning, must be finally decided all claim to poetical honours.[15]

Second, traditional criticism has fully understood that the interests and priorities of such an audience have never been and can never be defined for good and all; that they are subject to historical change not merely in the sense of being supplemented but of being utterly transformed:

> the collaborators are individuals who are interested in literature, convinced that it matters, and intelligent about it, and the collaboration is an interplay of personal judgments. Where the interest is widely enough spread, the outcome of the interplay will be something approaching a consensus as to what English Literature...is – for us....The 'for us' is of course a crucial emphasis. Here it leads immediately to the observation that 'we' shall not be naïve enough to suppose ourselves representative in any final way. As the inner sense of stress, tension and human need changes, English Literature changes – not merely (I mean) by accretion; the contour map, the chart of organic structure, changes.[16]

But the two aspects highlighted by Johnson and Leavis themselves beg the question: for what is the common reader, after all, and how can an inner sense of human need change if a large number of white, male, bourgeois literary critics are packing the committee? What I want to suggest is that the 'we' habitually used by traditional literary criticism is a complex gesture towards a consensus about literature, certainly, but also something else: a recognition that each work of literature itself does more than predicate or assume an audience; it creates an audience by exactly the same dialectical means as those it employs to surprise its author.

To reiterate a passage quoted in Chapter 1:

> The 'truth' of the work lies in its undoing of the hierarchies or categories of our everyday understanding; it offers us a truth not of assertion but of process, of experience, of contestation. Thus it undoes, among many other prepossessions, our ordinary notions of what living or effective truth is and how it is recognised.[17]

If this is true for the writer it is true for the reader. If 'the internal action or plot of the story or poem, in all its manifestations, contains, reveals, and indeed in large part *is* the drama of the writer's relationship to his unfolding conception', then 'one of the things we do when we read the work is enact on our side an analogous drama: the drama of our relationship to what has been [and what is being] unfolded.'[18] And drama is the right word, because the work of literature does not seek merely to establish a relationship of any kind whatever with its readers; it establishes a relationship with them which is analogous to the relationship it establishes with its author, and which is analogous, in fact, to the relationship typically found between dramatic centres of consciousness within works of literature themselves. In other words, works of literature seek to establish holistic, *gestalt*, human relationships (however partial, however contingent, and however fleeting) both internally and externally.

This preamble is necessary for a point best illustrated by the chapter on reading in a book of Jonathan Culler's. In *On Deconstruction*, Culler turns quite explicitly to the 'who, we?' question as I have adapted it. He does not discuss *Lolita* and the particular issues that novel raises, but he does bring up similar questions where what he calls 'reading as a woman' is concerned. There are, he believes, three phases or 'moments' in feminist criticism: the first, where women's experience is set alongside men's by way of a supplement (women seeing things in *Jane Eyre*, for example, that men have typically missed, or women rediscovering neglected works by women authors); the second where women acknowledge that they, too, have 'missed' aspects of the female literary heritage because they have been alienated from their own experience by the ubiquity of patriarchal attitudes; and the third, most radical, phase where women entirely reject and disown 'the system of concepts or procedures of male criticism' as being 'in complicity with the preservation of male authority'.[19] The first of these phases is clear enough, whereas the third is one in which the male critic can hardly claim competence – except to serve as an example of course. The second phase has the most immediate implications for the 'who, we?' question and its relation to the autonomy of literature, and it is this phase that I want to discuss here.

Culler has a test case just like *Lolita*. His is the opening chapter of *The Mayor of Casterbridge*, where 'the drunken Michael Henchard sells his wife and infant daughter to a sailor for five guineas at a country fair' (*OD* 43). It seems obvious that a woman reader will react differently to a male one presented with the same passage, though Culler in fact says more than this. It is his belief that 'the reader's *experience*', and not merely their measurable, critical reaction (elicited by discussion, say, or personal reflection), will be different. But this conclusion is contradicted by feminist criticism itself in its second phase. Women readers may read in a state of false consciousness: women, as Culler himself puts it, 'can read, and have read, as men' (*OD* 49). So powerful, so ubiquitous, and so unquestioned are patriarchal attitudes in most literature (let alone canonical literature like Hardy's novels), that women find themselves actually disavowing their gender and falling in with those attitudes out of habit and indoctrination. 'The most insidious oppression', Culler points out, 'alienates a group from its own interests as a group and encourages it to identify with the interests of the oppressors, so that political struggles must first awaken a group to its interests and its "experience"' (*OD* 50). And this is one of the tasks feminist criticism has set itself in its second phase: 'through the postulate of a woman reader, to bring about a new experience of reading and to make readers – men and women – question the literary and political assumptions on which their reading has been based' (*OD* 51).

However desirable the end the difficulty of bringing it about is clear. Feminist critics are going to have problems with this postulated woman reader that are directly comparable with those presented by the postulated 'general reader' belonging to Samuel Johnson and others. (What about the lesbian woman reader, or the black one?) But they also add a new problem all their own. On the one hand, 'the problem is precisely that women have not been reading as women' (*OD* 51) when they turn up *The Mayor of Casterbridge*, say, or *Madame Bovary*. On the other, they must simply be 'awakened'. But can readers be awakened while they have their noses in books? Can a 'new experience of reading' be brought about not just in terms of 'reaction', but in terms of the very 'experience' itself?

Two related sets of points arise. The first is that 'women can read, and have read, as men', not only because of the omnipresence of patriarchalism, but also because that omnipresence is focused and distilled by the reading in hand. In just the same way the possibility must exist that men can read and have read as women, or that all of us, men and women both, have read *Lolita* as paedophilic child-abusers, because that novel itself demands to be read in such a fashion (to a certain extent at least). Like *The Mayor of Casterbridge*, *Lolita*, by virtue of 'our relationship to what has been unfolded' in it, is able to undo the hierarchies or categories of our everyday understanding just far enough to allow us to partake in things we might otherwise reject immediately. Whatever our waking reason and reflection may say about Humbert's pursuit of Lolita, we really would be disappointed and baffled if he were to abandon that pursuit and transform himself into a model father. In exactly the same way, such is our interest in allowing Hardy to initiate and maintain his narrative – such is our contribution to and complicity in that process – that we will accept acts of connubial brutality that are otherwise unthinkable. Individual works of literature have the capacity to 'create' or elicit the readers they need by breaking down orientations of every conceivable kind. This is a very simple idea, and hardly a new one, but it is of great importance to the autonomy of literature.

The evidence I want to introduce in support of this idea is not of a positive kind; nor does it come from an altogether unimpeachable source, since Jonathan Culler is a male. But in fact what I have to say is less to do with feminism than with the critical attitude Culler himself adopts in his account of reading (though feminist and other critics may adopt the same attitude, and indeed they frequently do). What is strange is that Culler, who uses his book to hand out demerits for lack of literary sophistication left, right and centre – to Irving Howe, Cleanth Brooks, and Norman Mailer, but also to Geoffrey Hartman, Stanley Fish, and Frank Lentricchia – should himself, despite his vantage point in deconstruction, retain so homespun a theory of readership. In taking a new reading response for a new reading experience, for example, he tends to make two kinds of points. First, he uses a great many active verbs in describing the new, desirable, and politically self-conscious style of reading he prefers; verbs which are active but also instrumental: 'to read as a woman is to *avoid* reading as a man, to *identify* the specific defenses and distortions of male readings and *provide correctives*'; the woman reader must '*escape the limitations* of male readings … by *developing questions and perspectives* which would enable a woman to read as a woman'; to achieve this 'is not to repeat an identity or an experience that is given but to *play a role she constructs* with reference to her identity as a woman'.[20] The active verbs are chosen to suggest ways (or 'moves' or 'reading strategies') in which readers might overcome the false consciousness works of literature instil. But these active verbs are what a psychologist would call compensatory. Such terminology attempts to achieve critically, by second order consent, what is virtually impossible to achieve as a matter of first-hand experience. Or to put it the other way, and to borrow Goldberg's expression, it is 'rather like a surgeon in front of his instruments deciding which of them you're going to use on the patient'. If the first chapter of *The Mayor of Casterbridge* requires us to enter into Henchard's peculiar auction, enter it we will, though we may rationalize our complicity (or reject it) at leisure after the event. Moreover, alarming as it may sound, our identities as women, men, or anything else, appear to play a very small role in this process.

The second strand to Culler's argument is closely related to this last point. In the second phase of feminist criticism, he suggests, 'the problem is precisely that women are led to identify with male characters, against their own interests as women'. Confronting generically misogynist classic American fiction, from 'The Legend of Sleepy Hollow' to *Huckleberry Finn* and beyond, the woman reader 'is powerfully impelled by the structure of the novel to identify with a hero who makes women the enemy'. This time the emphasis is entirely different. Instead of a rousing list of active verbs, calling upon the woman reader to escape, provide, develop, construct, and so forth, we encounter an equally simplistic idea of the reader's relationship to a work of literature: identification. This time the reader is essentially *passive*; it is 'the structure of the novel' that has its wicked way on women readers of American fiction. I would not like to go so far as to say that identification never takes place in literature, but I think it is much rarer than some critics think, and infinitely less important. In any event, we are going to need a much more sophisticated term than this to describe what actually takes place in reading. On 'Rip van Winkle' I cannot comment; but certainly any reader who *identifies* with either Hardy's Henchard or Nabokov's Humbert has started off on the wrong foot where either novel is concerned. Men and women readers alike find themselves, at various times and in varying degrees, complicit with characters like these, certainly; but this neither requires nor implies identification. On the contrary, our complicity may and surely does make us loathe Henchard and Humbert more. Moreover, if, as Dan Jacobson suggests, the various hierarchies, categories, prepossessions, and ordinary notions which we carry around internalized within us (including categories of gender) experience a degree of lability in encountering Henchard, then what grounds for identification are there? Who or what could be said to be identifying with who in such a case? What 'selfhood' is it that 'defines itself' in opposition to another? And in what kinds of opposition? What role is it we can construct with reference to our identity? And if a woman can read as a man, in what sense can she be said to 'identify against herself' in the act of reading? Who, we, indeed?

The reader, then, like every other element associated with literature, is transformed by contact with it. We are not free to act upon a text (identify, escape, provide, develop, construct, etc.) without its acting upon us in kind. We do not, to quote Sam Goldberg again, approach literature like geologists, or even study it like anthropologists: we read it. Nor are the everyday categories we bring to the encounter so stable, or so passively inert, as to provide means for 'identification'. In Chapter 2 I discussed Emily Brontë's prickly attitude to story-telling in general and naïve acts of identification in particular. Her sister Charlotte came at the issue from the other side of the coin, but she, too, knew that certain aspects of fiction are not there to be turned on and off at the reader's convenience:

> When authors write best, or at least, when they write most fluently, an influence seems to waken in them which becomes their master, which will have its own way, putting out of view all behests but its own, dictating certain words, and insisting on their being used, whether vehement or measured in their nature; new moulding characters, giving unthought-of turns to incidents, rejecting carefully elaborated old ideas, and suddenly creating and adopting new ones. Is it not so? And should we try to counteract this influence? *Can we indeed counteract it?*[21]

To borrow Michael Riffaterre's phrase, works of literature do their best to 'compel reader responses' from us,[22] and so successful are they, as a rule, that critics can as often as not begin to assume, however tentatively, the existence of invisible readers who are similarly compelled. It is perfectly in order for Jonathan Culler and for feminist critics to ask questions like 'how should we read? what kind of reading experience can we imagine or produce? what would it be to read "as a woman"?' (*OD* 63). But these questions cannot be posed in a vacuum, or at our critical, reflective leisure. Moreover, we really address them not to ourselves at all, but to the works of literature in whose hands the answers actually lie.

5.4   Derrida again

The second 'unfriendly' objection, I fear, cannot be answered to anybody's satisfaction. Some readers will feel that this study is 'not good enough on the Theory': that it arises, demonstrably, from insufficient reading and knowledge in this area. This charge is one I can never rebut by assertion. Clearly, there are entire avenues of thought not so much as looked at here. On the other hand, I do not think that extra consideration of my American Aristotelians, or of the New Historicists, or of Hayden White and Paul Ricoeur, would lead to startling revelations about their attitude towards literature – though it is possible I am mistaken. But two intellectual figures have been discussed here who are on an entirely different plane from writers like those. Derrida and Freud could each demand a lifetime's study, and I am well aware that

I have insufficient expertise to say anything final about them. About Freud I think I have said as much as I can; but there are some important loose ends regarding Derrida that I am aware of, and so it might be best to end, as I began, with him. I want to suggest, in short, that if I am not good enough on the theory then Derrida (on one particular occasion at least: Joyce's *Ulysses*) is far from being good enough on those aspects of literature which resist theoretical determination.

I said in Chapter 1 that this study, like Derrida's work in general, laid some claim to being non-idealist. I said that literature was inexplicable in idealist terms; that its being so was what made Derrida's account of it so valuable; that 'the "I-don't-understand-therefore-it's-irrational-non-analytic-magical-illogical-perverse-seductive-diabolical" that has always signed the triumph of the old obscurantism' was something I wanted to avoid; that Derrida and I had a lot in common, indeed; that I, too, was interested in saying otherwise; and so forth.

Well: those who wish to turn the page on philosophy only end up doing philosophy badly. My claiming to avoid metaphysical-cum-oppositional-cum-idealistic modes of thought and habits of argument was exploded as a joke when I made such extensive use, on two occasions, of R.G. Collingwood, who is an idealist philosopher almost by definition. But even leaving Collingwood aside, is not the entire study devoted to the oppositional demarcation of literature from other institutional spheres?

I hope any reader will have seen that the position is not quite as simple as that. The argument presented here for literature's possession of its own activity has never involved the suggestion that institutional contamination does not exist. On the contrary, I have said that literature thrives on such contamination, and in that meeting and transforming it in fact is the very activity to which I refer. The alacrity with which literature meets contamination – positively goes out looking for it, indeed – is the fact that makes the entire purist proper/contaminant opposition an empty one, in my view, just as it was for Derrida. I have never suggested that because literature initiates a unique and irreplaceable dialogue with writers and readers about itself that such a dialogue necessarily either replaces or subordinates the dialogue it sustains with its philosophical, psychological, and historical context.

But I have in the end committed myself to a difference in kind and not a difference in degree between literature and history. Following Henry James I have argued that 'the reporter, however philosophic, has one law, and the originator, however substantially fed, has another', and that, *pace* Hayden White and Paul Ricoeur, 'the two laws can with no sort of harmony or congruity make ... a common household.'[23] Such a commitment is not only oppositional and idealistic in certain respects, it is also a commitment Derrida is explicitly asking his readers to reconsider philosophically, historically, critically, and ontologically:

> If I say, for instance, there is no difference of kind between difference of kind and difference of degree, what consequences will you draw out of that? You can draw two types of conclusion. First, that there are *only* differences of kind, since there is no difference of kind between difference of kind and difference of degree. So there *are* differences of kind, which would contradict the hypothesis. Second, that there are *only* differences of degree, since there is no difference of kind between difference of kind and difference of degree – which reproduces the previous contradiction. This is not a game. What I call 'differance' is precisely an attempt to avoid, or to overcome, this classical opposition between difference of kind and difference of degree. Differance is *at the same time* difference of kind and difference of degree – which means that it is neither one nor the other. Differance 'is' a difference (discontinuity, alterity, heterogeneity) *and also* the possibility and necessity of an economy (relay, delegation, signification, mediation, 'supplement', reappropriation) of the other as such: difference and in-difference with and without dialectics. Economy of the other, economy of the same. Let's take an example. When one says that the difference between nature and culture is not what philosophers think it is, a difference of kind (which implies a discontinuity), one implies that with some relays, delays, mediations, etc., there is *some* continuity – a continuity which is not a homogeneity, since there are different structures (which doesn't mean that the structural difference is a difference in essence, in the classical metaphysical sense). So when, for instance, one questions, and at a fundamental level, the concept or value of essence and its correlates such as attributes or accidents or qualities, and the concept of presence, which is implied in the concept of essence, then one deconstructs the *opposition* of essence and non-essence (that is, degree, etc.), and one has to reconsider the whole logic to which one refers in opposing difference of degree and difference in essence. And this is not a game, a formal game, because it has very concrete consequences in everything we analyse – in biology, in politics, in literature, and so on. Very briefly speaking, each time I work on anything, the first thing I have to acknowledge is that I'm not satisfied with a difference of kind and a difference of degree. And the logic of

the supplement, the logic of the *pharmakon*, the logic of the hymen, is each time a way of disturbing the order of this opposition. A supplement is at the same time something you add as simply something more, another degree, *and* something which reveals a lack in the essence, in the integrity of an entity, so what I call the logic of the supplement is the principle of disorder at work in this very opposition. That's what I'm doing all the time, and it's not what *I* am doing, it is the principle of contamination or disorder which is at work everywhere; and the firm distinction between difference of kind and difference of degree is a reaction, a terrible reaction, in order to master this principle of disorder. If you can really separate difference of kind and difference of degree then you can master everything.[24]

This is not a game; I am not seeking to overcome the objection that I have not read enough Derrida by ostentatiously introducing the longest quotation I could find. Nor do I even think there is much to add to this impressive statement, in which there is neither one word too many or too few. Derrida's stated aim of reaching 'an additional or alternative dimension beyond philosophy and literature'[25] or beyond the kind of thinking implied in such an opposition, could hardly be made clearer. I can only suggest first, that this study lays no claim to 'mastering' the difference between either literature and, say, history, or the difference between differences of kind and degree; my view is that literature and history confront the same world, only react in different ways to that encounter. Second, that this study may have spoken of the 'different structures' to be found in literature and history as if they *were* differences in essence. It seems I am both profoundly in agreement with Derrida and profoundly in disagreement with him. '[I]f you want to speak of someone, and especially if you want to condemn him in totality, without qualification and without appeal, read, read as much and as thoroughly as possible, with vigilance and honesty.'[26] I have not wished to condemn Derrida at all, least of all without qualification and without appeal. 'Honest' I think I have been; but be that as it may, it is hard for any reader to be as thorough or as vigilant as his work demands.

'In turning from philosophical questions (about differences of kind and differences of degree) to literary–critical ones I feel on firmer ground.' That is how I might have started this paragraph; and that is how I must start it despite Derrida's warnings about the intellectual oppositions such a statement could be said to take for granted.

The summary of Derrida's position I have just quoted is an explicit and valuable one. Nor is it by any means the only passage of particular help and interest to traditional literary theory:

> Why is the *figure of the biodegradable* so provocative? Both useful, from a heuristic point of view, but essentially limited in its relevance? In the most general and novel sense of this term, a *text* must be '(bio)degradable' in order to nourish the 'living' culture, memory, tradition. To the extent to which it has some sense, makes sense, then its 'content' irrigates the milieu of this tradition and its 'formal' identity is dissolved. And by formal identity, one may understand here all the 'signifiers,' including the title and the name of one or more presumed signatories. And yet, to enrich the 'organic' soil of the said culture, it must also resist it, contest it, question and criticize it enough (dare I say deconstruct it?) and thus it must not be assimilable ([bio]degradable, if you like). Or at least, it must be assimilated as unassimilable, kept in reserve, unforgettable because irreceivable, capable of inducing meaning without being exhausted by meaning, incomprehensibly elliptical, secret. What is it in a 'great' work, let's say of Plato, Shakespeare, Hugo, Mallarmé, James, Joyce, Kafka, Heidegger, Benjamin, Blanchot, Celan, that resists erosion? What is it that, far from being exhausted in amnesia, increases its reserve to the very extent to which one draws from it, as if expenditure augmented the capital? This very thing, this singular event that, enriching the meaning and accumulating memory, is nevertheless not to be reduced to a totality or that always exceeds interpretation. What resists immediate degradation is this very thing, the text or in the text, which is no longer on the order of meaning and which joins the universal wealth of the 'message' to unintelligible singularity, finally unreadable (if reading means to understand and to learn to know), of a trace or a signature. The irreplaceable singularity, the event of signature, is not to be summed up in a patronymic name, because it is the work itself. The 'proper name' in question – which has no meaning and is not a concept – is not to be reduced to the appellation of civil status. What is more, it is proper to nothing and to no one, reappropriable by nothing and by no one, not even by the presumed bearer. It is this singular impropriety that permits it to resist degradation – never forever, but for a long time. Enigmatic kinship between waste … and the 'masterpiece.'[27]

Again, I can have nothing to add to such a passage except by way of commendation. That each work of literature is a 'singular impropriety' seems to me both a good joke and a statement of fact. But why is it then that when Derrida turns to such singular improprieties his response is often a disappointing one? For that is what his pieces of work on individual works of literature seem to me. In the previous section I criticized Jonathan Culler for taking too simple-minded an approach to the matter of readers and gender. Derrida addresses the issue in similar terms. 'There must be refinements,' he argues,

> both around the concept or the law of 'phallocentrism' and in the possible plurality of readings of works that remain singular. At the moment we are in a slightly 'crude' and heavy-handed phase of the question. In polemical argument, there is too much confidence in the assumed identities of the signatories, in the very concept of sexual identity, things are dealt with too generally, as if a text were this or that, in a homogenous way, for this or that, without taking account what it is in the status or the very structure of a literary work – I would rather say in the paradoxes of its *economy* – which ought to discourage these simplistic notions.[28]

Here a claim is made which moves from the theoretical sphere to that of the 'absolutely singular performance': towards 'the very structure of a literary work'. But Derrida often does not appear interested in the economies of individual works of literature. (Or, rather, as I intimated in Chapter 1, he seems interested only in certain aspects of such economies: their dependence on other economies, above all.) He has said of himself as a younger man that 'I was interested by the possibility of fiction, by fictionality, but I must confess that deep down I have probably never drawn great enjoyment from fiction, from reading novels, for example, beyond the pleasure taken in analyzing the play of writing, or else certain naive movements of identification.'[29] It is this preponderance of the theoretical generalization over the absolutely singular performance that I have in mind. Only a critic more concerned with fiction*ality* than with fiction, it seems to me, could assume that 'the play of writing' is some divorceable and abstractable element in literature, and could be content with Jonathan Culler-style 'naive movements of identification'.

It is hard to see how a critic capable of the passage from 'Biodegradables' quoted above could have so little to say, in the end, about *Ulysses*, for example. In 1984 Derrida was invited to speak at the Ninth International James Joyce Symposium in Frankfurt; the result was a long and digressive paper (which his editor gallantly suggests mimes Joyce's own fictional procedure), 'Ulysses Gramaphone: Hear Say Yes in Joyce'.[30] The paper had its origin in an issue no reader of Joyce's novel could regard as marginal or unimportant: the ultimate meeting of Stephen and Bloom, which is the key-stone of the narrative, is clearly both a coincidence and an event planned and orchestrated by Joyce himself. Moreover, this is how *Ulysses* itself depicts the meeting of the two men: we are to recognize it as both sheer serendipity (to Stephen and Bloom themselves) and sheer necessity (to us and to Joyce, now that we know each of the characters better than he knows himself). 'With Joyce', as Derrida puts it,

> luck is always taken in hand by the law, by meaning, by the program, according to the overdetermination of figures and ruses. And yet the chance nature of meetings, the randomness of coincidences lends itself to being affirmed, accepted, yes, even approved in all their fallings-out. In all their fallings-out, that is to say, in all the genealogical chances that set adrift the notion of legitimate filiation in *Ulysses* and no doubt elsewhere. ('UG' 258)

Derrida then goes on to find in the personal history of his involvement with the Frankfurt conference a multiplied instance of the apparent randomness of coincidence. The paper is in part concerned with the word 'yes' in *Ulysses*; some time before delivering it Derrida found, in Ohio (itself mentioned in *Ulysses*), a brand of yoghurt called YES, with the fetching slogan, 'Bet You Can't Say No to Yes'. Tokyo is also mentioned in *Ulysses*, and Derrida had been there, too, while drafting the paper. Looking for postcards (they, too, form one of the themes of his discussion) he finds himself staring at two books on a newsagent's shelf: *16 Ways to Avoid Saying No*, and *Never Take Yes for an Answer*. Stranger yet, when Jean-Michel Rabaté, Derrida's contact at the Frankfurt conference, asked him over the phone for the title of his future talk it transpired that the one Derrida spontaneously chose bore a striking similarity to the title of a chapter in Rabaté's new book – about Joyce, needless to say.

These are funny instances of something profound about *Ulysses*, and instances of something about which our feelings are ambivalent: the novel's encyclopedism, summed up by Joyce's famous comment that his ingenuity had left incidents, allusions, echoes and assorted red herrings within the book which would 'keep the professors busy for centuries'. There are plenty of other imaginative authors who absorb an enormous amount of academic interest; none (except Shakespeare and, more puzzlingly, Samuel Beckett) on anything like the scale of James Joyce. Where Joyce is concerned there is what Derrida calls a 'declared project of keeping generations of university scholars at work for centuries of babelian edification' ('UG' 280). And that is no coincidence, but itself the direct result of something in Joyce, and in *Ulysses* in particular. The 'declared project' is Joyce's own, not simply that of his tireless interpreters. The conference Derrida addressed represented, he said, a research institution 'prepared to use not only means of transport, of communication, of organizational programming allowing an accelerated capitalization, a crazy accumulation of interest in terms of knowledge blocked in Joyce's name … but also modes of archivization and consultation of data unheard of' where other famous authors are concerned ('UG' 280–1). The occasion at Frankfurt was an intimidating one, therefore, not simply because Derrida was an outsider, nor because his Joycean competence was at a lower level than that of his audience, but as a result of a peculiarly knowing kind of foreknowledge on Joyce's own part. 'Joyce experts', he suggested, 'are the representatives as well as the effects of the most powerful project for programming over the centuries the totality of research in the onto-logico-encyclopedic field, all the while commemorating his own, proper signature.' 'The effects of his preprogramming, you know better than I,' he told his audience, 'are admirable and terrifying, and sometimes of intolerable violence.'

> One of them has the following form: nothing can be invented *on the subject* of Joyce. Everything we can say about *Ulysses*, for example, has already been anticipated, including … the scene about academic competence and the ingenuity of metadiscourse. We are caught in this net. All the gestures made in the attempt to take the initiative of a movement are found to be already announced in an overpotentialized text that will remind you, at a given moment, that you are captive in a network of language, writing, knowledge, and *even narration*. ('UG' 281)

Once is chance; twice is coincidence; the third time (as the Mafia say) is enemy action. Just as everything involved in Derrida's coming to speak at Frankfurt (from some yoghurt in Ohio to some management primers in a Tokyo newsagent) 'was already pre-dicted and pre-narrated' by what he calls 'a hypermnesic machine', so everything said and done by the Joyce institution 'has been signed in advance' by the inscrutable, omniscient novelist ('UG' 281). What looks like chance is revealed to be necessity. Like Bloom and Stephen themselves, 'We are caught in this net' – or so it appears. So it is that Derrida seeks to hoist the Joyce institution on its own petard: it, too, is the victim of both necessity and chance:

> Once one recognizes that, in principle, in *Ulysses* the virtual totality of experience – of meaning, of history, of the symbolic, of languages, and of writings, the great cycle and the great encyclopedia of cultures, scenes, and affects, in short, the sum total of all sum totals – tends to unfold itself and reconstitute itself by playing out all its possible combinations, with a writing that seeks to occupy all the spaces, well, the totalizing hermeneutic that makes up the task of a worldwide and eternal institution of Joyce studies will find itself confronted with what I hesitatingly call a dominant effect, a *Stimmung* or a *pathos* ... ('UG' 291)

This dominant effect of the Joyce-institution will be familiar to anyone who takes to reading about *Ulysses* as well as in it. The guides, the keys, the companions, the gazetteers, the explicatory diagrams and tables – not to mention the biographical studies, monographs, exegetical notes, conference papers, and symposia by the score – have proliferated ever since the novel's publication, and at an ever-increasing rate since Joyce himself authorized a schematic table of the novel's contents, reproduced by Frank Budgen in 1930. It is a dominant effect, certainly, within Joyce studies; it is also a contaminatory one. But that is not the half of it. The onto-logico-encyclopedic overpotentialization is there in *Ulysses* itself, and in Joyce's understanding of it; it has the potential to contaminate *Ulysses*, and it has the potential to contaminate us, whether we are inside the Joycean institution or not. (The other crowd-puller apart from Derrida himself at the Ninth International Symposium was the 'corrected text' of *Ulysses*, edited, not to mention computer generated, by Hans Walter Gabler: an edition which has gone on to become one of the most sizable white elephants in academic publishing history.) Taken to an extreme,

> We can imagine that there will soon be a giant computer of Joycean studies. ... It would capitalize all publications, coordinate and teleprogram all communication, colloquia, theses, papers, and would draw up an index in all languages. We would be able to consult it any time by satellite or by 'sunphone,' day and night, taking advantage of the 'reliability' of an answering machine. 'Hello, yes, yes, what

are you asking for? Oh, for all the occurrences of the word *yes* in *Ulysses*? Yes.' It would remain to be seen if the basic language of this computer would be English and if its patent would be American, given the overwhelming and significant majority of Americans among the trustees of the Joyce Foundation. ('UG' 286)

Derrida's attitude to this variety of contamination is one we might call ambivalent, were it the case that he had given equal consideration to both sides of the issue. Certainly he is happy to send one or two squibs past the ears of the Joycean community, regarding the intimidatory effect it inherits and passes on. 'When you call on incompetents, like me … ' , he asks, 'is it not both to humiliate them, and because you expect from these guests not only news, good news come at last to deliver you from the hypermnesic interiority in which you go round in circles like hallucinators in a nightmare, but also, paradoxically, a legitimacy?' ('UG' 284). In seeing himself as he does ('I do not belong to your large, impressive family'; 'Joyce remains a stranger to me'), Derrida clearly situates himself, to a certain degree at least, outside this vicious circle of interiority. Yet he is also reflexively aware that his thinking about Joyce, and the paper he has to give, together owe an immense amount to the onto-logico-encyclopedic impulse. In the absence of the giant computer or the internet, Derrida re-read *Ulysses*, 'first in French, then in English, pencil in hand, counting the *oui*'s and then the *yes*es and sketching out a typology' ('UG' 288). He also counted up the postcards, the telephone conversations, the anagrams of *oui* (IOU, for example) and *yes* (HELY'S, for example) and the homonyms of I (eye, ay), not to mention the references to circumcision, perfume, and the prophet Elijah. He provides typological footnotes on *yes* in general and those English expressions translated by *oui* in particular. He does all these things in the belief that encyclopedic work of this kind (present in his encounters with yoghurt and Japanese books, present also in Joyce himself and in *Ulysses*, and the inspiration for countless pieces of typologically oriented literary criticism), which he calls 'the machine of filiation … ready to domesticate, circumcise, circumvent anything', is a form of 'yes-laughter' necessarily complemented by another, 'a completely different music … the vowels of a completely different song' ('UG' 294).

So there is a completely different music available to be played: by somebody if not by Derrida, Hans Walter Gabler, or the symposiasts gathered together in Frankfurt. But if we ask what the other music *is* that is nearly drowned out by business as usual in the onto-logico-encyclopedic institution of Joyce studies, the answer is very much as the argument advanced in Chapter 1 might lead us to expect. Where we might have hoped to find discussed by Derrida those elements in Joyce and in *Ulysses* which could be said to resist the lure of overpotentialization, we find only a kind of gap or space of pure alterity:

> I can hear this too, very close to the other one, as the yes-laughter of a gift without debt, light affirmation, almost amnesic, of a gift or an abandoned event, which in classical language is called 'the work,' a lost signature without a proper name that reveals and names the cycle of reappropriation and domestication of all the paraphs only to delimit their phantasm, and does so in order to contrive the breach necessary for the coming of the other, whom one can always call Elijah, if Elijah is the name of the unforeseeable other for whom a place must be kept, and no longer Elijah, the great operator, Elijah, the head of the megaprogramotelephonic network, but the other Elijah: Elijah the other. ('UG' 294–5)

It can only seem astonishing, I think, that the other *Ulysses* Derrida is groping for here is so incompletely realized by him: so almost completely *un*realized. That prodigious novel, fully capable of absorbing and returning all the institutional contamination Joyce-studies can float, throw, launch, beam, or radiate towards it, has to all intents and purposes disappeared and been replaced by an abstraction, a 'gift without debt', a 'light affirmation', able only to do some revealing and some naming of the forces of appropriation within and around it – forces which, it is worth recalling, the critic here has made use of as and when it suits him (pencil in hand, counting the yeses), all the while insisting on his status as outsider or guest, poised on an Archimedean promontory outside the institution concerned.

'What of the Joycean institution', Derrida asks at the beginning of his lecture, 'and what should I think of the hospitality with which it honors me today in Frankfurt?' ('UG' 263). In all that follows it never occurs to him to ask what *Ulysses* itself might 'think of' or have to say about such things, and the Joycean institution in particular. In fact the novel is allowed to materialize only as the supine provider for the encyclopedic enterprise: yes, *oui*, postcards, circumcision, the prophet Elijah, and so on, ad infinitum. The other Elijah, as Derrida calls it – the aspect of the novel which does not merely reveal or name but actually, actively, and radically criticizes that encyclopedic enterprise – is itself ultimately smothered. How? By being described in terms that amount to another manifestation of the contaminatory encyclopedism we started with:

> A differential vibration of several tonalities, several qualities of yes-laughters which do not allow themselves to be stabilized in the indivisible simplicity of one sole sending, of self to self, or of one sole consigning, but which call for the counter-signature of the other, for a *yes* which would resound in a completely other writing, an other language, an other idiosyncrasy, with an other stamp. ('UG' 305)

In fact there is no need for *Ulysses* to resound in such a way in order for it to appraise and to criticize the tendency to encyclopedism in itself and in its readers. Far from its being impossible to invent anything on the subject of Joyce, his very biodegradability carries with it something 'unassimilable, kept in reserve, unforgettable because imperceivable, capable of inducing meaning without being exhausted by meaning' – and that is the freedom the novel accords to Bloom, to Stephen, to Joyce, and to us. The chance and the necessity of encyclopedism, bound up with each other as they are, are met in the book not by a kind of vacuous, ever-to-be-anticipated alterity concomitant with the everlasting yea, or by 'the indivisible simplicity of one sole sending, of self to self, or of one sole consigning', but by a series of things much more substantial, demanding, and ineluctable: dramatic events, developments, and revelations which form a web of human understanding, as opposed to a chain of coincidence. Despite the novel's bulk, the web of understanding woven in *Ulysses* is immensely fragile and elusive – so much so as to be positively an embarrassment to Joyce-studies, which normally prefers to locate the novel's significance elsewhere. But the ephemeral nature of what it is Bloom and Stephen and Joyce and we ourselves come to see in *Ulysses* is nothing for literature to be ashamed of. (We do not come to see any more in the *Odyssey*, or *Hamlet*, or *War and Peace* — despite Tolstoy's many suggestions and interpretations along the way.) Given the extent to which consciousness is burdened, in *Ulysses* and in other works of literature, but also outside them ('Bet You Can't Say No to Yes'), the fact that Joyce's novel can even point to areas where understanding is lacking is remarkable enough. The web of understanding extends, painfully slowly and tentatively it is true, over Bloom's dead father and dead son, over his very-much alive wife, over Stephen's dead mother, over Ireland's history and political situation in 1904, over Catholicism and Judaism and the demands they make even on those no longer believers, on the role and function of the artist, and over experiences such as death and love. There is nothing final about such understanding, but there is more to it than what Derrida calls 'legitimate filiation' – if there were not, we all might as well give up the ghost. Neither is there anything of great intellectual weight: Bloom is no more worth listening to, in this respect, than Emma Woodhouse or Enobarbus or J. Alfred Prufrock. Ultimately, that is to say, it is a moot point whether the web of understanding spun by works of literature spreads over us, and if so for how long: whether *Madame Bovary* or the 'Wife of Bath's Tale' gives us readers something we can take away and make use of. Perhaps all that *Ulysses* or any other work of literature does is encourage us in the belief, for better or for worse, that understanding does exist, if only we could find it. In any event, what Derrida calls 'a completely other writing' is neither called for in Joyce's novel, nor is it present, because it is the encyclopedism which *itself* suggests an antidote; very far from 'an other idiosyncrasy' arriving from outside like Elijah, the overpotentialization of *Ulysses* itself makes clear both to Joyce and the novel's other readers that other elements in the novel must be deployed or instituted to counter its effects.

In fact therefore it is not true, as I said earlier, that what is chance to Bloom and Stephen is simply necessity to us, though from the privileged viewpoint given us by Joyce that will often seem to be the case. (That is one of the genuine challenges of the book: not to join in the encyclopedic jamboree in a spirit of superiority, but to overcome the Siren-like seduction it extends to us – by which I mean to see the encyclopedic impulse as it should be seen, an element vitally necessary in terms of providing the steep historical and cosmic irony which surrounds the two heroes but also as a feature which is demonstrated to have its limits, morally and humanly speaking.) Not even Joyce has complete control over his hypermnesic machine: the autonomy of literature forbids it. In that respect, Bloom and Stephen are free to make as much sense of their experience as the limits of their intelligence and sensitivity allow; but even they have inklings or intimations of its significance.

Those inklings come to a sad and funny climax in the 'Ithaca' episode of *Ulysses*, where Joyce deliberately contrasts the two tired but animate men with the galactic, social, and mechanical structures which surround but which can never encompass them. Here, we might imagine, is the moment of triumph for the encyclopedic attitude. But paradoxically enough the more the impersonal is asserted, the more humane the men become; the more emphatically Joyce abandons the subcutaneous realist enterprise (the 'stream of consciousness' and so on) the more graphic and complete becomes our understanding of Bloom's and Stephen's minds and attitudes. The Socratic, onto-logico-encyclopedic, and interrogatory voice cannot even stifle Joyce's habitual linguistic exuberance and his humour, let alone the two men who are the favoured objects of those things:

> What advantages attended shaving by night?
> A softer beard: a softer brush if intentionally allowed to remain from shave to shave in its agglutinated lather: a softer skin if unexpectedly encountering female acquaintances in remote places at incustomary hours: quiet reflections upon the course of the day: a cleaner sensation when awaking after a fresher sleep since matitutinal noises, premonitions and perturbations, a clattered milk-can, a postman's double knock, a paper read, reread while lathering, relathering the same spot, a shock, a shoot, with thought of aught he sought though fraught with nought might cause a slower rate of shaving and a nick on which incision plaster with precision cut and humected and applied adhered which was to be done.[31]

The more insistently the encyclopedic voice scrapes away at them, the more irreduceable the men become:

> Reduce Bloom by cross multiplication of reverses of fortune... and by elimination of all positive values to a negligible negative irrational unreal quantity. Successively, in descending helotic order: Poverty: that of the outdoor hawker of imitation jewellery, the dun for the recovery of bad and doubtful debts, the poor rate and deputy cess collector. Mendicancy: that of the fraudulent bankrupt with negligible assets paying 1s. 4d. in the £, sandwichman, distributor of throwaways, nocturnal vagrant, insinuating sycophant, maimed sailor, blind stripling, superannuated bailiff's man, marfeast, lickplate, spoilsport, pickthank, eccentric public laughingstock seated on bench of public park under discarded perforated umbrella. Destitution: the inmate of Old Man's House (Royal Hospital), Kilmainham, the inmate of Simpson's Hospital for reduced but respectable men permanently disabled by gout or want of sight. Nadir of misery: the aged impotent disfranchised ratesupported moribund lunatic pauper. (855)

Nothing, in fact, could be further from the triumph of encyclopedism than the 'Ithaca' chapter. What happens there, surely, is that the personal and the impersonal are illuminated by each other: yes, Bloom and Stephen are two humans surrounded and encapsulated (hailed and interpellated, even, as Althusser would say) by forces ultimately far beyond their comprehension, and we in the gods above Joyce's shoulder look down on them accordingly. But not only do they remain humans notwithstanding; their humanity is positively revealed and (implicitly) asserted by virtue of this very fact. We are bound to be struck by how little the pair of them know, on the one hand, but by how much they silently, hesitantly, incompletely understand, on the other. The water in Bloom's tap may flow 'From Roundwood reservoir in county Wicklow of a cubic capacity of 2,400 million gallons, percolating through a subterranean aqueduct of filter mains of single and double pipeage constructed at an initial plant cost of £5 per linear yard', etc., but he it is who makes the cocoa. Moreover every act of understanding *is* that: it is not supplied externally by force of revelation, nor does it spring ready made from the colossal process surrounding Bloom and Stephen. Bloom knows it is coincidence, not information or intuition, that has Stephen mention the name of the hotel in which Bloom's own father committed suicide (801). He sees the past and the future as what they are, not as repositories of encyclopedic significance:

The irreparability of the past: once at a performance of Albert Hengler's circus in the Rotunda, Rutland square, Dublin, an intuitive particoloured clown in quest of paternity had penetrated from the ring to a place in the auditorium where Bloom, solitary, was seated and had publicly declared to an exhilarated audience that he (Bloom) was his (the clown's) papa. The imprevidibility of the future: once in the summer of 1898 he (Bloom) had marked a florin (2s.) with three notches on the milled edge and tendered it in payment of an account due to and received by J. and T. Davy, family grocers, 1 Charlemont Mall, Grand Canal, for circulation on the waters of civic finance, for possible, circuitous or direct, return.
Was the clown Bloom's son?
No.
Had Bloom's coin returned?
Never. (816–17)

Indeed, as we approach Bloom's particular and overriding obsession, his wife Molly – and only as we approach her – the personal and the impersonal, the humane and the encyclopedic, begin to merge:

> What did his limbs, when gradually extended, encounter?
> New clean bedlinen, additional odours, the presence of a human form, female, hers, the imprint of a human form, male, not his, some crumbs, some flakes of potted meat, recooked, which he removed.
> If he had smiled why should he have smiled?
> To reflect that each one who enters imagines himself to be the first to enter whereas he is always the last term of a preceding series even if the first term of a succeeding one, each imagining himself to be first, last, only and alone, whereas he is neither first nor last nor only nor alone in a series originating in and repeated to infinity.
> (863)

Clearly Molly here is turning into the infinite and abstract woman, and every one of her lovers into the infinite and abstract man, 'in a series originating in and repeating to infinity'. But though Bloom (and therefore we the readers) can see her that way, she is Molly, too; only she (as Bloom acknowledges) can lay claim to the list of men her husband then provides, 'and so each and so on to no last term'. (Indeed, needless to say, the list she provides during her soliloquy will be at variance with Bloom's.) In a moment of encyclopedic comprehension Bloom abandons the idea of retribution (assassination, duel, divorce, 'exposure by mechanical artifice', and so on) and, while remaining 'a conscious reactor against the void of incertitude', sees that in that context his and Molly's problems are small indeed (866): 'the futility of triumph or protest or vindication: the inanity of extolled virtue: the lethargy of nescient matter: the apathy of the stars.'

Bloom and Stephen, 'competent, keyless citizens' as they are, have 'proceeded energetically from the unknown to the known through the uncertitude of the void' (818). We, too, are free to make as much sense of their meeting as we can, knowing as we ought to do that no interaction of luck and necessity, or chance and overdetermination alone could begin to explain what it is we witness. It is not the case that, as Derrida believes, 'all the gestures made in the attempt to take the initiative of a movement are found to be already announced' in Joyce's novel; neither is it the case that 'the virtual totality of experience' has unfolded and reconstituted itself in *Ulysses* 'by playing out all its possible combinations'. There is still plenty for us to do, however fragile appears the reward for making sense of Bloom's and Stephen's encounter. What Derrida calls 'an other idiosyncrasy' would be of no constructive help at all in that exercise, nor does it arise: the solution must be born of the problem. The resistance must arise from the contamination, or it fails to answer.

Notes

Introduction

1 J. Hillis Miller, 'Presidential Address 1986. The Triumph of Theory, the Resistance to Reading, and the Question of the Material Base', 283, *PMLA* 102: 3 (May 1987), 281–91.

2 In one sense Hillis Miller missed the point about 'the turn to history' and the contemporary discussion of literature as 'cultural product'. Institutionalists – in particular New Historicists – have proved themselves very careful and patient readers, after all: only they are looking for something different from Hillis Miller. They might also accuse him of a degree of naïvete when he talks about reading 'with nothing taken for granted beforehand'. In what un-historical neverland or highly favoured institutional niche, they might ask, can a person read with *nothing taken for granted*? Surely the real point is a different one: that literary critics may talk and write about culture, history, society, etc., at great length and with great sophistication, but that in itself is no guarantee that they will make the study of literature count in our society. It does not follow that because you talk about society you have a social impact. Indeed, as I suggested *vis-à-vis* Stephen Greenblatt and Cardinal Wolsey's hat, it might be argued that New Historicism (for example) is as 'academic' a variety of English study as any other. Does it not value Elizabethans' responses to Shakespeare over that of living, modern-day people? The critics Hillis Miller describes as responding to 'a demand to be ethically and politically responsible in our teaching and writing, to grapple with realities rather than with the impalpabilities of theoretical abstractions' will have some of the social influence to which they aspire. It may not be as momentous as they hope, or as direct and uncomplicated, but it will be felt – and there is no suggestion that feminists, post-colonialists, and others should give up their work. But the explicit turn to culture and society is not the only way the study of literature counts; it may not even in fact be the most important way. Critics should have enough faith in literature to acknowledge that it does not always require to be *made* to count, by the professoriate, at any rate: it itself is a reality to be grappled with, and often enough it counts of its own accord as it has always done, simply by finding its readers. Literature always finds its readers under circumstances of greater or lesser institutional control, whether as a set text at university or a book you find on a park bench, certainly: but that control does not entirely determine the nature of the reading experience.

1 Institutionalism and Ideality

1 Jacques Derrida, 'The Time of a Thesis: Punctuations', trans. Kathleen McLaughlin, 37, in Alan Montefiore (ed.), *Philosophy in France Today*

(Cambridge: Cambridge University Press, 1983), 34–50; referred to below as 'TT'.

2 Jacques Derrida, *Positions*, trans. and ed. Alan Bass (London: Athlone, 1987), 51.

3 Jacques Derrida, *Limited Inc*, trans. Samuel Weber and Jeffrey Mehlman (Evanston: Northwestern University Press, 1988), 93–4.

4 Jacques Derrida, 'Some Statements and Truisms about Neologisms, Newisms, Postisms, Parasitisms, and other Small Seismisms', trans. Ann Tomiche, 85, in David Carroll (ed.), *The States of 'Theory': History, Art, and Critical Discourse* (New York: Columbia University Press, 1990), 63–94.

5 Derek Attridge, ' "This Strange Institution Called Literature": An Interview with Jacques Derrida', trans. Geoffrey Bennington and Rachel Bowlby, 44, in Jacques Derrida, *Acts of Literature*, ed. Attridge (London: Routledge, 1992), 33–75; referred to below as 'TSI'.

6 It might be suggested that Michel Foucault has done at least as much as Derrida to inculcate an institutional view of literature; and I would agree. 'Genealogy', he wrote in 'Nietzsche, Genealogy, History', 'seeks to reestablish the various systems of subjection: not the anticipatory power of meaning, but the hazardous play of dominations.' (*The Foucault Reader*, ed. Paul Rabinow (London: Penguin, 1986), 83.) Moreover, it is Foucault's view that 'the universe of discourses' is one encompassed, determined, and articulated by 'the juridical and institutional system' of power operating in any given culture (ibid. 113), and his influence on New Historicism in particular has been extensive. But it seems to me that Foucault is a less interesting institutionalist than Derrida. His 'hazardous play of dominations' remains fundamentally a politico-cultural phenomenon as opposed to a literary–critical one. So I will not discuss his work further here.

7 It is hard to provide adequate bibliographical evidence of this repudiation of the ideality of literature in contemporary criticism: not because little such evidence exists but because there is so much of it. To list names, books, and journal articles would be invidious, I think. It might suggest that only some strictly limited number of individuals hold such a view. What I can point to are such instances as Richard Rorty's notion, considered in Chapter 2, of 'a seamless, undifferentiated "general text" '; Freud's idea, considered in Chapter 3, that 'very many imaginative writings are far removed from the model of the naïve day-dream; yet I cannot suppress the suspicion that even the most extreme deviations from that model could be linked with it through an uninterrupted series of transitional cases'; and the New Historicists' animadversions on the word autonomy, considered in Chapter 4. This will seem a rather disparate bundle to present as evidence, but I hope readers will find it coherent when it is properly introduced in the chapters to follow.

8 Harold Bloom, *The Western Canon: The Books and School of the Ages* (New York: Harcourt Brace, 1994), 10–11.

9 Gerald Dworkin, *The Theory and Practice of Autonomy* (Cambridge: Cambridge University Press, 1988), 7.

10 Ibid. 5, 6. Moral–philosophical discussions of autonomy are available, but insofar as they see autonomy as solely 'a feature of persons' (ibid. 6), such discussions are of strictly limited use where this study is concerned. In discussing autonomy as a human attribute, philosophers are bound to

consider concepts like will, liberty, responsibility, and independence. Were such concepts to be introduced in a discussion of the autonomy of literature, the critical law of diminishing returns would soon begin to operate. Works of literature, as we shall see in Chapter 3, may seem to act *like* human beings in some important respects, but fully-fledged consciousnesses they are not. Dearden's emphasis on activity as the basis of ontological autonomy is, of course, itself highly anti-Platonic and Aristotelian: 'The purpose of living', as Aristotle wrote in *Poetics*, Chapter 6, 'is an end which is a kind of *activity*, not a *quality*' (trans. T.S. Dorsch; my italics); what is true of living, is true of literature also, in this respect.

11 Geoffrey Bennington and Jacques Derrida, *Jacques Derrida*, trans. Bennington (Chicago: University of Chicago Press, 1993), 253–4.

12 Jacques Derrida, 'No Apocalypse, Not Now (Full Speed Ahead, Seven Missiles, Seven Missives)', trans. Catherine Porter and Philip Lewis, 27, *Diacritics*, 14: 2 (Summer 1984), 20–31.

13 Pierre Macherey, *A Theory of Literary Production*, trans. Geoffrey Wall (London: Routledge and Kegan Paul, 1978), 52.

14 I am well aware that the word 'traditional' is a contestable one, and I do not use it here in an honorific sense. There are many traditions of literary criticism, and an admirer of Derrida or Foucault has as much right to claim the term as I have: neither of those writers is free from tradition.

15 Macherey, *A Theory of Literary Production*, 53.

16 Ibid.; my italics.

17 Ibid.

18 See, e.g., John Casey, *The Language of Criticism* (London: Methuen, 1966), Richard Wollheim, *Art and Its Objects* (Harmondsworth: Penguin, 1970), and Roger Scruton, *Art and Imagination: A Study in the Philosophy of Mind* (London: Routledge and Kegan Paul, 1974).

19 Jacques Derrida, 'The Law of Genre', trans. Avital Ronell, 225, in *Acts of Literature*, 221–52.

20 Jacques Derrida, 'At this Very Moment in this Work Here I Am', trans. Ruben Berezdivin, 427, in Peggy Kamuf (ed.), *A Derrida Reader: Between the Blinds* (New York: Columbia University Press, 1991), 403–39.

21 I am grateful to Alex Segal for pointing out these examples in Wimsatt and Beardsley's and Leavis' work. See Alex Segal, ' "The Intentional Fallacy" Deconstructed', in John Barnes (ed.), *Border Crossing: Studies in English and Other Disciplines* (Bundora, Vic.: La Trobe University Press, 1991), 100–7, and id., 'The Pen and the Voice: Deconstruction, Leavis and Phonocentrism', *Meridian*, 13: 2 (Oct. 1994), 171–83. In fact I think the example from Leavis fails to support this line of argument; but other examples from other critics could be found, no doubt.

22 Attridge, *Acts of Literature*, 3.

23 Ibid. 25.

24 F.R. Leavis, 'The Responsible Critic: Or the Function of Criticism at Any Time', 296, in id. (ed.), *A Selection from 'Scrutiny'*, 2 vols (Cambridge: Cambridge University Press, 1968), ii. 281–316.

25 Again, it is difficult to provide a bibliographical summary of so widespread a tendency in traditional criticism. But see Leavis on Joseph Conrad's conservatism in Chapter 3, section 3.3, below.

26 See Derrida, *Limited Inc*, 115.
27 Derrida, 'Some Statements and Truisms', 89.
28 Derrida, *Positions*, 68.
29 'What I should be tempted to denounce as a lure – i.e. totalization or gathering up', Derrida asks Derek Attridge, ' – isn't this what keeps me going?' ('TSI' 34). It is a lure he is not always able to resist, at least where other people are concerned. Some of the remarks Derrida makes about the 'metaphysical' tradition may be too sweeping; but that does not stop him making them.
30 Derrida's 'steno-telegraphic band', 'Border Lines' (trans. James Hulbert, in Harold Bloom, et al., *Deconstruction and Criticism* (New York: Seabury Press, 1979), 75–176), is one example of this element in his work.
31 It was Derrida who, in his thesis-defence, asked (like Sartre and many others before him) what Etienne Balibar and Pierre Macherey call 'the old idealist question': what is literature? For Macherey that question itself 'revives... an idealist and conservative aesthetic. If I had a single clear idea when I began my work, it was that we must abandon this kind of question because "what is literature" is a false problem. Why? Because it is a question which already contains an answer. It implies that literature is *something*, that literature exists as a *thing*, as an eternal and unchangeable thing with an essence.' (Balibar and Macherey, 'On Literature as an Ideological Form', trans. Ian McLeod, John Whitehead, and Ann Wordsworth, 86, 98, in Robert Young (ed.), *Untying the Text: A Post-Structuralist Reader* (London: Routledge and Kegan Paul, 1981), 79–99.) Like Derrida, I am happy to have it implied that literature is a thing; I do not think it follows that it is an eternal and unchangeable one.
32 Jacques Derrida, 'The Principle of Reason: the University in the Eyes of its Pupils', trans. Catherine Porter and Edward P. Morris, 11, *Diacritics*, 13: 3 (Fall 1983), 3–20; referred to below as 'PR'.
33 Martin Amis, *London Fields* (London: Jonathan Cape, 1989), 359.
34 Derrida, 'No Apocalypse, Not Now', 27.
35 Jacques Derrida, 'Biodegradables: Seven Diary Fragments', trans. Peggy Kamuf, 847, *Critical Inquiry*, 15 (Summer 1989), 812–73.
36 *Letters of John Keats*, ed. Robert Gittings (Oxford: Oxford University Press, 1970), 12.
37 Isaac Babel, *You Must Know Everything: Stories 1915–1937*, trans. Max Hayward (New York: Carroll and Graf, 1984), 211–12.
38 Nadezhda Mandelstam, *Hope Against Hope: A Memoir*, trans. Max Hayward (London: Collins Harvill, 1970), 71.
39 Thomas Mann, *Joseph and his Brothers*, trans. H.T. Lowe-Porter (London: Penguin, 1978), vi.
40 Dan Jacobson, *The Beginners* (New York: Macmillan, 1966), 146.
41 In point of fact the second line produced the first: 'Under the brown fog' produced 'Unreal'. In his draft Eliot originally had 'Terrible City'. The whole little passage then duly produces its twin in 'The Fire Sermon': 'Unreal City/ Under the brown fog of a winter noon/Mr Eugenides, the Smyrna merchant/Unshaven, with a pocket full of currants...'.
42 Dan Jacobson, *Adult Pleasures: Essays on Writers and Readers* (London: André Deutsch, 1988), 23–4. In an earlier version of this essay the passage continued: 'The "truth" of the work lies in its undoing of the hierarchies or

categories of our everyday understanding; it offers us a truth not of assertion but of process, of experience, of contestation. Thus it undoes, among
many other prepossessions, our ordinary notions of what living or effective
truth is and how it is to be recognised.' (Id., 'The Uselessness of Literature',
64, *Quadrant*, 26: 3 (Mar. 1982), 61–4.)
43 George Eliot, *Middlemarch*, ed. Rosemary Ashton (London: Penguin, 1994),
    291–2.
44 Jacques Derrida, *Writing and Difference*, trans. Alan Bass (London: Routledge
    and Kegan Paul, 1978), 11.
45 Ibid.
46 Jacques Derrida, *Of Grammatology*, trans. Gayatri Chakravorty Spivak
    (Baltimore: Johns Hopkins University Press, 1976), 158.
47 Derrida, *Writing and Difference*, 11.
48 If you wish to answer the question 'what is literature?' you will have to
    make theoretical, oppositional distinctions between literature and its fellow-
    institutions. That is unavoidable. In fact, Derrida is clearly interested in try-
    ing to find out how far a critic can go without making such distinctions.
    But you will also have to do justice to the holistic nature of the material
    under consideration by attempting to respond to it in kind, practically. You
    can answer the question either by keeping a foot in both camps or by work-
    ing your way, like Derrida, towards a position prior to or beyond the pair of
    them. One approach alone will not do.
49 'TSI' 40, 53. Derrida might draw support for such a view from Philippe
    Lacoue-Labarthe and Jean-Luc Nancy's *The Literary Absolute: The Theory of
    Literature in German Romanticism*, trans. Philip Barnard and Cheryl Lester
    (New York: State University of New York Press, 1988). '[A]lthough it is
    not entirely or simply philosophical,' Lacoue-Labarthe and Nancy write,
    'romanticism is rigorously comprehensible (or even accessible) only on a
    philosophical basis, in its proper and in fact unique … articulation with the
    philosophical.' In particular 'it is because an entirely new and unforeseeable
    relation between aesthetics and philosophy will be articulated in Kant that
    a "passage" to romanticism will become possible' (Ibid. 29). Literature,
    therefore, in the words of the translators, 'as the object of a duly legitimated
    and institutionalized discipline, is thoroughly determined as a response to a
    certain philosophical "crisis." The received notion of literature, in other
    words, which assumes in particular that literature is different from or exter-
    nal to philosophy in various ways (and can thus perennially bemoan
    "external" incursions on the part of philosophy or "theory" into properly
    literary problems) is in fact philosophical through and through.' (Ibid. xiv)
    At a certain level of abstraction this is no doubt true; but then at a certain
    level of abstraction everything (Romanticism included) is 'philosophical
    through and through'. Nor would I deny that the institution of criticism
    underwent great change in the era Lacoue-Labarthe and Nancy discuss. Those
    who wish to turn the page of philosophy, Derrida has remarked, only end
    up doing philosophy badly *(Writing and Difference*, 288), and this study is
    doubtless guilty in this respect. But when philosophers like Richard Rorty
    and Alasdair MacIntyre (and, it may be, Lacoue-Labarthe and Nancy) wish
    to turn the page of literary criticism are they not liable to find themselves
    in similar difficulties?

50 Derrida has suggested – in a way that is bound to remind us of Schiller's notions of the naïve and the sentimental – that the '"twentieth-century modernist, or at least nontraditional texts"' on which he has spent most of his time (e.g. Mallarmé, Joyce, Celan, Bataille, Artaud, and Blanchot) 'all have in common that they are inscribed in a *critical* experience of literature' ('TSI' 41). The implication being that some works of literature are not so inscribed. What such works would look like we can only guess – or rather, we know what such works look like, but they are not works of literature.

51 S.L. Goldberg, 'Shakespeare's Centrality', 5, *Critical Review*, 18 (1976), 3–22; my whole argument here owes a great deal to this essay of Goldberg's.

52 F.R. Leavis, *English Literature in Our Time and the University* (London: Chatto and Windus, 1969), 122.

53 See Vàclav Havel, *Letters to Olga, June 1979–September 1982*, trans. Paul Wilson (London: Faber and Faber, 1988), 282: 'the playwright himself ends up being suprisingly bound by the world he creates. ... he soon finds himself miraculously caught up in the rules of his world, and ultimately becomes the first "victim" of his own creation. The sovereign ruler becomes the humble subject, the re-creator a mere handmaiden of the miracle of re-creation. It would seem that Being, more transparently here than anywhere else, is in command of its own re-creation by the creator.' Passages parallel to this, from *Dr Zhivago* and from Charlotte Brontë's correspondence, are to be found in Chapters 3 (section 3.2) and 5 (section 5.3).

54 T.S. Eliot, *'The Waste Land': A Facsimile and Transcript of the Original Drafts, Including the Annotations of Ezra Pound*, ed. Valerie Eliot (London: Faber and Faber, 1971), 111.

2 'A New Spin on the Old Words': Criticism and Philosophy

* See Richard Rorty, *Essays on Heidegger and Others: Philosophical Papers, Volume 2* (Cambridge: Cambridge University Press, 1991), 99 (referred to below as *H&O*): 'The stages "in the history of Being" which Heidegger recounts are marked ... by people ... pretending to say the same old thing while subversively putting a new spin on the old words.'

1 See, e.g., Terry Eagleton, 'The End of English', *Textual Practice*, 1: 1 (Spring 1987), 1–9; Stanley Fish, 'Profession Despise Thyself: Fear and Self-Loathing in Literary Studies' in id., *Doing What Comes Naturally: Change, Rhetoric, and the Practice of Theory in Literary and Legal Studies* (Durham, NC: Duke University Press, 1989), 197–214; David Bromwich, 'Literature and Theory' in id., *A Choice of Inheritance: Self and Community from Edmund Burke to Robert Frost* (Cambridge, Mass.: Harvard University Press, 1989), 264–91; Alvin Kernan, *The Death of Literature* (New Haven: Yale University Press, 1990); and Bernard Bergonzi, *Exploding English: Criticism, Theory, Culture* (Oxford: Oxford University Press, 1990).

2 F.R. Leavis, 'The Responsible Critic: or the Function of Criticism at Any Time', 299, in id. (ed.), *A Selection from 'Scrutiny'*, 2 vols (Cambridge: Cambridge University Press, 1968), ii. 281–316.

3 Richard Rorty, *Contingency, Irony, and Solidarity* (Cambridge: Cambridge University Press, 1989), 26; referred to below as *CIS*.

4 In place of what he calls 'an altar to Literature', Rorty says he would prefer 'to have no high altars, and instead just have lots of picture galleries, book displays, movies, concerts, ethnographic museums, museums of science and technology and so on – lots of cultural options but no privileged central discipline or practice' (*H&O* 132): remarks which sit oddly with his intellectual privileging of literary criticism. Whereas it is true many in the Western world already possess the panoply of cultural options Rorty describes, or something like it, it is to our credit that we find it quite insufficient as a moral and intellectual structure. It would appear that we cannot live in the midst of a range of cultural options without enquiring as profoundly as we can into the sources of their value. Our notion of the 'comfortableness of human association' (see Rorty's remarks on Dickens, below) is simply not that platitudinous. For example: we are belatedly becoming aware that the ethnographic museums of the West mark the tombs of those fragile cultures in Africa, the Pacific, and elsewhere that we have destroyed or are in the process of destroying. Such places are matters of cultural life and death to the present-day inhabitants of the Torres Strait or the Amazon; for Rorty they are merely a cultural option.

5 One example from a rather unexpected source might be given here. In chapter 12 of *Ulysses* ('Nausicaa'), Gerty MacDowell reveals her legs to Bloom during a firework display: 'And then a rocket sprang and bang shot blind and O! then the Roman candle burst and it was like a sigh of O! and everyone cried O! O! in raptures and it gushed out of it a stream of rain gold hair threads and they shed and ah! they were all greeny dewy stars falling with golden, O so lovely! O so soft, sweet, soft!' In chapter 46 of Thackeray's *Pendennis* ('Monseigneur S'amuse'), the eponymous hero shares a remarkably similar experience with a venturesome and sexually inexperienced young woman at a firework display in Vauxhall Gardens: 'He was engaged with Fanny. How she wondered! how happy she was! how she cried Oh, oh, oh, as the rockets soared into the air, and showered down in azure, and emerald, and vermilion. As these wonders blazed and disappeared before her, the little girl thrilled and trembled with delight at Arthur's side – her hand was under his arm still, he felt it pressing him as she looked up delighted.'

6 F.R. Leavis, *The Great Tradition: George Eliot, Henry James, Joseph Conrad* (Harmondsworth: Penguin, 1962), 13.

7 In the writing of a novel, poem, or play, these criteria are moral and aesthetic at one and the same time: that is why neither of these terms is very good for describing them. Furthermore these criteria are not standards aimed at; they are means by which the writer decides how he or she can progress with the material already established. When new material is added those criteria disappear, being no longer relevant. Something similar takes place in the mind of readers as their successive interpretative guesses ('moral' and 'aesthetic') are superseded in the act of reading.

8 *H&O* 78–9. To do justice to the Victorians it is worth pointing out that the points made here are by no means new. T.H. Lister, reviewing Dickens' first four books in 1838, suggested that 'the tendency of his writings is to make us practically benevolent – to excite our sympathy in behalf of the aggrieved

and suffering in all classes; and especially in those who are most removed from observation. He especially directs our attention to the helpless victims of untoward circumstances, or a vicious system...' (Stephen Wall (ed.), *Charles Dickens: A Critical Anthology* (Harmondsworth: Penguin, 1970), 47).

Walter Bagehot, writing in 1858, described Dickens as the most obvious manifestation of a kind of 'sentimental radicalism', itself a reaction to the political harshness of the Regency: 'The vice of the then existing social authorities and of the then existing public had been the forgetfulness of the pain which their own acts evidently produced' (ibid. 136–7).

9 Dickens, Rorty might argue, understood the family to be itself an institution, and one no less powerful in its influence over society than the Circumlocution Office – indeed much more so. This is undeniably true. But I do not think changing an institution of this kind (and by these means serving human liberty) could ever be separated from the search after private perfection.

10 Vladimir Nabokov, 'On a Book Entitled *Lolita*', 305, in id., *Lolita* (London: Weidenfeld and Nicolson, 1959), 301–7.

11 Marcel Proust, *Remembrance of Things Past*, trans. C.K. Scott Moncrieff and Terence Kilmartin, 3 vols (London: Penguin, 1983), i. 597; my italics.

12 *Lolita*, 110–11.

13 For Nabokov, pornography 'connotes mediocrity, commercialism and certain strict rules of narration': 'Obscenity must be mated with with banality because every kind of aesthetic enjoyment has to be entirely replaced by simple sexual stimulation' ('On a Book Entitled *Lolita*', 303). Pornography is, as a rule, mediocre and commercial; but it hardly follows that writing which is not mediocre and commercial cannot, *ipso facto*, have a pornographic effect. Neither does the 'aesthetic enjoyment' obtainable from Nabokov's novels (however that might be defined, if indeed it can be defined in isolation) offer any protection whatsoever against 'simple sexual stimulation' (however *that* might be defined). 'Thus, in pornographic novels,' Nabokov goes on, 'action has to be limited to the copulation of clichés. Style, structure, imagery should never distract the reader from his tepid lust. The novel must consist of an alternation of sexual scenes. The passages in between must be reduced to structures of sense, logical bridges of the simplest design, brief expositions and explanations, which the reader will probably skip but must know they exist in order not to feel cheated' (ibid.). Terms like 'style, structure, and imagery' are as poor in terms of sanitary protection as they are in terms of critical effectiveness.

14 See, e.g., the passage: 'Unless it can be proven to me...that in the infinite run it does not matter a jot that a North American girl-child named Dolores Haze had been deprived of her childhood by a maniac...I see nothing for the treatment of my misery but the melancholy and very local palliative of articulate art' (*Lolita*, 275–6); 'the smothered memories, now unfolding themselves into limbless monsters of pain' Humbert refers to in chapter 32 of the second part of the novel, and which he also calls 'icebergs in paradise' (ibid. 277); and finally, that limpid, delicate, painterly, and self-admiring passage, of which Nabokov was himself particularly proud, on Humbert's hearing the noise of a playground while on his travels towards the end of the novel, itself ending: 'I stood listening to that musical vibration

from my lofty slope, to those flashes of separate cries with a kind of demure murmur for background, and then I knew that the hopelessly poignant thing was not Lolita's absence from my side, but the absence of her voice from that concord' (ibid. 299). It is true that immediately after the death of Lolita's mother and before collecting Lolita from her summer camp Humbert is assailed, as he puts it, 'by all sorts of purely ethical doubts and fears' (ibid. 104). These 'ethical fears' are that Lolita may have received news of her mother's death from some other source, that she is being brought home by others as a result, and that, as he has not applied for guardianship, his 'daughter' will be taken from him by the authorities. One influx of guilt only occurs early in part two of the novel, and it illustrates the retrospective quality I have in mind: 'And I catch myself thinking today that our long journey had only defiled with a sinuous trail of slime the lovely, trustful, dreamy, enormous country that by then, in retrospect, was no more to us than a collection of dog-eared maps, ruined tour books, old tyres, and her sobs in the night – every night, every night – the moment I feigned sleep' (ibid. 172).

15 'On a Book Entitled *Lolita*', 305.

16 Alasdair MacIntyre, *After Virtue: A Study in Moral Theory*, 2nd edn (London: Duckworth, 1985), 142; referred to below as *AV*.

17 Charles Taylor, *Sources of the Self: The Making of the Modern Identity* (Cambridge, MA: Harvard University Press, 1989), 47.

18 Ibid. 52–3.

19 Ibid. 105–6.

20 Hayden White, *The Content of the Form: Narrative Discourse and Historical Representation* (Baltimore: Johns Hopkins University Press, 1987), 173.

21 Emily Brontë, *Wuthering Heights*, ed. David Daiches (Harmondsworth: Penguin, 1965), 76; referred to below as *WH*.

22 Charles Dickens, *Barnaby Rudge* (Oxford: Oxford University Press, 1954), 276; my italics.

23 Taylor, *Sources of the Self*, 97.

24 George Eliot, *Middlemarch*, ed. Rosemary Ashton (London: Penguin, 1994), 824.

25 Martha Nussbaum, *Love's Knowledge: Essays on Philosophy and Literature* (New York: Oxford University Press, 1990), 45; referred to below as *LK*.

26 After all of which, it may come as a surprise that – in so far as these ideal types have any value at all – Richard Rorty regards himself as more a Nietzschean than an Aristotelian (see *H&O* 159). A *Nietzschean*? Richard Rorty? No doubt he has benefited a great deal from Nietzsche's scepticism about truth: it being an army of metaphors and so forth. But what has he done with that scepticism? Domesticated it; gentrified it out of recognition. At least for Nietzsche the truth was an *army* of metaphors, implying some kind of intellectual and moral struggle; for Rorty it is a mere conversation, a matter of switching vocabularies or selecting a self you can be happier with. Imagine what Nietzsche would have made of that!

27 See S.L. Goldberg, *Agents and Lives: Moral Thinking in Literature* (Cambridge: Cambridge University Press, 1993), ch. 2, *passim*.

28 Dan Jacobson, *Adult Pleasures: Essays on Writers and Readers* (London: André Deutsch, 1988), 21.

29 See *The Selected Letters of D.H. Lawrence*, ed. James T. Boulton (Cambridge: Cambridge University Press, 1997), 222, 321.
30 *The Complete Notebooks of Henry James*, eds Leon Edel and Lyall H. Powers (New York: Oxford University Press, 1987), 141.
31 Henry James, *Selected Letters*, ed. Leon Edel (Cambridge, MA: Harvard University Press, 1974), 414.
32 Henry James, *The American Scene*, ed. John F. Sears (London: Penguin, 1994), 100.
33 Henry James, *The Critical Muse: Selected Literary Criticism*, ed. Roger Gard (London: Penguin, 1987), 53–4.
34 Ibid. 505, 497–8.
35 Daniel Defoe, *Moll Flanders*, ed. G.A. Starr (Oxford: Oxford University Press, 1971), 194.

3 'These Shafts Can Conquer Troy, These Shafts Alone': Criticism and Psychoanalysis

* See *The Pelican Freud Library*, xiv. *Art and Literature*, ed. Albert Dickson (London: Penguin, 1985), 398 (referred to below as *PFL* xiv). 'We may say in all modesty that to-day even the more obtuse among our colleagues and contemporaries are beginning to realize that no understanding of neurotic states can be reached without the help of psychoanalysis. "These shafts can conquer Troy, these shafts alone" as Odysseus confesses in the *Philoctetes* of Sophocles.'
1 Thomas Mann, 'Freud and the Future', 414, in id., *Essays of Three Decades*, trans. H.T. Lowe-Porter (London: Secker and Warburg, n. d. [1947]), 411–28.
2 R.G. Collingwood, *An Autobiography* (Oxford: Oxford University Press, 1978), 90.
3 Ibid. 94.
4 It is sometimes said that Freudian psychology, in positing the existence of the unconscious, has dethroned that notion of subjectivity previously adhered to in Western rationalist thought. Apparently, this raises what Paul Ricoeur calls 'the novel problem of the lie of consciousness and consciousness as a lie' (*The Conflict of Interpretations: Essays in Hermeneutics*, ed. Don Ihde (Evanston: Northwestern University Press, 1974), 99). As a result of Freud's discoveries, Lacan felt, 'the very centre of the human being was no longer to be found at the place assigned to it by a whole humanist tradition' (*Écrits: A Selection*, trans. Alan Sheridan (London: Tavistock, 1977), 114). The conscious mind, as Freud memorably put it, is no longer master in its own house, and the subject is merely another instance of the myth of presence. 'Logic', Jacques Derrida maintains, 'obeys consciousness, or preconsciousness, the site of verbal images, as well as the principle of identity, the founding expression of a philosophy of presence' (*Writing and Difference*, trans. Alan Bass (London: Routledge and Kegan Paul, 1978), 207). Here are the post-structuralist hermeneutics of suspicion going at full pelt: presumably, if consciousness is a lie, and these are conscious statements, they must be unreliable ones. In Derrida in particular we see an old ruse: instead of *deconstructing* the Cartesian conscious/unconscious opposition, he for tactical reasons

occupies the term normally de-privileged in Western metaphysics – in this case the unconscious – in order to take pot-shots at logic, identity, presence, and the rest.

5 Collingwood, *An Autobiography*, 94, 95.

6 I am not suggesting for one moment that moral philosophy either can or should 'pick up where it left off', before the advent of psychoanalysis. Quite clearly, Freud has altered our moral topography for good and all, and an attempt to reconstitute what Jacques Derrida calls 'the good old discourse of the Enlightenment' would be, in his words, 'a sort of shameful, botched restoration', of no use to anybody. (See Jacques Derrida, 'Let Us Not Forget – Psychoanalysis', trans. Geoffrey Bennington and Rachel Bowlby, 4, *Oxford Literary Review*, 12 (1990), 3–7.)

7 It could be argued that this chapter might have been devoted to the literary theories associated with Jacques Lacan rather than those associated with Freud himself, in so far as these two sets of theories can be distinguished. I take little account of Lacan in what follows, for two reasons. First, I think it is fair to say that, despite some auspicious beginnings, Lacanian theory has not yet achieved the degree of penetration and currency among literary critics (past and present) that Freudian theory has done. This no doubt has much to do with the notorious difficulty of Lacan's work and the fact that much of it still awaits publication. Second, as the reader will discover in due course, there is another post-Freudian psychoanalytical development that I do wish to discuss in some detail and which is, alongside ego psychology and Lacan, one of the three most important such developments: object relations.

8 Emile Benveniste, 'Remarks on the Function of Language in Freudian Theory', 65, in id., *Problems in General Linguistics*, trans Mary Elizabeth Meek (Coral Gables: University of Miami Press, 1971), 65–75.

9 *The Pelican Freud Library*, iv. *The Interpretation of Dreams*, ed. Angela Richards (Harmondsworth: Penguin, 1976), 368; referred to below as *PFL* iv.

10 Freud often discussed types of mental orientation that remind us of characters from literature: those 'wrecked by success', for example, like Lady Macbeth, or Heathcliff after the ruin of the Lintons and the Earnshaws. His discussion of Lady Macbeth and her husband in 'Some Character-Types Met With in Psychoanalytic Work', e.g., is very convincing indeed. The 'germs of fear which break out in Macbeth on the night of the murder do not develop further in *him* but in *her*', he writes, astutely; 'what he feared in his pangs of conscience is fulfilled in her; she becomes all remorse and he is all defiance' (*PFL* xiv. 307–8).

11 Lionel Trilling, *The Liberal Imagination: Essays on Literature and Society* (Oxford: Oxford University Press, 1981), 50.

12 Richard Wollheim, *On Art and the Mind* (Cambridge, MA: Harvard University Press, 1974), 333.

13 Elizabeth Dalton, *Unconscious Structure in 'The Idiot': A Study in Literature and Psychoanalysis* (Princeton: Princeton University Press, 1979), 10.

14 *The Pelican Freud Library*, xi. *On Metapsychology: The Theory of Psychoanalysis*, ed. Angela Richards (London: Penguin, 1984), 151.

15 David Archard, *Consciousness and the Unconscious* (London: Hutchinson, 1984), 25.

16 S.L. Goldberg, 'Shakespeare's Centrality', 10, *Critical Review*, 18 (1976), 3–22.
17 Trilling, *The Liberal Imagination*, 43.
18 Dan Jacobson, *Adult Pleasures: Essays on Writers and Readers* (London: André Deutsch, 1988), 16.
19 Joseph Conrad, *Heart of Darkness* (Harmondsworth: Penguin, 1973), 39.
20 Hanna Segal records this example of the suspension of disbelief: 'She dreamt that she was driving in her car to work. There was some anxiety at this point in the dream because the electric current was cut off, but she realized that she had a battery torch of her own and that the battery was in working order. When she arrived at work, she waited for a doctor to turn up to help her; but when he turned up he had a broken arm in a sling and was useless. She slowly realized that the work she was supposed to carry out was the opening up of an enormous mass grave. She started digging alone by the light of her little torch. Gradually, as she dug, she realized that not all the people buried in this grave were dead. Moreover, to her great encouragement, those who were still alive immediately began to dig with her. At the end of the dream, she had a very strong feeling that two things had been achieved; one was that anyone who was still alive had been rescued from this mass grave, and had become her helper; and, secondly, that those people who were dead could now be taken out of the anonymous grave and (this seemed extremely important to her in the dream) could now be buried properly with their names on the grave. At some point in the dream, she thought that all the victims in the grave were women.' (*Introduction to the Work of Melanie Klein* (London: Karnac, 1988), 93–4.)
21 Michael Riffaterre, *Fictional Truth* (Baltimore: Johns Hopkins University Press, 1990), xvii.
22 Jane Austen, *Emma*, ed. Ronald Blythe (London: Penguin, 1966), 331.
23 Charles Dickens, *Bleak House* (Oxford: Oxford University Press, 1948), 22.
24 Charlotte Brontë, *Jane Eyre*, ed. Q.D. Leavis (Harmondsworth: Penguin, 1966), 311; in what follows I pass over the phallic elements of Bertha's 'swelled and dark', 'bloodshot' face: elements which may explain Jane's fascination with it as well as her revulsion.
25 Ibid. 261.
26 D.W. Winnicott, *Playing and Reality*, (Harmondsworth: Penguin, 1974), 124.
27 Archard, *Consciousness and the Unconscious*, 19.
28 Ibid. 21–2; my italics.
29 Ibid. 22.
30 Michael Polanyi, *Personal Knowledge: Towards a Post-Critical Philosophy* (London: Routledge and Kegan Paul, 1962), 122.
31 Ibid. 129.
32 It is a revealing aspect of Freud's thought and his legacy that it has proved hard for his commentators to say exactly where such processes belong in his account of the unconscious: 'if what may be called a "moment of insight" ... sometimes occurs', writes Jean Laplanche, '– the resurgence of a forgotten memory, a sudden illumination – it may be said that this phenomenon, which is unquestionably conscious in the descriptive sense, does not allow us to decide whether it belongs topographically to the conscious system' (Jean Laplanche and Serge Leclaire, 'The Unconscious: A Psychoanalytic Study', 128, *Yale French Studies*, 48 (1972), 118–75).

33 Richard Wollheim, *Freud*, 2nd edn (London: Fontana, 1991), xv.

34 Marion Milner, *On Not Being Able to Paint* (New York: International Universities Press, 1957), 71–2. Milner expands the point later: 'the naming of it [a sketch] to oneself as a potato or a jug or a human face could completely shatter one's awareness of the rhythmic relations in the scribble. Or rather, as soon as a scribble became recognisable objects the whole rhythmic pattern of it could become violently altered and pushed in another direction' (ibid. 76).

35 Virginia Woolf, *To the Lighthouse* (Everyman's Library Series, London: J.M. Dent, 1938), 182.

36 Milner, *On Not Being Able to Paint*, 72.

37 Ibid. 73–4.

38 Ibid. 73.

39 Woolf, *To the Lighthouse*, 98.

40 Ibid. 203–4.

41 Hanna Segal, *The Work of Hanna Segal; A Kleinian Approach to Clinical Practice: 'Delusion and Artistic Creativity' and Other Psychoanalytic Essays* (London: Free Association Books, 1986), 213; referred to below as *WHS*.

42 Hanna Segal, *Dream, Phantasy and Art* (London: Routledge, 1991), 30; referred to below as *DPA*. This account of fantasy 'continually interacting with perception' is one that should be compared with Marion Milner's account of drawing ('restraining conscious attention, or rather, a quick willingness to have it and then forgo it') quoted above. This interaction is also (in the most general sense) itself one of the 'dialogues', mentioned in Chapter 1, which help constitute literature.

43 *WHS* 43. 'For our continued influxes of feeling are modified and directed by our thoughts,' Wordsworth wrote in the preface to *Lyrical Ballads*, 'which are indeed the representatives of all our past feelings'.

44 Trilling, *The Liberal Imagination*, 54.

45 See 'Delusion and Artistic Creativity', in *WHS* 207–16.

46 Psychoanalytic critics, as we might expect, have often had recourse to this old story. 'In moments of high inspiration,' Kurt Eissler writes, 'the artist is in a state of excitement and reduced reality-testing ... so immersed in the onrush of internal imagery as to be, in effect, immune to the reality that surrounds him – very much as though he were in the grip of an acute psychosis' (Eissler, *Discourse on Hamlet and 'Hamlet': A Psychoanalytic Enquiry* (New York: International Universities Press, 1971), 547). This passage might be compared with one from an entirely different source: 'After two or three stanzas and several images by which he himself was astonished, his work took possession of him and he experienced the approach of what is called inspiration. At such moments the correlation of forces controlling the artist is, as it were, stood on its head. The ascendancy is no longer with the artist or the state of mind he is struggling to express, but with the language, his instrument of expression. Language, the home and dwelling of beauty and meaning, itself begins to think and speak for man, and turns wholly into music, not in the sense of outward, audible sounds but by virtue of the power and momentum of the inward flow. Then, like the current of a mighty river polishing stones and turning wheels by its very movement, the flow of speech creates in passing, by the force of its own laws, rhyme and rhythm

and countless other forms and formations, still more important and until now undiscovered, unconsidered, and unnamed.' (Boris Pasternak, *Dr Zhivago*, trans. Max Hayward and Manya Harari (London: Collins, 1961), 427.) The point being that the inversion of 'the correlation of forces controlling the artist' Pasternak's poet experiences may imply all sorts of things, but not psychosis. Still less does it suggest any form of *immunity* to reality.

47 Joseph Conrad, *Lord Jim* (Harmondsworth: Penguin, 1949), 138.

48 *DPA* 89. Hard evidence for this specific idea is difficult to find. Though he sailed as a senior officer in many more, Conrad commanded only two vessels: the barque *Otago* between January 1888 and March 1889; and a Congo paddle-steamer, the *Roi des Belges*, which he took charge of for a matter of days in September 1890, during the captain's illness. Though there is evidence of depression in the Congo and of first-command nerves on the *Otago*, there is none to suggest that Conrad started writing on either of these trips. His first novel, *Almayer's Folly*, was started, it would appear, not on board ship at all but in a state of idleness, in London, in Autumn 1889. The MS was carried round the world for years before being completed in 1894, and chapters were added on ship and on shore as circumstances permitted; as Conrad was often depressed when idle, he no doubt turned to his novel during lulls on sea or land. (In *A Personal Record* he mentions working on the book while second mate on the *Adowa*, icebound at Rouen.) Of course, Conrad may have written something on board the *Otago*, but we do not know. In her account Hanna Segal mentions a letter of Conrad's, linking first command, depression, and first writing, but she gives no provenance or date. The point she makes, however, about the presence of solitude, responsibility, and depressive anxiety in both captaincy and authorship is a fair one. In the preface to *A Personal Record*, for example, Conrad speaks of that book's 'presenting faithfully the feelings and sensations connected with the writing of my first book and with my first contact with the sea' (*A Personal Record*, ed. Zdzislaw Najder (Oxford: Oxford University Press, 1988), xxi).

49 Joseph Conrad, *The Shadow-Line: A Confession*, ed. Jacques Berthoud (London: Penguin, 1986), 124. At the climax of *his* despair, and with 'Loneliness … closing on him', Lord Jim, Marlow believed, 'tried to write – to somebody – and gave it up' (*Lord Jim*, 307).

50 *The Shadow-Line*, 125.

51 Joseph Conrad, 'The Secret Sharer', 89, in id., *Twixt Land and Sea: Three Tales* (Harmondsworth: Penguin, 1978), 85–130; referred to below as 'SS'.

52 'SS' 96. Leggatt's 'doubleness' is psychological not physical. The captain himself admits 'He was not a bit like me, really' ('SS' 99).

53 *The Selected Melanie Klein*, ed. Juliet Mitchell (London: Penguin, 1986), 143.

54 Mr Burns, the chief mate in *The Shadow-Line*, is similarly hirsute: 'his red moustaches captured one's eyes exclusively, like something artificial' (*The Shadow-Line*, 99). In *The Mirror of the Sea*, Conrad mentions his first mate on the *Otago*, Charles Born, memorable for 'a red moustache, a lean face, also red, and an uneasy eye'. On the *Otago*'s leaving Bangkok, Conrad goes on, 'a bit of manœuvering of mine among the islands of the Gulf of Siam had given him an unforgettable scare. Ever since then he had nursed in secret

a bitter idea of my utter recklessness' (*The Mirror of the Sea*, ed. Zdzislaw Najder (Oxford: Oxford University Press, 1988), 18–19).

55 'SS' 127–8. '[W]hatever the ship', Conrad reminds us, 'it is in the forepart of her that her chief mate feels most at home', or should feel most at home in the proper order of things (*The Mirror of the Sea*, 17). To send the mate foreward is thus to take control.

56 *Heart of Darkness*, 66–7.

57 *The Shadow-Line*, 111.

58 *Lord Jim*, 83.

59 *The Pelican Freud Library*, vi. *Jokes and their Relation to the Unconscious*, ed. Angela Richards (Harmondsworth: Penguin, 1976), 302; referred to below as *PFL* vi.

60 Henri Bergson, *Le rire: Essai sur la signification du comique* (Paris: Presses Universitaires de France, 1940), 14.

61 Ibid. 4, 39.

62 Ibid. 44, 8.

63 *A Personal Record*, xvii, 98–9; the westward winter voyage round the Horn, Conrad's editor lugubriously reminds us, is one Conrad himself never made. He took the easier route: eastwards, in summer.

64 Ibid. 36, 18.

65 Ibid. xix ('It rests notably, among others, on the idea of Fidelity') and Conrad, 'Books', 9, in id., *Notes on Life and Letters* (London: J.M. Dent, 1949), 3–10.

66 *A Personal Record*, 94.

67 See F.R. Leavis, '*The Shadow-Line*' and ' "The Secret Sharer" ' in id., '*Anna Karenina' and Other Essays* (London: Chatto and Windus, 1967), 92–110 and 111–20. Critics of Leavis often and rightly remind us of the emotional and intellectual investment he made in concepts like 'standards', 'continuity', and tradition. What they tend to ignore is that Leavis also made something of a habit of revealing the inadequacy of such concepts for conservative writers like Swift ('The positives disappear'), Pope ('his creativeness is not merely a matter of his being able to realize an ideal Augustan order'), and Johnson ('his limitations appear when the training begins to manifest itself as unjustifiable resistance'). (These remarks bearing on 'the essential tendency of the Augustan tradition' are all made in *The Common Pursuit*.) He comes to similar conclusions when discussing *The Rainbow* in his book on D.H. Lawrence. The implication being, that Leavis is neither the simpleminded nor the authoritarian defender of tradition-as-inertia that he is often represented as being.

68 *The Shadow-Line*, 83.

69 'SS' 91. Jim is similarly over-confident before the *Patna* runs aground: 'A marvellous stillness pervaded the world, and the stars, together with the serenity of their rays, seemed to shed upon the earth the assurance of everlasting security' (*Lord Jim*, 19).

70 Conrad, 'Tradition', 201, in *Notes on Lives and Letters*, 194–201.

71 Leavis, ' "The Secret Sharer" ', 114.

72 See Marlow on 'going home', the need to 'render an account' in so doing, and the unavoidable obligation 'to meet the spirit that dwells within the land, under its sky, in its air, in its valleys, and on its rises, in its fields, in its waters and its trees – a mute friend, judge, and inspirer. Say what you like,

to get its joy, to breathe its peace, to face its truth, one must return with a clear consciousness' (*Lord Jim*, 169). ('Conscience' is the word we expect to meet at the end of this passage, of course: 'consciousness' is the word we get.) Given the unforgiving form of this moral absolute, it is no wonder so many of Conrad's heroes, like he himself, chose to stay away. On one occasion Conrad did describe a return to Poland ('Poland Revisited', in *Notes on Life and Letters*, 141–73): a trip which, he felt, made 'the order and continuity of his life' since leaving that country appear 'to his conscience as a series of betrayals' (ibid. 149). The brief account of his father's death and funeral to be found in that essay evokes the silence and abstemiousness of the young Conrad, without 'a single tear to shed' for his father and 'nothing in my aching head but a few words, some such stupid sentences as, "It's done," or, "It's accomplished" ': 'I could see again the small boy of that day following a hearse; a space kept clear in which I walked alone, conscious of an enormous following...' (ibid. 169).

4 'A Province of Truth': Criticism and History

1 R.G. Collingwood, *The Idea of History* (Oxford: Oxford University Press, 1961), 236; referred to below as *IH*.
2 *IH* 242. On the basis of what has been said in Chapter 3 it will be obvious where I would want to revise Collingwood's account here. It is not exactly the novelist's *aim* that characters and incidents be *shown* 'developing in a manner determined by a necessity internal to themselves'. The fact is that they inevitably do develop in this way if they develop at all.
3 *IH* 246. The fact that this aim can never be wholly achieved is a problem of historical knowledge, and there is nothing in it to make a historian give up his work. As Collingwood says, 'this separation between what is attempted in principle and what is achieved in practice is the lot of mankind, not a peculiarity of historical thinking' (*IH* 247). The only difference between Collingwood and ourselves where this principle is concerned is that we are more sceptical, indeed more cynical, about the historian's ability to act on it. Many in Collingwood's time were reluctant to believe that the truth of history could be of the same order as the imagination of the novelist; many nowadays are reluctant to believe that the imaginative constructions and narratives of historians can bear any relation to the truth.
4 David Bromwich, *A Choice of Inheritance: Self and Community from Edmund Burke to Robert Frost* (Cambridge, MA: Havard University Press, 1989), 280.
5 'Jane Austen is by common consent', Marilyn Butler writes, 'an author remarkably sure of her values' (Butler, *Jane Austen and the War of Ideas*, rev. edn (Oxford: Oxford University Press, 1987), 1). I do not believe we can hold such a view of the person who wrote *Mansfield Park* or *Emma*, novels which, bossy as they undoubtedly can be, are so out of a profound and manifest sense of insecurity. Still, such a view is subtlety itself compared with Terry Eagleton, for whom Butler's study 'sheared coolly through decades of diplomatic Trillingesque talk about Austen's "tensions" and finely-tuned ambivalences and actually said that, well, when you get down to it, she's just a straight *Tory*' (quoted in ibid. xvii).

6 Stephen Greenblatt, 'Towards a Poetics of Culture', 1, in H. Aram Veeser (ed.), *The New Historicism* (New York: Routledge, 1989), 1–14.

7 Marilyn Butler, 'Against Tradition: The Case for a Particularized Historical Method', 25, in Jerome J. McGann (ed.), *Historical Studies and Literary Criticism* (Madison: University of Wisconsin Press, 1985), 25–47.

8 Jerome J. McGann, *The Beauty of Inflections: Literary Investigations in Historical Method and Theory* (Oxford: Oxford University Press, 1985), 9; referred to below as *BI*.

9 Marilyn Butler, *Romantics, Rebels and Reactionaries: English Literature and its Background 1760–1830* (Oxford: Oxford University Press, 1981), 185.

10 Veeser, 'Introduction', xiii, in *The New Historicism*, ix–xvi.

11 Stephen Greenblatt, 'Shakespeare and the Exorcists', 164, in Patricia Parker and Geoffrey Hartman (eds.), *Shakespeare and the Question of Theory* (New York: Methuen, 1985), 163–87; referred to below as 'SE'.

12 Butler, *Jane Austen and the War of Ideas*, xii.

13 Occasionally such vocabulary becomes overtly horticultural. For Marilyn Butler, 'most influence criticism ignores minor writing, reviewing, newspaper articles, the intellectual ambience which is the actual seedbed of intellectual discussion' (Butler, 'Against Tradition', 29). To which 'influence criticism' can only ask three questions: how simple or self-evident a relation is there between 'intellectual discussion' and literature?; if such a relationship can be substantiated, how much of any particular work of literature would it explain?; and, finally, what metaphorical sleight of hand on Butler's part permits the vague 'thinness' of *ambience* (atmosphere) to be at once transformed into the thick, generative loam of 'seedbed'?

14 This is not simply a matter of theory, needless to say; in a book about pedagogical practice, Gerald Graff says again and again (and again) how crucial it is to 'teach the cultural text'. 'Current schools of criticism', he writes, 'disagree over whether anything like an objective reconstruction of the relevant context of any text is possible, just as they disagree over how much real-world referentiality and authorial agency can be ascribed to any text and how broadly the "relevant context" should be defined. ... But despite these substantive and important disagreements, there is considerable agreement on at least one point: that meaning is not an autonomous essence within the words of a text but something dependent for its comprehension on prior texts and situations.' (*Professing Literature: An Institutional History* (Chicago: University of Chicago Press, 1987), 256.)

15 Butler, 'Against Tradition', 43–4. This is the first of a list of five principles of Butler's historical method: a method which, she reminds us, 'might be put to any ideological use' (ibid. 43), like Tupperware.

16 Butler writes of Jane Austen: 'A genre is an established code, a medium of communication already learnt by writer and reader; to participate with Austen, we have to be ready to re-learn the code her first readers already knew' (*Jane Austen and the War of Ideas*, xxxi). Notice this peremptory *have*. Butler admits that 'a great novel, a *Tristram Shandy* or an *Emma*, can also be understood on our terms: each has a vitality that transcends its genre' (ibid. 3). But in so far as a novel is good (never mind great) it will inevitably transcend and transform its genre, and force its readers to learn entirely new 'codes'. This was a point made by Wordsworth when, in the

advertisement to *Lyrical Ballads*, he spoke of 'that most dreadful enemy to our [reading] pleasures, our own pre-established codes of decision'.

17 Butler, *Romantics, Rebels and Reactionaries*, 185.

18 Jerome J. McGann, *Social Values and Poetic Acts: The Historical Judgment of Literary Work* (Cambridge, MA: Harvard University Press, 1988), 75; referred to below as *SV*.

19 Leavis, 'The Responsible Critic: or the Function of Criticism at any Time', 292–3, in id. (ed.), *A Selection from 'Scrutiny'*, 2 vols (Cambridge: Cambridge University Press, 1968), ii. 281–316; my italics. Leavis' essay is best read in this edition, as it preserves the entire debate between himself and F.W. Bateson concerning the latter's idea of 'the final context' in which poems 'need to be read' (ibid. 291). Bateson anticipated the New Historicists in many respects, and so, even though he and Leavis battled it out in 1953, their exchange is a *locus classicus*.

20 Veeser (ed.), *The New Historicism*, xi.

21 Historical *idées reçues* are common amongst New Historicists. None that I have read have gone so far as to produce for current consumption that canard familiar to every British history pupil, 'The middle classes were rising ... ', but Marilyn Butler, for example, does inform us in all seriousness that 'The middle of the eighteenth century was a period of growing insight into the subjective mind' (*Jane Austen and the War of Ideas*, 7), as if 'the subjective mind' was some kind of separate (and unhistorical) phenomenon better or worse understood in different historical eras.

22 The apparently hyper-significant relationship between events in nature and in human affairs, regarded by some commentators as an Elizabethan World Picture internalized by Shakespeare, is often enough shown by him to be either a product of hindsight, or trivial, or both. A representative instance is *Macbeth* II. iv., where Ross and 'an Old Man' discuss the awesome portents of the nights preceding Duncan's murder. Among these terrifying incidents are a falcon being killed by a mousing owl the previous Tuesday, and some horses breaking out of their stables and indulging in acts of equine cannibalism. It could be argued that one of the things the play as a whole suggests is the danger of such superstitious thinking.

23 'SE' 164; my italics. As regards the absolute disjunction of the literary and the nonliterary, when Leavis came to thinking about reform of the English Tripos at Cambridge, here are some of the issues he thought students of the seventeenth century might address in their studies: the background in religious history; Calvinism to Puritan individualism; Church and State; the causes of the Civil War; the social, literary, and cultural changes during the Restoration; the social–economic correlations of literary history; the rise of the Press; and so on and so forth – not a 'purely literary' issue in the whole list. (F.R. Leavis, *Education and the University: A Sketch for an 'English School'* (London: Chatto and Windus, 1948), 52–3.)

24 McGann quotes some comments by an earlier critic, Milman Parry, to the effect that: 'The literature of every country and of every time is understood as it ought to be only by the author and his contemporaries. ... The task, therefore, of one who lives in another age and wants to appreciate that work correctly, consists precisely in rediscovering the varied information

and complexes of ideas which the author assumed to be the natural property of his audience' (*SV* 121). All I can say about such a view of literature is that some readers never grow out of it.

25 Quoted in Leavis, 'The Responsible Critic', 280.

26 Ibid. 291.

27 Ibid. 294, 307.

28 Ibid. 294.

29 Butler, 'Against Tradition', 44.

30 Leavis, 'The Responsible Critic', 293. As we have seen, it was the notion of context 'as something determinate' that concerned Leavis in historicism. Similarly, Jacques Derrida writes at the beginning of 'Signature Event Context', with speech–act theory in mind, 'does the notion of context not conceal, behind a certain confusion, philosophical presuppositions of a very determinate nature? Stating it in the most summary manner possible, I shall try to demonstrate why a context is never absolutely determinable, or rather, why its determination can never be entirely certain or saturated' (Derrida, *Limited Inc* (Evanston: Northwestern University Press, 1988), 3). See ibid. 64; my italics: 'even in the ideal case ... there must already be a certain element of play, a certain remove, a certain degree of independence with regard to the *origin*, to *production*, or to intention in all its "vital," "simple" "actuality" or "*determinateness*," etc.'

31 Leavis, 'The Responsible Critic', 295.

32 See the essay of that name in Richard Wollheim, *Art and Its Objects*, 2nd. edn (Cambridge: Cambridge University Press, 1980), 157–66.

33 Jacques Derrida, 'Before the Law', 187, in id., *Acts of Literature*, ed. Derek Attridge (New York: Routledge, 1992), 181–220. See id., 'Declarations of Independence', trans. Tom Keenan and Tom Pepper, 13, *New Political Science*, 15: 2 (Summer 1986), 7–15: 'How is a State made or founded, how does a State make or found itself? And an independence? And the autonomy of one which both gives itself, and signs, its own law? Who signs all these authorizations to sign?'

34 Michael Riffaterre, *Fictional Truth* (Baltimore: Johns Hopkins University Press, 1990), 6–7, 84.

35 Ibid. 54.

36 Hayden White, ' "Figuring the Nature of the Times Deceased": Literary Theory and Historical Writing', 22, in Ralph Cohen (ed.), *The Future of Literary Theory* (New York: Routledge, 1989), 19–43.

37 Hayden White, *The Content of the Form: Narrative Discourse and Historical Representation* (Baltimore: Johns Hopkins University Press, 1987), x; referred to below as *CF*.

38 Hayden White, *Tropics of Discourse: Essays in Cultural Criticism* (Baltimore: Johns Hopkins University Press, 1978), 22; referred to below as *TD*.

39 Hayden White, *Metahistory: The Historical Imagination in Nineteenth-Century Europe* (Baltimore: Johns Hopkins University Press, 1973), 14–15, 5; referred to below as *Mh*.

40 White, 'Figuring the Nature of the Times Deceased', 25.

41 Edward Said, *Orientalism: Western Conceptions of the Orient* (London: Penguin, 1985), 104.

42   Ibid. 21–2.
43   Ibid. 24.
44   The number of foursomes White corrals into his scheme is truly remarkable. At various points we have Northrop Frye's (Romance, Comedy, Tragedy, and Satire), itself having murky origins in the four seasons; Karl Mannheim's (Anarchism, Conservatism, Radicalism, and Liberalism); Vico's (Metaphor, Metonymy, Synecdoche, and Irony), itself taken up by Kenneth Burke; two from Hegel (the birth, maturity, old age, and death of civilizations, but also the Universal, Pragmatic, Critical, and Conceptual kinds of reflective history); Classical drama's (*pathos, agon, sparagmos,* and *anagnorisis*), itself taken up by Marx; Stephen Pepper's 'four world hypotheses' (formism, organicism, mechanism, and contextualism); Droysen's four kinds of representation (Interrogative, Didactic, Discussive, and Recitative); Croce's varieties of nineteenth-century historical thought (Romantic, Idealistic, Positivistic, and 'New'); Eduard Fueter's varieties of the same thing (Romantic, Liberal, Realistic, and Scientific); Nietzsche's forms of historical consciousness (Antiquarian, Monumental, Critical, and 'Superhistorical'); two from Marx (the Elementary, Total, Generalized, and Money forms of exchange value, but also the Reactionary, Conservative, Utopian, and Scientific types of socialist consciousness); Piaget's four phases in infant development (sensorimotor, representational, operational, and logical); and last, but by no means least, Freud's four types of dream-work. The only two such groups White appears to have overlooked – both of which could be added to his scheme without much difficulty, no doubt – are the four historical stages of human subsistence developed by Scottish Enlightenment *philosophes* (hunting and gathering, nomadic, agricultural, and commercial), and the Fab Four themselves: John, Paul, George, and Ringo.
45   'Figuring the Nature of the Times Deceased', 24, 38, 34.
46   Paul Ricoeur, *Time and Narrative,* trans. Kathleen McLaughlin and David Pellauer, 3 vols (Chicago: University of Chicago Press, 1984–88), i. 82; referred to below as *TN.*
47   Paul Ricoeur, *Hermeneutics and the Human Sciences: Essays on Language, Action and Interpretation,* ed. and trans. John B. Thompson (Cambridge: Cambridge University Press, 1981), 289.
48   Ricoeur, *Hermeneutics and the Human Sciences,* 291.
49   Ibid. 296; my italics. The last word on Aristotle's unfortunate expression has, I think, been said by S.L. Goldberg: 'Who but a philosopher', he asks, 'would think it was *praising* poetry to call it more philosophical than history?' (*Agents and Lives: Moral Thinking in Literature* (Cambridge: Cambridge University Press, 1993), 150).
50   Jane Austen, *Northanger Abbey,* ed. Anne Ehrenpreis (Harmondsworth: Penguin, 1972), 202.
51   See ibid. 42, and Wordsworth's pref. to *Lyrical Ballads:* 'The principal object ... which I proposed to myself in these Poems was to chuse incidents and situations from common life, and to relate or describe them, throughout, as far as was possible, in a selection of language really used by men ... '.
52   George Eliot, *Middlemarch,* ed. Rosemary Ashton (London: Penguin, 1994), 341.
53   *Northanger Abbey,* 123.

5 Four Objections

1 Hayden White, *The Content of the Form: Narrative Discourse and Historical Representation* (Baltimore: Johns Hopkins University Press, 1987), 99.

2 F.R. Leavis, 'Literary Criticism and Philosophy', 213, in id., *The Common Pursuit* (Harmondsworth: Penguin, 1962), 211–22; my italics.

3 Richard Freadman, *Literature, Criticism and the Universities: Interviews with Leonie Kramer, S.L. Goldberg and Howard Felperin* (Perth, WA: The Centre for Studies in Australian Literature, University of Western Australia, 1983), 8.

4 Ibid. 11.

5 Isaiah Berlin, *The Hedgehog and the Fox: An Essay on Tolstoy's View of History*, rev. edn (London: Orion, 1992), 66.

6 Ibid. 75.

7 Ibid. 68.

8 See Louis Althusser, 'Ideology and Ideological State Apparatuses (Notes Towards an Investigation)', in id., *'Lenin and Philosophy' and Other Essays*, trans. Ben Brewster (London: New Left Books 1971), 123–73.

9 Louis Althusser, 'Marxism and Humanism', 234, in id., *For Marx*, trans. Ben Brewster (New York: Pantheon Books, 1969), 221–47; referred to below as 'MH'.

10 Ideology, writes Althusser, 'is indispensable in any society if men are to be formed, transformed and equipped to respond to the demands of their conditions of existence' ('MH' 235). No doubt; but in performing this function is ideology itself not bound to be transformed, and to transform the conditions of existence of which it is the product?

11 See Althusser, 'Ideology and State Ideological Apparatuses', 162–3.

12 Pierre Macherey, *A Theory of Literary Production*, trans. Geoffrey Wall (London: Routledge and Kegan Paul, 1978), 3–4; my italics; referred to below as *TLP*.

13 Jerome McGann, *The Beauty of Inflections: Literary Investigations in Historical Method and Theory* (Oxford: Oxford University Press, 1985), 280.

14 Jacques Derrida, *Margins of Philosophy*, trans. Alan Bass (Brighton: Harvester, 1982), 136. I have done some more bending of Derrida here. In asking this question, Derrida had in mind the unity of the individual subject as prescribed by Western metaphysics, an issue which is connected to the more strictly literary–critical question I am going to pursue, no doubt.

15 Samuel Johnson, *Lives of the English Poets*, ed. Arthur Waugh, 2 vols (London: Oxford University Press, 1906), ii. 485. 'The *Church-yard*', Johnson goes on, 'abounds with images which find a mirrour in every mind, and with sentiments to which every bosom returns an echo.'

16 F.R. Leavis, *English Literature in our Time and the University* (London: Chatto and Windus, 1969), 7.

17 Dan Jacobson, 'The Uselessness of Literature', 64, *Quadrant*, 36: 3 (Mar. 1982), 61–4.

18 Dan Jacobson, *Adult Pleasures: Essays on Writers and Readers* (London: André Deutsch, 1988), 16.

19 Jonathan Culler, *On Deconstruction: Theory and Criticism after Structuralism* (London: Routledge and Kegan Paul, 1983), 63, 61; referred to below as *OD*.

20 *OD* 52, 54, 58, 64; my italics.

21 Brontë to George Henry Lewes, 12 Jan. 1848; quoted in Juliet Barker, *The Brontës* (London: Weidenfeld and Nicolson, 1994), 547; my italics.
22 See Michael Riffaterre, 'Compelling Reader Responses', in Andrew Bennett (ed.), *Reading Reading: Essays on the Theory and Practice of Reading* (Tampere: Tampere English Studies, 1993), 85–106.
23 Henry James, 'Honoré de Balzac', 353, in id., *The Critical Muse: Selected Literary Criticism*, ed. Roger Gard (London: Penguin, 1987), 349–72.
24 Jacques Derrida, 'Some Questions and Responses', 258–9, in Nigel Fabb, Derek Attridge, Alan Durant, and Colin MacCabe (eds), *The Linguistics of Writing: Arguments Between Language and Literature* (Manchester: Manchester University Press, 1987), 252–64.
25 Richard Kearney, *Dialogues With Contemporary Continental Thinkers: The Phenomenological Heritage* (Manchester: Manchester University Press, 1984), 122.
26 Jacques Derrida, 'Biodegradables: Seven Diary Fragments', trans. Peggy Kamuf, 840, *Critical Inquiry*, 15 (Summer 1989), 812–73.
27 Ibid. 845.
28 Derek Attridge, ' "This Strange Institution Called Literature": An Interview with Jacques Derrida', 59, in Derrida, *Acts of Literature*, ed. Derek Attridge (London: Routledge, 1992), 33–75.
29 Ibid. 39
30 Trans. Tina Kendall, rev. Shari Benstock and Derek Attridge, *Acts of Literature*, 256–309; referred to below as 'UG'.
31 James Joyce, *Ulysses* (London: Penguin, 1992), 787. All references are to this edn.

Index

activity, in and of works of literature, 7, 16, 19, 35–41, 46–8, 64, 105–6, 107, 108, 109, 112, 116, 136, 143–4, 156, 160, 163, 168, 175, 194, 198, 203, 223, 240 n 10, 254 n 2, 255 n 16
Althusser, Louis, 236
  'Ideology and Ideological State Apparatuses', 206, 208
  'Marxism and Humanism', 206–9, 259 n 9
Amis, Martin, *London Fields*, 31
Archard, David, *Consciousness and the Unconscious*, 103, 113–14
Aristotelianism, North American neo-, 79–80
Aristotle, *Poetics*, 67, 241 n 10
Arnold, Matthew, 195–6
  'Sohrab and Rustum', 156–7
Attridge, Derek, 22
  ' "This Strange Institution Called Literature": An Interview with Jacques Derrida', 15, 22, 43, 227, 242 n 29, 244 n 50
Austen, Jane, 30, 31–2, 58, 159–60, 254 n 5, 255 n 16
  Emma, 109–10, 158
  Northanger Abbey, 198–200
  Pride and Prejudice, 73
autonomy, literary–theoretical, 15–20, 28, 33, 35–6, 48, 146, 153, 157, 160, 176–7, 194, 197–8, 202, 203, 205–6, 207, 211–12, 214, 220

Babel, Isaac, *You Must Know Everything*, 36
Balibar, Etienne, and Pierre Macherey, 'On Literature as an Ideological Form', 242 n 31
Bateson, F.W., 170–1, 256 n 19
Bennington, Geoffrey and Jacques Derrida, *Jacques Derrida*, 16

Benveniste, Emile, 'Remarks on the Function of Language in Freudian Theory', 98–9
Bergson, Henri, *Le rire*, 138–9
Berlin, Isaiah, *The Hedgehog and the Fox*, 204–8
Bloom, Harold, *The Western Canon*, 15
Bromwich, David, 'Literature and Theory', 150–1
Brontë, Charlotte,
  on authorial compulsion, 222
  Jane Eyre, 38, 64, 111–12, 214–15, 250 n 24
Brontë, Emily, *Wuthering Heights*, 69–72, 75–6
Butler, Marilyn,
  Jane Austen and the War of Ideas, 153, 254 n 5, 255 n 16, 256 n 21
  'Against Tradition', 152, 154, 171, 255 n 13
  Romantics, Rebels and Reactionaries, 153, 154
Byron, George Gordon Lord, 160
  Don Juan, 213

Carlyle, Thomas, 'On History', 33
chance, in literary production, 37–8
Collingwood, R.G., 119, 162, 181, 189, 193, 223
  and re-enactment, 173–5
  An Autobiography, 96–7
  The Idea of History, 146–50, 173–5
  The Principles of Art, 16
complicity, among readers of literature, 62–3, 218–22
Conrad, Joseph, 128–30, 252 n 48
  and conservatism, 140–2
  and humour, 136–9
  and tradition, 139–42
  Heart of Darkness, 107, 136
  Lord Jim, 137, 253 n 72

Conrad, Joseph – *continued*
  The Mirror of the Sea, 252 n 54,
    253 n 55
  Notes on Life and Letters, 140, 142,
    254 n 72
  A Personal Record, 140–1, 252 n 48
  'The Secret Sharer', 128–35, 137,
    142, 252 n 52
  The Shadow-Line, 129–30, 136–7,
    141–2
'contamination', literary-theoretical;
    see Derrida and 'contamination'
'context', as literary–theoretical
    principle, 153–5, 158, 167–9,
    171–5, 196, 255 n 14, 257 n 30
Culler, Jonathan, *On Deconstruction*,
    218–22

Dalton, Elizabeth, *Unconscious
    Structure in 'The Idiot'*, 101–2
deconstruction, 3–4, 13, 26–7, 167
Defoe, Daniel, *Moll Flanders*, 92–3
Derrida, Jacques (*see also* Attridge,
    Derek; Bennington, Geoffrey; and
    Kearney, Richard), 12–15, 21–30,
    32, 34, 40–42, 222–38, 243 nn 48
    and 49
  and 'contamination', 21–6, 28–33,
    223, 230–4, 238
  'At this Very Moment in this Work
    Here I Am', 21
  'Before the Law', 176–7
  'Biodegradables', 34, 225, 226
  'Border Lines', 242 n 30
  'Declarations of Independence',
    257 n 33
  'Force and Signification', 41
  'The Law of Genre', 21
  'Let Us Not Forget –
    Psychoanalysis', 249 n 6
  Limited Inc, 12–13, 257 n 30
  Margins of Philosophy, 215
  'No Apocalypse, Not Now (Full
    Speed Ahead, Seven Missiles,
    Seven Missives)', 17, 31
  Of Grammatology, 44
  Positions, 12, 24
  'The Principle of Reason', 29–33

'Some Questions and Responses',
    224–5
  'Some Statements and Truisms
    about Neologisms, Newisms,
    Postisms, Parasitisms, and other
    Small Seismisms',13, 24
  'The Time of a Thesis', 12–15, 25
  Writing and Difference, 40, 243 n 49,
    248 n 4
  'Ulysses Gramaphone', 227–33
'dialectical relationship', of author
    and text, reader and text, text
    and context, 35–7, 46–8, 104,
    106, 108–11, 115–19, 143–4,
    171–2, 218, 223, 245 n 73,
    251 n 46
Dickens, Charles, 30, 59, 147, 160,
    211, 246 n 9
  Barnaby Rudge, 73
  Bleak House, 111
Dickinson, Emily, 'Because I could not
    Stop for Death', 160–3
Donne, John, 'Satire 4', 165
Dostoevsky, Fyodor, *Crime and
    Punishment*, 175
Dworkin, Gerald, *The Theory and
    Practice of Autonomy*, 16

Eagleton, Terry, 153, 254 n 5
Eissler, Kurt, *Discourse on Hamlet and
    'Hamlet'*, 251 n 46
Eliot, George,
  'The *Antigone* and Its Moral', 64
  Middlemarch, 35, 39–40, 68–9,
    77–8, 199
Eliot, T.S.,
  'The Love Song of J. Alfred
    Prufrock', 78, 193–4
  'Tradition and the Individual
    Talent', 45–8
  The Waste Land, 38, 48, 242 n 41
essentialism, literary–theoretical, 20

Foucault, Michel, 240 n 6
Freadman, Richard, *Literature,
    Criticism, and the Universities*, 204
Freud, Sigmund, 60, 95–120, 122–3,
    135, 178

Freud, Sigmund – *continued*
  and wish-fulfilment, 101, 102–5,
    125, 143
  Art and Literature, 95, 98, 99–100,
    101, 116, 249 n 10
  The Interpretation of Dreams, 99, 100,
    102, 106–8
  Jokes and their Relation to the
    Unconscious, 137–8
  On Metapsychology, 103

'general text', the literary–theoretical,
  55, 65, 75, 76, 169, 181, 212–3
Goldberg, S.L. (*see also* Freadman,
  Richard), 204, 220–1
  Agents and Lives, 82, 258 n 49
  'Shakespeare's Centrality', 44–5, 104
Graff, Gerald, 24
  Professing Literature, 255 n 14
Greenblatt, Stephen,
  'Towards a Poetics of Culture', 152
  'Shakespeare and the Exorcists',
    153, 163–9

Havel, Vaclav, *Letters to Olga*, 244 n 53
historicism, literary–theoretical, 4–6,
  154, 169–75, 256 n 23

ideality, literary–theoretical, 12–15,
  240 n 7
'identification', in works of literature,
  126–7, 220–1, 227
inspiration, in literary production, 37–8
institutionalism, literary–theoretical,
  6–7, 14–15, 17, 24, 28, 32–3, 41,
  42–4, 176–7, 184, 210, 240 n 6
'intermittence', psychological, 114–16

Jacobson, Dan,
  Adult Pleasures, 38–9, 85, 106, 217
  The Beginners, 37
  'The Uselessness of Literature', 217,
    242 n 42
James, Henry, 30, 32, 83, 199
  The Ambassadors, 90–1
  The American Scene, 91–2
  Complete Notebooks, 91
  'Honoré de Balzac', 223–4

  preface to *The Awkward Age*, 36
  preface to *The Princess*
    Casamassima, 84, 92
  preface to *The Wings of the Dove*, 62
  The Princess Casamassima, 89
  Selected Letters, 91
  Selected Literary Criticism, 92
Johnson, Samuel, *Lives of the English*
    Poets, 216
Joyce, James,
  Ulysses, 30, 57, 100, 233–4, 245 n 5
  'Ithaca', 234–8
Kearney, Richard, *Dialogues With*
    Contemporary Continental Thinkers,
    225
Keats, John, 160, 211
  Letters, 36
Klein, Melanie (see also 'positions'),
  120, 122, 131

Lacan, Jacques, 249 n 7
  Écrits, 248 n 4
Lacoue-Labarthe, Philippe, and Jean-
  Luc Nancy, *The Literary Absolute*,
  243 n 49
Laplanche, Jean, and Serge Leclaire,
  'The Unconscious', 250 n 32
Larkin, Philip, 'A Study of Reading
  Habits', 200
'latency', psychological (*see also*
  'intermittence'), 113–15
Lawrence, D.H., 30, 32, 159, 160
  Selected Letters, 86
Leavis, F.R., 1, 27–8, 174, 204
  and conservatism, 253 n 67
  English Literature in Our Time and the
    University, 46, 217
  Education and the University, 256 n 23
  The Great Tradition, 58
  'Literary Criticism and Philosophy',
    203
  'Reality and Sincerity', 22
  'The Responsible Critic', 23, 51,
    158, 170–2, 256 n 19
  '"The Secret Sharer"', 141–2
  '*The Shadow-Line*', 141
liberal humanism, literary–theoretical,
  6, 10, 24, 80–6, 167, 210, 216–17

McGann, Jerome J., 169, 170, 194
  The Beauty of Inflections, 152–62,
    213
  Social Values and Poetic Acts, 155–8,
    175
Macherey, Pierre, *A Theory of Literary
    Production*, 18–19, 200, 209–11
MacIntyre, Alasdair, 63–78, 79, 88, 195
  After Virtue, 63–5, 67–8, 74–6
Mandelstam, Nadezhda, *Hope Against
    Hope*, 36
Mann, Thomas,
  'Freud and the Future', 95, 96
  Joseph and His Brothers, 36
Marvell, Andrew, 'Horatian Ode', 172
Melville, Herman, *Moby-Dick*, 81–2
Miller, J. Hillis, 'Presidential Address
    1986', 4–7, 213, 239 n 2
Milner, Marion, *On Not Being Able to
    Paint*, 117, 118, 126,
    251 nn 34 and 42

Nabokov, Vladimir, 60
  on pornography, 246 n 13
  Lolita, 60–62, 215–16, 246 n 14
  'On a Book Entitled *Lolita*', 62,
    246 n 13
New Criticism, the, 1, 4
New Historicism, 4–6, 15, 42, 145–6,
    150–69, 170–1, 175, 176,
    239 n 2, 256 n 21
Newman, Cardinal John Henry, *The
    Idea of the University*, 17, 50–1
Nietzsche, Friedrich, 172, 247 n 26
Nussbaum, Martha, 78–94
  Love's Knowledge, 78–9, 82–90

object relations, in psychology, 120–8

Parry, Milman, 173, 256 n 24
Pasternak, Boris, *Dr Zhivago*, 251 n 46
Piercy, Marge, *Woman on the Edge of
    Time*, 199
Plato, 65, 79–80, 89
Polanyi, Michael,
  and 'incubation', 115–7, 123, 126
  Personal Knowledge, 115
Pope, Alexander, 'Epistle to
    Burlington', 108–9

'positions' (Kleinian: paranoid–
    schizoid and depressive), 120–22,
    130, 135
post-structuralism, 1–4, 248 n 4
Proust, Marcel, *Remembrance of Things
    Past*, 57, 60

Richardson, Samuel, *Clarissa*, 176
Ricoeur, Paul, 189–99
  and the '*Gegenüber*', 192–7
  The Conflict of Interpretations, 248 n 4
  *Hermeneutics and the Human
    Sciences*, 197
  Time and Narrative, 189–97
Riffaterre, Michael,
  'Compelling Reader Responses', 222
  Fictional Truth, 109, 177
Rorty, Richard, 51–63, 66, 79, 82, 84,
    88, 139, 183, 196, 247 n 26
  Contingency, Irony, and Solidarity,
    52–61
  Essays on Heidegger and Others, 49,
    52, 53, 55, 58–9, 66, 245 n 9,
    247 n 26

Said, Edward, *Orientalism*, 183–5
Segal, Alex,
  '"The Intentional Fallacy"
    Deconstructed', 241 n 21
  'The Pen and the Voice', 241 n 21
Segal, Hanna, 127–8, 135–6, 143
  Dream, Phantasy and Art, 122–3,
    124, 126, 127, 129
  *Introduction to the Work of Melanie
    Klein*, 250 n 20
  The Work of Hanna Segal, 121–6,
    128, 143
Shakespeare, William, 45, 166
  Hamlet, 82, 87–8, 92, 99–100, 105,
    166
  1 Henry IV, 169
  King Lear, 77, 92, 163–9
  Macbeth, 166, 249 n 10, 256 n 22
Sinyavsky, Andrei (a.k.a. 'Abram
    Tertz'), 199
Solzhenitsyn, Alexander, 27, 172
Sophocles, *Antigone*, 64–5
'story-telling animal', man as, 65–78
structuralism, 1, 178–9, 181

Taylor, Charles, 63–78, 79, 88
  Sources of the Self, 66–8, 76–8
Thackeray, William Makepeace,
  Pendennis, 245 n 5
Tolstoy, Leo, 80, 83–4, 204–5, 207
Trilling, Lionel, *The Liberal
  Imagination*, 97, 100, 104, 126

Veeser, H. Aram, *The New Historicism*,
  153, 164
volition, in works of literature, 36–9,
  109, 110, 240 n 10

White, Hayden, 178–89, 195
  and four-part intellectual structures,
    185, 257 n 44
  The Content of the Form, 67, 178,
    186–8, 191, 198, 202

'Figuring the Nature of the Times
  Deceased', 178, 188
Metahistory, 179–80, 182–3, 185–6
Tropics of Discourse, 178–82, 185–8
Winnicott, D.W., *Playing and Reality*,
  112
Wollheim, Richard,
  Art and Its Objects, 176
  Freud, 116
  On Art and the Mind, 100
Woolf, Virginia, *To the Lighthouse*,
  117–19
Wordsworth, William, 90, 198,
  255 n 16
  preface to *Lyrical Ballads*, 105, 251,
    258 n 51
  The Prelude, 121, 125